Old Rights and New

THE RIGHTS EXPLOSION

Robert A. Licht, series editor

The Framers and Fundamental Rights

Is the Supreme Court the Guardian of the Constitution?

Old Rights and New

Old Rights and New

Edited by Robert A. Licht

The AEI Press

Publisher for the American Enterprise Institute
WASHINGTON, D.C.

1993

This book was funded in part by a grant from the National Endowment for the Humanities.

Distributed by arrangement with

University Press of America
4720 Boston Way
Lanham, MD 20706

3 Henrietta Street
London WC2E 8LU England

Library of Congress Cataloging-in-Publication Data

Old rights and new / edited by Robert A. Licht.
    p.   cm.—(The Rights explosion)
  Includes bibliographical references and index.
  ISBN 0-8447-3775-5 (cloth).—ISBN 0-8447-3776-3 (paper)
  1. Civil rights—United States.   I. Licht, Robert A.   II. Series.
KF4749.052   1993
342.73'085—dc20
[347.30285]   93-16577
                                                                                              CIP

The AEI Press
Publisher for the American Enterprise Institute
1150 17th Street, N.W., Washington, D.C. 20036

Printed in the United States of America

Contents

Editor and Authors

ROBERT A. LICHT is resident scholar and director of constitutional studies at the American Enterprise Institute. Mr. Licht taught philosophy at Bucknell University and liberal arts at St. John's College in Annapolis. He has been a visiting scholar at the Kennedy Institute for Ethics and a National Endowment for the Humanities fellow at AEI. He is the author of "On the Three Parties in America" and "Reflections on Martin Diamond's 'Ethics and Politics: The American Way' " and the editor of the other two books in The Rights Explosion series: *The Framers and Fundamental Rights* (AEI Press, 1992) and *Is the Supreme Court the Guardian of the Constitution?* (AEI Press, 1993).

DANIEL J. ELAZAR is professor of political science at Temple University in Philadelphia, where he directs the Center for the Study of Federalism, and president of the Jerusalem Center for Public Affairs, an independent institute. Professor Elazar also holds the Senator N. M. Paterson Professorship in Intergovernmental Relations at Bar Ilan University in Israel. He is the author of more than fifty books, including *The American Partnership: American Federalism, a View from the States*.

WILLIAM A. GALSTON is currently professor at the School of Public Affairs, University of Maryland at College Park, and senior research scholar at the university's Institute for Philosophy and Public Policy. He served as director of economic and social programs at the Roosevelt Center for American Policy Studies before joining the University of Maryland's faculty in 1988. Professor Galston is the author of *Liberal Purposes: Goods, Virtues, and Diversity in the Liberal State*.

LEON R. KASS is Addie Clark Harding Professor in the College and the Committee on Social Thought, the University of Chicago, and Adjunct Scholar of the American Enterprise Institute. Author of *Toward a More Natural Science: Biology and Human Affairs*, he has written widely on ethical and philosophical issues raised by biomedical advance. His contribution to this volume was prepared while he was the William H. Brady, Jr., Fellow at AEI.

HARVEY C. MANSFIELD, JR., is the Frank G. Thompson Professor of Government at Harvard University. He has written widely on American political institutions and practices and on the works of Edmund Burke, Machiavelli, and other political philosophers. He is most recently the author of *Taming the Prince: The Ambivalence of Modern Executive Power*.

ERIC SCHNAPPER is assistant counsel, NAACP Legal Defense and Educational Fund, where he is responsible for most noncriminal Supreme Court litigation, for Washington lobbying, and for voting, employment, and consumer litigation. He is also a lecturer at Columbia University Law School. His most recent publication is "A *Monell* Update: Clarity, Conflict, and Complications," in *Civil Rights Litigation Handbook*.

SUSAN SHELL is associate professor of political science at Boston College. She is the author of *The Rights of Reason: A Study of Kant's Philosophy and Politics* and of articles on theories of justice and on the current status of American education. Her essay on Idealism appeared in *Confronting the Constitution*, edited by Allan Bloom.

HENRY SHUE is the Wyn and William Y. Hutchinson Professor of Ethics and Public Life and the first director of Cornell's new Program on Ethics and Public Life. He is a founder of the Institute for Philosophy and Public Policy and the author of *Basic Rights*.

Old Rights and New

1

Introduction

Robert A. Licht

This volume poses, in the form of a question, a modest disjunctive proposition as regards rights, a foundation of the American regime: Has an intellectual upheaval occurred, which may be philosophically fathomed, but from which political recovery is unlikely if not impossible? Or, at long last, have we truly begun to make progress in "human rights" and begun to fulfill the promise of the American founding?

This is the second, and central, volume in the series "The Rights Explosion." The first volume, *The Framers and Fundamental Rights*, inquires into the meaning of rights as the framers of the Constitution understood them and as we understand the framers. The third and final volume, *Is the Supreme Court the Guardian of the Constitution?*, addresses the implicit question of the constitutional function of the Supreme Court in the light of the leading role it has assumed in the expansion of personal and group rights.

Today, rights are the territory where the political wars—the war between limited republican government and the centralized, social democratic state—and the so-called cultural wars of Eurocentrics versus the prophets of the New Age—intersect. This territory is not a vacation destination.

The United States was the first nation founded explicitly on the idea that governments are instituted among men to secure universal, individual, *natural* rights. Today, thanks to the success of our Constitution—that is, to the genius of the framers—we are sufficiently secure in our rights and flourishing in our liberties that we think of our founding principles as our ancient birthright. That is, our founding principles have become our *nomoi*, laws and customs, our governing opinions and most deeply held prejudices. But a brief reflection suggests just how paradoxical this is.

Natural rights, the American *nomoi*, are by definition antinomian. I mean by this dark assertion three things:

• They are not dependent on custom (one meaning of *nomos*), precisely because they are natural, or decisively prior to and alongside of custom.

• They are not dependent on law (the other meaning of *nomos*), because they become visible only in the absence of law and civil society.

• Because natural rights are talismans of human insecurity, they point to those aspects of human nature that are in tension with or lurk underneath the surface of civil society: the will to self-liberation and self-assertion, "spiritedness," as it has been called, but also cunning and violence.

Securing natural rights, or liberties, requires the establishment of civil society, in which we surrender our unlimited claims of right for the sake of security in them, as Harvey Mansfield points out in chapter 5. Nevertheless, although such a society makes lawful the claims that exist prior to the law, it cannot altogether domesticate them. If one requires a "proof text" of this assertion, he need seek no further than James Madison's *A Memorial and Remonstrance:*

> The religion . . . of every man must be left to the conviction and conscience of every man; and it is the right of every man to exercise it as these may dictate. This right is in its nature an unalienable right . . . because the opinions of men, depending only on the evidence contemplated by their own minds, cannot follow the dictates of other men. . . . In matters of Religion, no man's right is abridged by the institution of Civil Society.[1]

This notion of the natural right of conscience—a right to rebellion, a right not "to follow the dictates of other men"—animates the First Amendment and thus is carried into the bosom of the law itself. It is also a guiding principle in the design of the unamended Constitution, particularly with regard to the formation of majorities.

Again, it is Madison who instructs us, in the celebrated *Federalist* 10, where the tendency toward a tyranny of the majority—"majority faction"—may be overcome by the "extended republic." The extended republic (or better, perhaps, the empire of liberty, since each state is itself an extended republic) is composed of a multiplicity of sects and interests. These motile and protean sects and interests, through the combination of representation and interlocked federal and national governments, constantly coalesce, divide, and re-form into *constitutional* majorities. Thus the government avoids domination by a factional majority based upon an exclusionary vision of the public good. Stability is owed to motion and change.

Madison saw deeply into the problem that founding a regime on natural rights must present to a lawgiver. The doctrine of natural rights guaranteed that in the long run, in principle, a society built upon that foundation could not depend simply upon the stability of custom and religion. A government of liberty based on securing natural rights, must primarily place its trust in the soundness of the design of its institutions—that government be obliged to obey itself. This design must in turn take advantage of the good fortune of the potential wealth and extent of the nation and the natural self-interest of men to exploit and develop it.

This self-interest must in turn take advantage of the good fortune (or ill-fortune, as it may have turned out) of a philosophic and scientific tradition to understand itself and promote its prosperity. Finally, as Madison readily acknowledged but could not, by his own principles, place in the first category, free government must depend upon character and virtue. That is to say, in this last matter we are in the hands of custom, or good fortune simply, because these qualities by design are consigned to the private sphere for their cultivation and nurture.

Now the danger to liberty, according to the Anti-Federalists, was the inclination toward absolute monarchy, or the centralization of power in a national government. Madison, however, feared both majority faction and the centrifugal tendencies of federations. Although absolute monarchy is now a quaint relic, the centralization of power assuredly is not. Today we must ask the question of whether the danger to liberty comes from the *Madisonian*, or centralizing, side of the controversy together with a transformed understanding of rights, that is from the very principles of the regime itself. But perhaps Madison himself may not have appreciated and foreseen that the antinomian doctrine of rights, having become the *nomos* of constitutionalism, would develop a life of its own that would transform the regime and threaten its dynamic stability.

The idea of "natural" rights has been all but abandoned—along with the distinction between natural and civil rights it implied—to be replaced by the considerably less transparent, less sober idea of "human rights." This transformation is complex and not well-understood. Several contributors to this volume, combining a tacit Hegeli-

3

anism with a dogmatically skeptical rationalism, believe there has been not a transformation but an evolution based on the progress we have made in our understanding of rights. Above all, they argue, it is a matter of understanding the basic concept of rights, getting rights right, as it were, and of being scrupulous and rigorous in the use of the various forms of argumentation of contemporary analytic and moral philosophy and jurisprudence.

Other contributors, however, believe that something more is afoot in this transformation of the idea of rights—something considerably darker and a grave threat, not only to the American regime, but to the idea of liberty itself.

Constitutionalism in America is founded upon the autonomy of natural reason, the liberty of conscience, and a certain givenness of social and religious custom. In retrospect, it may seem but a small step from this to the increasingly dominant notion of individual moral autonomy. Prospectively, however, viewed from the founding, this transformation represents a formidable philosophic and social development. It was not merely a small step from Madison's faith in reason and the ability of the sovereign people to judge the fitness and character of political leaders and their policies to the idea that such judgments—as we say, "value judgments"—cannot be rational.

In the United States, however, this evolution has now been accomplished in the name of rights. The "given" quality of social and religious custom, together with a trust in rationality, both long assaulted by the intellectual classes, have been breached.

Synopses of the Chapters

In this introduction, I offer the reader a brief guide to the battlefield and to the places where the combatants—the authors—have taken a stand. The summary presentation begins with the polar positions of Harvey C. Mansfield, Jr., and Henry Shue. William A. Galston's mediating overview of the subject follows. This is followed by Susan Shell's inquiry into the use and abuse of the moral philosophy of Kant in the contemporary rights debate. Daniel J. Elazar's reflection on the political and constitutional consequences of the idea of human rights follows. We return to jurisprudence in Eric Schnapper's critical review of the Supreme Court's evolving interpretation of civil rights and affirmative action. We then look at Leon R. Kass's inquiry into the effect of the new understanding of rights on the practice of medicine and its social consequences, an area perhaps at the root of modernity itself—the mastery and possession of nature. I offer, finally, my own brief reflections on some of the positions taken in these pages.

Harvey C. Mansfield, Jr., on Responsibility versus Self Expression. "From the beginning," writes Mansfield, "America has been a society whose government is devoted to the protection of rights, but fairly recently . . . a new conception of rights has taken hold." This new conception has altered our moral bearings, and there has been a "change in moral climate, from responsibility to self-expression."

The old rights were the "rights of man," understood as the rights of "certain beings with a fixed nature and with alterable laws and customs." Thus, human nature is "partly fixed, partly alterable." Rights pertain to the fixed part, "so they are inalienable." Since rights are not "taken away by bad laws," they cannot be "granted by good ones."

A right is a permission "to do a range of things that an individual is able to do." This is also a right *not* to do something. Although granted by nature, "it is actuated by self-permission." This presupposes that the individual is competent to judge for himself and to assert his right if he chooses, and that it is possible to assert it. "There is no right not to have rain on the Fourth of July."

The discovery of the rights of man depended on a hypothesis: "By imagining how men would be in a state of nature prior to the establishment of laws and customs," it became possible to see "what one's rights are." Thus, "men would have equal rights . . . to the extent . . . that no one group of them would have a clear title to rule other men." Further, because "prior to laws and custom men would live in penury and mutual distrust, their first concern would be for their lives." Thus men would have equal rights to life and to the liberty that protects life, as well as to "the pursuit of the happiness with which . . . a tenuous life is occupied."

The pursuit of happiness will in practice be the pursuit of property, since it serves as a guard for life and liberty. Security of property requires laws and customs. And so "men must leave the state of nature and form civil society." Doing so, "they exchange natural rights for civil rights. Natural rights are the rights on which civil society is founded; civil rights are the ones it secures."

The Constitution of the United States was established for the sake of securing these natural rights to life, liberty, and the pursuit of happiness, "but the rights actually secured . . . are civil rights." They are "more specific" (as in the Bill of Rights) than natural rights, but are "therefore also more limited." Natural rights are "unlimited but useless . . . ; civil rights are effectual but limited."

It is the right to consent—"to a government with the power to make and enforce laws"—by which natural rights are exchanged for civil rights. Consent is a "key right" that "makes all other rights effectual by joining them to government." The principal security for the civil rights established by government is the form of government it constructs. "With such constitutional provisions as the separation of powers and federalism, the ruling majority should be a *constitutional* majority . . . respectful of the rights of minorities and mindful of the common good," rather than a "factious, willful majority."

This older conception of rights has "two other, opposite qualities. They are formal, and they are connected to interests." By formal, Mansfield indicates that there is a difference between "the formal possession of a right and its actual exercise." Government secures only the former. But, while rights are formally equal, "they are in practice necessarily unequal." Because of luck and natural differences of ability, some will exercise their rights more successfully than others. This gap "is an inevitable feature of any society based on rights." To force the gap completely closed would suffocate the rights intended to be secured and contravene the right of consent.

The other quality of rights, "interests," are "opposite to the formality of rights, since they describe how one can expect rights actually to be exercised." "Our interest derives from our human nature, but it is not confined . . . to the state of nature." They therefore carry over into civil society and activate our civil rights: "Just as the natural right to life is sustained by the natural desire of self-preservation, so the civil right to acquire property is activated by our interest in an improved standard of living." This fact gains supporters for a regime of rights because they profit from it.

But what is the connection between the American regime of rights and the idea of responsibility? "Responsibility is the rights-based transformation of what used to be called duty or virtue." It is of human origin and democratic, and it may be defined as "the act of voluntarily taking charge of a situation in order to improve it." Although "responsibility is not identical to rights or interests, it is not antithetical either."

As regards interests, "one's concrete interest may be attached to a position in which he is made responsible for certain actions," and "he may then believe that responsibility is [a] duty, in a sense not requiring devotion to something higher." The notion of responsibility may be a key American contribution to liberal democracy and to the theories of rights and interests, which are "too theoretical to suffice by themselves."

Finally, a right requires "at least the ability to claim it"—that is, a certain competence. "One must, as we say, 'stand up for' one's rights," and also stand up for others in a like situation. Thus there is a certain "aristocratic sense of honor and generosity" present in the exercise of responsibility. "Through . . . responsibility liberal democracies recapture the love of the noble and the concern for the whole."

Mansfield argues that *every* essential quality of rights as understood above "is denied or radically modified in the new rights that are claimed today"; that they derive from "a fixed human nature," they are equal, they belong to competent individuals, and they are protected by private property. Rights are divided into natural and civil, and their key is the right of consent; they are constitutional, formal, connected to interests, and responsible."

The theoretical origin of the new rights is a clue to their abandonment of the connection of rights and interests. The new rights "were born in Friedrich Nietzsche's doctrine of the creative self." The course of the passage to America of this thought has not yet been fully told. One source of its passage to these shores, however,

> is the historicism taken from German philosophy that was decisive in American pragmatism, for the pragmatists influenced the progressives and the progressives were the predecessors of the New Deal. Pragmatism is not as American as apple pie.

Because this movement intellectually abandoned human nature, it lost the "rational ground of rights" and thus moved, in part unwittingly, toward Nietzsche's unfixed self, which defines itself by self-expression. "The creatives are not obliged to respect the rights of other selves . . . that are inchoate, malleable, or conformist. . . . Nonetheless, . . . the creatives may decide to devote themselves to equal rights," and they become "*equalizers* of those whose rights are equalized."

Such creative beings "are open-ended in fact and not merely in their formal potentialities. . . . The element of sobriety supplied by the notion of interest to a rights-based society is forgone."

As regards competence, it is no longer a requirement for rights. "The disabled are induced to dwell on their disabilities rather than encouraged to make do with their abilities." And, since none of us have all the abilities we would like, we are all, in a sense, disabled. "The shift from competence to disability transforms a right from a permission requiring other people's respect into a duty to be fulfilled by others." So doing, it subverts true charity.

In general, the new rights "do not include the right of private property. Under the old rights, private property is the guardian of a self whose individuality is already secure." But under the new rights, property gives to the self an unacceptable identity of "rapacity."

Private property depends on the formality of rights, but "promoters of the new rights . . . denounce any discrepancy between the formal right and its actual exercise."

The distinction between natural and civil rights also disappears under the new rights. "We now speak of human rights, which as such have no necessary relationship to civil society." They do not have to pass through a form of government for their securing, and they "owe nothing to a free government and are indifferent to its survival. . . . The new rights have the security of civil rights and the amplitude of natural rights, as if we could have our cake and eat it too."

Nor do the new rights "give effect to the right of consent standing between natural and civil rights. . . . The realm of politics is lost from sight." The new rights are effectively postconstitutional. "Since self-expression is the norm, the new rights have little to do with self-government."

The self-creating individuals "do not know their own selves, much less others'; so they have no basis for respecting others' rights." Too busy trying to live by their own doctrine, they cannot "be bothered with persuading others and seeking their consent." For such persons, rights become wants. "When rights are wants, those who have the wants are no longer required to claim their rights, to fight for them." Others, the elites, will see to it that government will "step in to guarantee those rights," thereby exercising them better than individuals do for themselves. Rights then become entitlements, "secure from responsibility to what the common good may require."

> A society of entitlements is a static society of defensive special interests. The new rights transform citizens into government dependents—restless, suspicious, ungrateful, passive, and incompetent.

Most important, "the right of privacy actually reflects the government's decision to define the private . . . because [it] defines the private, it intrudes on the private."

The new rights create an environment where rights are equalized at the extreme, and the extreme exercise of a right comes to be the only exercise; . . . thus responsibility is disjoined from moderation."

Henry Shue on Implied Protections and Protections Presupposed— Or, Not Every Right That Looks New Is New. Henry Shue takes sharp exception to Mansfield's argument. To call a right new "is frequently a sneer," he alleges. While rights are often dismissed as "new," "an old right is implied to have been discovered in the nature of things." There are "better reasons than supposed newness to resist the proliferation of rights claims and the rights inflation produced by illegitimate coinage of rights." What is needed to determine the legitimacy of a rights claim is "a consensus upon the concept of a right and a consensus upon the standards for the adequate protection of a right."

What appears to be Mansfield's argument—"to specify . . . a list of features distinctive of the old rights and then to declare the new rights to be illegimate *because* they lacked the features common to the old"—is not an argument at all. "What is needed is an argument to show that each of the features shared by the old rights is a necessary condition of being a right."

The old rights, moreover, cannot be considered complete unless we are willing to say we have learned nothing new about human social nature since 1800. Would "John Locke, Alexander Hamilton, and James Madison have learned nothing from Charles Darwin, John Stuart Mill, Fyodor Dostoyevsky, Sigmund Freud, or Max Weber about which rights need protection"?

Mansfield argues that the work of Friedrich Nietzsche is the historical pivot of conceptions of rights. But Shue asserts that "current debates about rights have virtually nothing to do with Nietzsche. . . . British jurisprudence, as exemplified by H. L. A. Hart, . . . has been more influential than American pragmatism." And John Rawls, whom Mansfield cites, is influenced by Immanuel Kant, not Nietzsche.

Mansfield's general thesis seems to be that "rights which are fundamentally Nietzschean are new and rights uncorrupted by Nietzsche are old." But "the *bête noir* of those who are exercised about new rights" is the right of privacy. Its American origins cannot be traced back to Nietzsche, however, but to the classic 1890 article by Samuel D. Warren and Louis D. Brandeis. For them, the right of privacy is that of "an inviolate personality."

But the central question is, What is a right? Mansfield calls it a "permission to do a range of things that an individual is able to do." But this cannot be adequate. "If a right were only a permission, it would be hard to imagine any good reason for governments to have been instituted. . . . Rights ground demands for protection, often institutional and sometimes governmental." Generalizing, "a morally grounded right may or may not require legally enforceable protection, but it does require effective protection."

"A permission and a right are quite distinct. . . . It can make perfect sense to protect a right, but there is nothing to protect in the case of the permission." Further, "rights entail correlative duties upon other parties, and permissions do not." It thus appears that Mansfield is confusing "being at liberty . . . with enjoying a right to liberty." The former is the case when no one contests one's permission, the latter when there are third parties able to enforce or protect one's rights. What is key is the "implemented right," provided by social institutions. It is these "institutionalized protections that distinguish genuine rights from the mere permissions considered by Mansfield."

The issue, then, is how "one can responsibly go about considering whether to institute new forms of protection for rights . . . that will sometimes but not always involve recognizing additional rights." To do this it is necessary to look at the *"forms* that good arguments . . . take." A right to physical security, for example, is perhaps the most basic there is. Every person has a "moral right" to physical security.

A case in point is the question of whether a man coercing his wife to have sex with him is guilty of the crime of rape. "If a . . . state where marital rape is impossible by definition chooses to grant legal protection" to a wife against such coercion by her husband, "is the legislature creating a new right? . . . It turns out to be very difficult . . . to argue that . . . marital rape is both a new idea and a bad idea." A woman is not a slave to her husband, and she retains "a basic right to the security and integrity of her own body."

The basis of moral rights is "determined at a given time by the facts of human social interaction at that time. . . . The precise articulation of the rights awaits philosophical, political, and legal insight, arising from attempts to build principled consensus." We may say that "recognized rights can *imply* genuine rights that have not yet been recognized, and recognized rights can *presuppose* genuine rights that have not yet been recognized" (emphasis added).

Since human society changes, and "rights are based upon the nature of society, some genuinely new rights might well become necessary as society changes." Because new medical technology, for example, has created "undreamed-of possibilities for the cruel, unusual, and gratuitous infliction of pain and suffering by doctors . . . unwilling to exercise any judgment" in its use, it becomes reasonable to recognize a "right to die." Here people are not exercising a Nietzschean new right, but "simply responding to new threats with new protections."

Nevertheless, "although rights need not be old in order to be legitimate, some rights that appear to be new . . . entail or are entailed by rights that are indisputably old." Such rights are not the result of changed circumstances, but of having "newly realized that certain measures were needed all along." Here it is useful to draw an analogy between "forms of reasoning about moral rights and forms of reasoning about constitutional rights."

The famous constitutional metaphor of Justice William O. Douglas that "specific guarantees in the Bill of Rights have penumbras, formed by emanations from those guarantees" has been much ridiculed. But the sentence has been improperly read by Judge Robert Bork to read: "Specific guarantees in the Bill of Rights create penumbras that help give the specific guarantees life and substance." On this basis, according to Bork, Justice Douglas "somehow created a general but wholly undefined 'right of privacy' that . . . lies outside any right or 'zone of privacy' to be found in the Constitution." But properly read, as Richard Mohr has argued, this is the richest reading of the sentence:

> Specific guarantees [in the Bill of Rights] have penumbras that are formed by emanations from those *general* guarantees that help give the specific guarantees life and substance.

Thus, the First, Third, and Fourth Amendments "are themselves the penumbras of an underlying general right of privacy!" The right against having soldiers quartered in one's home was thus a *prospective* protection of privacy. Therefore, the right of privacy is an *old* right. This conforms to a form of reasoning found in "all theoretical areas . . . backwards from *explicandum* to *explicans*," or reasoning to presuppositions.

Shue argues that he is not trying to "prove" a right to privacy, but rather to show "two general ways one can reasonably move to new formulations of what may or may not be new rights." This is neither a denial of "abiding human interests" nor an exercise in Nietzschean self-expression. The form of argument that shows implied rights reasons "downstream," whereas the form of argument that shows prospective rights reasons "upstream"; that is, in the first case from the general to the specific, and in the second, from the specific to the general. But in truth, reasoning is also dialectical, moving in both directions. "Theory construction has no algorithms, and one of the algorithms it does not have is, Always reject new conceptions."

William A. Galston on Philosophy and History—The Evaluation of Rights in American Thought. William Galston steps back from the confrontation between "old" and "new" to find a perspective from which a middle ground may come into view.

Historically, "the post-Reformation wars of religion serve as a useful point of departure." Cruelty, the prime vice of those wars, and the fear that it aroused were taken as subjects of political thought by humanist writers such as Montaigne. In the words of Judith Shklar, fear is "irreducible," and "it can be both the beginning and an end of political institutions such as rights." This can be seen in the Eighth Amendment to the Constitution's prohibition against cruel and unusual punishment.

The wars of religion also focused "on the value of life and the formulation of rights of self-preservation" by Thomas Hobbes and John Locke. Both the Declaration of Independence and the Fifth Amendment reflect this.

Religious intolerance caused the development of "doctrines of toleration, rights of religious conscience, and the conception of a sphere of privacy, free from government interference." The First Amendment, indeed "American constitutionalism generally," has been greatly influenced by these doctrines. Protestantism itself, with its emphasis on the "fundamental equality of human beings" and its derivative consensual theory of political legitimacy, or consent, is another great source of rights thinking.

Then there is the general "breakdown of feudal and aristocratic systems," and the rise of "an enormously powerful revision of medieval property theory . . . in which full-blown property rights were grounded in self-ownership and labor" made its appearance and is reflected in the work of Locke. The Fifth and Fourteenth Amendments certainly reflect his heritage. In more recent times, the teachings of Immanuel Kant on individual autonomy and dignity and the tradition of "liberal individuality, shaped in response to the rise of liberal societies," have had their complex influence.

Thus there are thus "three great historical events—religious conflict, the attenuation of feudal-aristocratic economies, and the rise of liberal societies—" that have created the categories of the contemporary discussion of rights. Politically, "rights are constitutive of liberalism," and the critique of rights, in general, reflects "broader reservations about liberalism itself." Broadly speaking, however, the critiques fall into three categories:

• The first is a critique made from within the liberal tradition; it observes that the problem lies not with the conception of rights, but with the failure of liberal regimes to realize them. This critique must be substantially accepted by defenders of rights.

• Second is a more radical line, which "takes issue with standard conceptions of rights." This focuses primarily on economic welfare rights. This critique is perhaps the "most perplexing" to defenders of rights, "especially when proposed new rights come into practical conflict with older ones": for example, "welfare rights can clash with established property rights," and broad rights of free expression may clash with "the right of women and minorities not to be degraded."

• The third, most radical critique "questions the entire category of rights as a way of describing and justifying political life." This may be rejected, while conceding "that rights form only a part of a comprehensive political morality and do not function well if applied in abstraction from the other aspects of that morality."

Galston turns next to moral theory: "Many of the political disagreements over rights find reflection . . . within the debates . . . of modern moral philosophy. Perhaps the best known of these is the conflict, real or alleged, between individual rights and collective ends."

This often takes the form of a conflict between proponents of utilitarianism and those of personal liberty. Galston observes that, "in the absence of a common denominator of value[,] . . . intuition and common sense in specific cases" must weigh the competing arguments. Proponents of rights theory ground their views on sentiments of personal inviolability and the idea of "self-ownership," or the notion that each person is the "morally rightful owner of himself," in the words of G. A. Cohen. Utilitarians, however, "are on strong ground when they insist . . . that the consequences (for others affected) of honoring an individual's right will at some level . . . appear intolerable."

This tension is evident as well between the Declaration of Independence and the Preamble to the Constitution, a tension further heightened by the Bill of Rights. Although it is "alleged that a rights-based regime is inherently defective in that it lacks shared purposes and a guiding conception of the common good," Galston believes this is "flatly mistaken" in one respect: "rights *are* shared ends" that promote the common good, as may be seen in an attentive reading of the Declaration of Independence.

Nevertheless, the problem of the common good returns on another level, because "no guarantee ensures that in practice the rights of each individual will be compatible with those of all the rest."

Another issue is the charge that "rights must give short shrift to . . . the claims of duty." Galston is not persuaded: "it is clear that many rights entail duties." Moreover, "rights can coexist with moral philosophies that give pride of place to duty," as in the thought, for example, of Immanuel Kant. Also, "some rights are simultaneously and equally duties"; opposition to tyranny, for example, is characterized in the Declaration of Independence "as both a right and a duty." Finally, however, rights cannot be "a complete and comprehensive moral theory," and this "moral incompleteness of rights extends far beyond duties," since "rights-based theories cannot do justice to supererogation, the virtues," and other morally significant actions.

Another approach to the foundation and content of rights is to look first at what function rights perform. The common theme among various thinkers is that rights offer *protection* to the individual. Galston carefully outlines the variations on this theme.

Turning from the function of rights directly to their content, Galston divides the field in two: general (or philosophical) and particular rights. As regards the former, "it must suffice to say that several influential but mutually incompatible proposals have surfaced." H. L. A. Hart, on the one side, has argued that there is an "*ur*-right: the equal right of all to be free." On the other, Dworkin dismisses a "general right to liberty," proposing in its place a fundamental "right to equal concern and respect." From this right particular liberties may be derived. Other candidates for fundamental rights put forward by legal and moral philosophers include "the right[s] to fair treatment, . . . not to be treated cruelly, and . . . not to be subjected to degradation or exploitation" (Joel Feinberg); and "the core human right . . . of participating . . . in the procedures by which deep conflicts are adjudicated" (Stuart Hampshire).

There is greater agreement, however, among contemporary thinkers on the question of particular rights, and five areas of agreement can be enumerated—although, as Galston makes clear, there are important areas of contention as well in each category:

- a right to life
- rights of personal protection—against slavery, cruel and unusual punishment, arbitrary searches, arrest, imprisonment, and confiscation: "invasions of religious, intellectual, and expressive freedom"
- rights to equal protection of the laws and the procedures of fair trial
- particular liberties, including travel, marriage, choice of profession, association, disposing of personal property
- rights of participation that help to secure and protect the other rights, including "fair access to citizenship; equal treatment of all citizens; free political speech"

There are also rights whose very existence is in doubt:

- Is there a right to privacy, such as in matters of sexual orientation, practice, and expression?
- Is there a right to property, "the modern form of [which] contest is rooted in the European conflict between classical liberalism and social democracy"?
- Are there welfare rights, or "guaranteed entitlements to basic levels of material provision and opportunity"?

Galston turns last to the question of who are the bearers of rights. Least controversial is the adult human being, but "matters become more complex when we move to . . . children, the handicapped, fetuses, animals, and even vegetation and inanimate nature." Another issue "heatedly debated in the United States . . . is whether groups as well as individuals may reasonably be regarded as rights-bearers." But the Declaration of Independence can be considered a "remote antecedent" of this issue insofar as a "people" "can invoke a right of separation."

Today, when liberalism is not engaged in "the grand seventeenth- and eighteenth-century contest with patriarchal monarchy and feudal aristocracy," the criticism of rights-based liberal society argues "that societies wholly preoccupied with claiming and exercising rights cannot provide scope for a fully rounded and worthy human existence." There is need to "flesh out the conception of 'rightness' that forms an indispensable complement to rights": that is, although I may have a right to do X, is X the "right thing to do?" Liberalism's future agenda, in Galston's view, must attend to questions of responsibilities, duties, and virtues, as well as those human associations, such as religion and the family, that are vital but are not "structured by the concept and practice of rights." In these concerns, "the discourse of rights gives way to the classic question of *paideia*[,] and . . . we must concern ourselves with the full range of influences on the formation of character in liberal societies."

Susan Shell on Kantianism and Constitutional Rights. As Galston observes, one of the greatest influences of moral philosophy on the idea of rights (and on modern constitutional jurisprudence) has been the writings of Immanuel Kant. Susan Shell examines this connection in depth and remarks that a "new attitude toward rights has made itself felt both on the bench and . . . among more liberal critics and students of the judiciary." This has been a reaction to "the conservative use to which legal realism was increasingly being put by the Court," which has been identified with the "*Lochner* era," when the

Court appealed "over the head of the Constitution, as it were, to an allegedly more fundamental standard of justice." An activist Court frustrated the democratic will in the name of fundamental rights, and it was not overly scrupulous in its fidelity to constitutional language.

The civil rights movement changed all that, however, and the formerly activist conservatives now found themselves in alliance with "advocates of judicial restraint and legislative deference." Now it was the liberals who "appealed over the heads of elected bodies to more fundamental principles." But what were those principles? The Holmesian skepticism and historicist criticism seemed "insufficient, given the new and expansive understanding of rights."

The philosophy of John Rawls seemed to break the impasse: "Here . . . was an intellectual approach that combined analytic rigor with interdisciplinary deference and the preferred political results." Immanuel Kant was considered to be the philosophic "Godfather" of this approach. Both Justice William Brennan's "constitutional ideal of human dignity" and Ronald Dworkin's "equal concern and respect" are echoes of this Kantianism.

"Kant's thought provides . . . a new understanding of the grounding of rights in and by an ideal constitution. . . . The upshot is at once a sanctification of rights and a desanctification of actual constitutions." This Kantianism in American constitutional jurisprudence exhibits three tendencies:

- the assimilation of constitutional rights and "human dignity": or, all rights are reducible "to a right to equal respect"
- an understanding that rights are detached from or "neutral toward competing conceptions of the good"
- an "injunction or invitation to 'aspire' to . . . civil and moral improvement"

The latter two, Shell contends, seriously mislead and distort the meaning of Kant's moral idealism. But "it is helpful to keep in mind that . . . his thought was welcomed by many as an antidote [to] utilitarianism and positivism."

John Rawls found a way to serve both "the claims of equality addressed by . . . earlier progressivism and [those] of the individual above the majority." He viewed rights as "independent of . . . any prior theory of the good." From Rawls's basic principle of justice as fairness, two other principles flow: individuals "would choose to guarantee . . . liberty, consistent with the equal liberty of others," and they "would choose to maximize the lot of the least fortunate." Talent and hard work are construed by Rawls as common assets that are distributed in a "morally arbitrary" way and convey "no implication as to the right of individuals to their fruit."

Shell observes that Rawls's critics were thick on the ground. But the greatest difficulty with his theory was "the essential baselessness of rights so understood. . . . What justified . . . real individuals in their claim to have rights at all?" His account of man in "the original position" detached rights "from the account of human nature, and in particular from the natural sense of desert (or spiritedness) in which it had both morally and psychologically been rooted." But without a "meaningful standard for desert," he also deprives his theory of "any positive concept of fairness. . . . Rawls's powerful claims on behalf of equality and his indignation at the cruelty of nature," which distributes its gifts arbitrarily, "leaves a tremendous void."

But this is a "curious inversion" of Kant, who grounded rights in "absolute dignity and self-worth." Rawls suggests that "a sense of self-worth is something we receive (and are indeed entitled to receive . . .) from others. Our sense of our own dignity and . . . our rights above society are themselves society's product." Nevertheless, the legal philosophers who followed Rawls used his work to find meaning in constitutional rights. Ronald Dworkin's concept of "equal concern and respect" describes "that to which individuals are, at bottom, constitutionally entitled." It is also "a frank admission of the dependence of an individual's sense of self-worth on the willingness of others to endorse or at least not condemn" their (arbitrarily) chosen way of life.

Dworkin has also argued for a notion of law as "integrity," which he associates with "the Kantian ideal of self-legislation." But the greatest use of integrity for Dworkin lies in its connection with equality and community. Dworkin argues that "law's constraints benefit society not just by providing predictability or procedural fairness . . . but by securing a kind of equality among citizens that makes their community more genuine." Dworkin's use of Kant "is a somewhat hazy commitment to equality . . . fleshed out, through the language of compassion that Kant himself would have abjured, as equality of 'concern.' " The individual, as Dworkin understands him, is no longer the individual of classical liberalism, whose fundamental need for security was the root of his natural rights, "but a fellow member of the communal hermeneutic circle, situated in a web of contextual, socially rooted meanings." The security of the individual is now understood as the "equal consideration in relation to and on the part of other members of the group"—that is, that "he or she counts and that others care."

Another legal scholar, David A. J. Richards, has used this line of reasoning to reconstruct the liberalism of the founders. He identifies the founders' "community of principle" with a "moral community of free and equal persons capable of respecting one another because they have been *guaranteed the resources to respect themselves.*" The Constitution, in this view, "aspires" to expand the community of "free and equal persons" by guaranteeing the resources of self-respect that make possible the respect of others. This "approach identifies fidelity to the Constitution with the pursuit of an egalitarian communitarianism."

Finally, this line of (allegedly) Kantian thought may be found in Supreme Court Justice Brennan's view of the Constitution as "aspirational" in its adaptability to evolving goals of "social justice, brotherhood, and human dignity." We can only be faithful to the founders' Constitution by accepting "the ambiguity inherent in the effort to apply [fundamental value choices] to modern circumstances," he asserts. The constitutional ideal of human dignity "will never cease to evolve." Shell remarks on the "vagueness of that ideal, along with its seemingly limitless adaptability to new historical circumstances."

Shell turns from these adaptations to their original in Kant's thought itself. Unlike the current communitarian assault on what they assume to be his individualism, "Kant was the first thinker to show compellingly that individuality and community . . . necessarily imply each other." Although each individual is "subjected to the law of [his] own making," individuals can have a "worldly existence only insofar as they engage interactively with other individuals. Morally, this takes the form . . . of a common will in whose necessitating dictates each individual participates." Man's moral freedom is what lifts him above the "economies of nature" and is the origin of his "absolute worth" or "dignity." In this "moral economy . . . no one can be a mere means to another," and it is because of this "moral community with others" that we are genuinely free.

But this community of free individuals is "an ideal of reason that cannot be identified with any actual human society." It is the ideal on which "the radical independence of the individual" rests. Thus, for Kant, human self-respect cannot be identified with the notion of "equal concern and respect" of others. "The community upon which Kantian individuality depends is not just a mutual admiration society. The right to respect flows from one's inherent worthiness."

The moral community, as an ideal of reason, has its counterpart in the juridical community "whose common will enjoins us to establish laws protecting persons" in the exercise of their freedom. This "community of right," as an idea, "provides for the greatest liberty of each [to be] consistent with the greatest liberty of all the rest." The ideal constitution for this community entails "republican self-government and the separation of legislative, executive, and judicial powers," as well as "intellectual and religious freedom, combined with strict protection of property rights along free market lines." For Kant, the fact that human beings are equal as "subjects of the state" is "perfectly compatible" with individual "physical or mental" inequality.

This interplay between the real and the ideal "suggests the relative insignificance of political activity to his conception of individual freedom." Thinkers and writers are the instruments of a progressive realization of moral community, "not politicians and civil servants." The "juridical community of means will gradually transform itself . . . into an ethical 'kingdom of ends.' "

Kant is also no friend of the relativist argument that "the state should be neutral toward competing ways of life because no way of life is ascertainably the best." Kant insists that the best way of life ensures that "rights as such have . . . genuine meaning or rational foundation." Kant also argues, however, that it is the responsibility of the state "to ensure that each is free to pursue his ends . . . consistent with the equal freedom of others," and to this extent his thought approaches the relativism with which he is charged.

But this position should not be confused with today's "value neutrality." "When Kant says that the laws of right have nothing to do with 'the ends men have by nature,' he does not mean that happiness has nothing to do with justice." There is a "supreme good" that humanity strives for: "happiness conjoined with virtue, or worthiness to be happy." This end, however, is on a cosmic scale; on a "human scale [concerning] the due that we owe to and are owed by other human beings," Kant's requirements are more modest. Indeed, in some ways they converge with those of Hobbes. "If the problem of politics can be solved for a nation of devils if only they are intelligent, there is good reason to suppose that man's baser impulses . . . may ultimately serve moral ends," and that these "moral efforts will not be futile, supported as they are by the workings of man's animal nature."

Indeed, "for Kant a starving man, so long as he has not been robbed or defrauded of his property, has only nature or himself to blame." On the basis of the Kantian principle of "freedom of contract in the name of human dignity," "contemporary efforts to treat welfare benefits as entrenched rights ultimately threaten the very private sphere upon which meaningful individualism hinges."

Kantian constitutionalism, which "differentiates the rational con-

19

stitution from its imperfect empirical embodiments, while . . . insisting on their underlying unity," entails a political progressivism by which actual governments approach the ideal. This finds a kinship in the American Constitution, which Abraham Lincoln called the "silver frame" surrounding the Declaration's "golden apple." There is an ideal, "underlying conception of justice, which judicial interpretation, however strictly it may want to adhere . . . to the simple intention of the founders, cannot ignore."

Nevertheless, there is an essential difference between Kantian constitutional aspiration and the Declaration's relation to the American Constitution. For Kant, constitutional rights "stem from the moral law grasped as a fundamental 'fact of reason,' " while for the framers, "rights stem from nature or nature's God, as mediated by the actual consent of the governed." Still, "some form of Kantianism" distinguished from the "morally neutered and historicized Kant currently in vogue" may perform a useful and evocative role.

Daniel J. Elazar on How Present Conceptions of Rights Shape the Protection of Rights in the United States. Daniel Elazar moves the discussion of the evolution of rights from moral philosophy to the social foundations of evolving political theory and practice.

> The changes that have taken place may have made late twentieth-century American civil society as different in its conceptions of rights from the founding generation's conceptions as the latter's were from the late medieval expressions of obligations and liberties.

The American tradition of rights goes back to the colonial foundings. The colonialists wished to protect "their individuality and their liberties," to which end they created constitutional documents that "proclaimed them publicly." The protection of rights, in their view, was "principally the acknowledgment and protection of liberties." This, however, embodied a "struggle between federal and natural liberty."

"Natural liberty is . . . the freedom of the state of nature," and "in the end it . . . leads to anarchy." Federal liberty, conversely, is "proper liberty," or "liberty to act according to the terms of the covenant *(foedus)* that calls the body politic into existence." A covenant, or pact, is the foundation of a "proper polity." It presupposes a shared moral sensibility and, if legitimate, it embodies liberty and equality. Violation of its terms is "a manifestation of anarchy," and is punishable. The polities established according to the principle of federal liberty will vary from one to another according to the particular terms of the agreement. The American civilization is informed by the tension between natural and federal liberty.

Federal liberty, from the Puritans to the eighteenth-century revolutionaries, the abolitionists, the populists, the progressives, and the civil rights movement of the 1950s and 1960s, has been based on a common belief "that people were not naturally free to commit certain wrongs." To violate this stricture was criminal and punishable under the Constitution. In this sense, federal liberty recognizes the relationship between obligation and right, and it may be said to bridge "premodern and modern conceptions of rights."

In the revolutionary period, for example, state bills and declarations of rights "reflected the hidden or open assumption that every individual was part of a community" and thus under certain obligations, as, reciprocally, was the community. "Natural law and rights meant a natural order." This was characteristically the Whig outlook and, to an extent, it differed from the contractarian philosophers. This sense of the relation of rights and obligations "has survived within the states."

Historically, in America, the idea of rights had by 1791 undergone two great transitions: "from the medieval conception of liberties to a modern conception of rights," and "from the idea that rights can best be protected through hortatory declarations to the idea that they can be protected through binding constitutional law." The unamended Constitution of 1787 thus assumed that "the best way to protect rights was through proper institutions." Although the Bill of Rights went beyond that idea, nevertheless, until the Civil War, rights thinking reflected the institutional view. "This was a period when the idea of natural rights gave way in prevailing opinion to that of constitutional rights, the task of institutions being the protection of the latter."

It was the state legislatures, in this period, that "did more for the protection of rights than courts." The Thirteenth, Fourteenth, and Fifteenth Amendments, which "provided new means for the enforcement of . . . rights through the courts as well as legislatures," were the culmination of this era. After this time the right of private property was raised in status—"reified"—as the preeminent right. Property rights "were defined to be the most important of all constitutional rights," and through them were all individual rights protected. In a sense, the way was cleared for this elevation of property rights because of the end of slavery, which institution had compromised those rights.

Property rights entailed emphasis on due process, or the notion that "taking," or "the improper removal of the bundle of powers and

21

opportunities that constituted property," was subject to higher, or extraconstitutional tests. At the same time, the right of contract, through the Fourteenth Amendment, was similarly elevated. In the first decades of the twentieth century, however, the elevation of property and contract rights was challenged, and "a new sense of individual rights began to develop, drawing on the Civil War amendments." In this transition the Supreme Court played a leading role, and "by the end of that generation the principle of civil rights was well established in jurisprudence."

The civil rights movement reached its apogee in the 1960s. "At the same time civil rights increasingly came to mean individual rights in the starkest sense." The individual was to be free of all constraints, except those "deemed absolutely necessary for the maintenance of law and order." Even these constraints were redefined, however, and "the maintenance of the social fabric"—which in colonial times had been paramount—"became distinctly secondary . . . in the face of individual rights challenges." When civil rights reached its greatest strength, it was already being replaced conceptually by the notion of human rights.

There are two elements to human rights. They require the least possible restraint by government on the individual, while at the same time requiring "public institutions to provide for the individual's welfare to the maximum possible extent." Thus human rights are a return to natural rights, but without nature. Human rights also "became the measure of the constitutionality serving as the measure of rights." Now the institutions of government were "defined as existing by virtue of their obligations to the individual. . . . Few rights flowed from those obligations, just as few obligations flowed from the rights of individuals."

This may be called the postmodern conception of rights. It includes liberties and entitlements, and "people are at liberty to do what they will, provided that they [do not] seriously infringe upon the rights of others to do the same." But the notion of a "serious" infringement appears to limit the needs of society. While the individual has maximal freedom, the institutions of government are "expected to guarantee . . . their basic needs and more." This is the element of entitlements in postmodern rights. The constitutional effect of these liberties and entitlements has required a shift from institutional arrangements to guarantees through "judicial fiat."

Elazar epitomizes the shift from modern rights—life, liberty, property, and the pursuit of happiness—to postmodern—welfare, expression, privacy—as a shift from Aristotelianism to Epicureanism. In other words, it is a shift from "a view of civil society as a comprehensive whole" to that of the "isolated individual." Pursuing this philosophic theme, Elazar seeks out the notions of "common humanity" on which all conceptions of right must rest.

The premodern conception of rights were as liberties and obligations, evident in the Bible and in classical thought as an "order that existed in the nature (or way) of things." Modern rights looked upon nature in the "empirical rather than the normative sense." Here too, however, "natural order includes obligations," and "natural rights were self-evident but had to be discovered if they were to be transformed into political realities." But natural law alone is not enough. Thus it was transformed into positive law "through covenants, compacts, constitutions, and consent" to overcome the disagreement about the source of the law, whether or not it was divine. Nevertheless, through consent, agreement about rights was possible and was embodied in the positive law.

> It is important to note the relationship between rights and consent. Rights may be authoritative, but in practice they have authority only when accepted by the consent of the governed. Thus consent is the bridge between abstract rights and concrete behavior of civil society.
> Modern natural rights had three dimensions: rights as justice, rights as liberties, and rights as exceptions.

To these, postmodern thought has added entitlements. But entitlements are now interpreted as property rights, since they are held to be a new form of property. Moreover, the "moral autonomy of the individual" becomes an "absolute." Morality is replaced by relativism, and "whatever the moral beliefs of the people happen to be will determine what rights" they have. "Under such circumstances, constitutionalism itself is challenged." Where the older view of constitutionalism was that the public good had "a veto over actions that went beyond a certain point," now "the most that a constitution will have is a vote."

Over against this radical individualism there has been a resurgence of "primordial groups in the postmodern world." This has led the postmodern declarations of rights to include, simultaneously, the "individual rights of welfare, expression, and privacy, and then [to] try to balance them with some provision for group rights as well." Elazar suggests that federalism might be a solution to this problem.

What is the future of postmodern liberalism? It has "challenged the very assumption that civil society exists as an actor in its own right." If individuals are not "able to have a collective expression through civil society . . . they will become isolated and alienated."

The end would seem to be "totalitarianism, a particularly virulent form of reified statism, which is likely to emerge in response to the human desire for order as well as freedom."

Eric Schnapper on New White Rights—The Transformation of Affirmative Action Jurisprudence. Eric Schnapper looks at the transformation of rights from within the jurisprudence of the Supreme Court. One area, he observes, that qualifies as "new rights" at least from the perspective of the framers is the emergence of *group rights* as a necessary complement to, or even completion of, civil rights. This issue evolved from programs of affirmative action and their attendant litigation.

In an interesting dissent from the dominant liberal notion of "fairness"—that is, that natural differences of ability can *not* be a basis of right or justice—Schnapper argues that race and gender may well be the basis of merit, or qualification, in certain circumstances. Thus there is a need for *greater* consideration of merit than the Court has to this point shown. Schnapper observes that "for more than forty years, objections to affirmative action have been grounded on an argument that such measures . . . are inconsistent with merit-based decision making." Yet although these obligations "are the mainstay of public criticism of affirmative action," in fact such arguments are largely absent from Supreme Court opinions. Moreover, a review of the cases of the past two decades demonstrates "the increasing indifference on the part of conservative justices to whether disputed affirmative action programs had in fact disadvantaged better qualified nonminority candidates."

The Court has not used merit-based arguments because of "the particular facts of those cases. . . . In actual litigation a judge cannot or should not hypothesize at will the facts that would best support a given ideology, but must deal instead with the contentions of the parties and with the evidence in the record." In practice, however, conservative justices have tried to find grounds other than merit for objecting to race-conscious measures. But "no one of these [grounds] has been embraced by a consistent bloc of votes, let alone a persistent majority."

Schnapper argues that in practice it would be better—"more sensible and predictable"—for assessing the legality of affirmative action programs if the Court returned to a consideration of "significant, identifiable differences in the comparative merit" of individuals. "Any legal analysis of a program ought to begin with an objective, fact-based inquiry into whether merit principles are significantly affected by the disputed practices." Moreover, to the extent that the

Court has insisted on colorblindness, this has had the potentially perverse effect of conferring "on less qualified whites a right to protection from merit-based selections."

A review of the declining relevance of merit considerations may begin with the celebrated *DeFunis* case of 1974. Mario DeFunis, a white applicant, claimed he had wrongfully been denied entrance to the University of Washington Law School in favor of a less qualified minority applicant. In that case, Justice William O. Douglas, in dissent, argued that "any state-sponsored preference to one race over another . . . is violative of the Equal Protection Clause." Yet he "refused to conclude that the race-conscious selection process . . . was unconstitutional." He argued that "it would be impossible to determine accurately the comparative qualifications of applicants without taking their race into account."

By this Douglas meant to indicate that race could be an important consideration in determining qualification for the study and practice of law. The Law School admissions test, for example, was of questionable validity for minorities: the undergraduate record of a minority applicant might show even greater aptitude for the law when motivation and perseverance were taken into account. Over the long run a minority lawyer may well exceed in achievement the more conventionally qualified candidates. Finally, and perhaps most important, the minority lawyer may serve his or her community better. "Douglas believed it was . . . necessary to take into account the race of an applicant in order to evaluate his or her qualifications in a . . . 'racially neutral' manner." But the actual record of the case had not relied on the actual qualifications for law school, and "for Douglas, actual merit was to be accorded controlling importance."

The *Bakke* case of 1978 was similar in that when it reached the Court, the case had no record of merit considerations as regards race. In this case "Alan Bakke challenged the special admissions program for disadvantaged racial minorities" at the University of California at Davis. Justice Lewis Powell, who controlled the outcome of the case, believed like Justice Douglas that racial classifications might be required for a "fair appraisal of each individual's academic promise in the light of some cultural bias in grading or testing procedures." Although the issue of whether the admissions tests to medical school might be culturally biased was "arguably relevant," however, Powell decided the case "consciously ignorant of whether [differences in actual ability] in fact existed" because of their absence from the record.

In 1981, the white plaintiffs in *Minnick v. California Department of Corrections* "challenged the use of racial considerations in hiring,

25

promotions, and assignments." The state "defended the use of racial considerations as part of its efforts to deal with violence in the prisons." The Supreme Court, following the suggestion of Justice Douglas in his dissent on *DeFunis,* remanded the case for additional evidence and findings to clarify the ambiguities in the record concerning the justification for the use of racial considerations. The majority of the Court "seemed willing to uphold race-based decisions that were related to actual qualifications" that is in this case the race of a prison guard was a consideration in controlling inmate violence.

In 1986 the issue emerged in an educational setting, in *Wygant v. Jackson Board of Education.* The school board of Jackson, Mississippi, responding to racial tensions in the schools believed to be the result of laying off a disproportionate number of minority teachers in previous years, adopted a new policy: "future layoffs, although otherwise based on seniority, would not reduce the proportion of minority teachers." Thus, "more senior white teachers would be laid off, while less senior blacks were retained." Here too, when the case reached the Supreme Court, there was no evidence in the record to justify the disputed race-conscious layoff rule. The school board argued before the Court that minority teachers "brought an additional and important qualification to their jobs," as role models for black students. This argument was rejected by a plurality. "If in this instance there was a conflict between merit and colorblindness, Powell and the rest of the plurality preferred colorblindness."

In 1982 the issue arose in reference to gender in *Mississippi University for Women v. Hogan,* where an all-female nursing school defended its exclusion of males on the ground that their inclusion would have a harmful effect on the education of the female students. The Court agreed that, if true, this would justify excluding men. That is, "sex would be a critical indicator of qualification." But Justice Sandra Day O'Connor, in her opinion for the Court, argued that "the uncontroverted record reveals that . . . the presence of men in the classroom would not affect the performance of female nursing students." In fact, however, the case had never gone to trial (it had been dismissed on the district level prior to trial), and "the record contained no support for the school's factual assertions."

The record of these cases indicates that "there has been a marked change in the basis of judicial objections to affirmative action. In the early years, conservatives often asserted . . . that race-conscious actions would always be inconsistent with merit-based decisions." But this is a question of empirically determined fact. "Initially the conservative justices attempted to avoid the potential tension between merit-based and colorblind decision making by refusing to undertake any inquiry into that empirical question." And in recent years they have taken the position that colorblindness is preferable "regardless of whether color-conscious decisions might . . . result in the selection of better qualified individuals." But "a rigid requirement of color-blindness would forbid the selection of the best qualified, and would thus confer on less qualified whites a right to protection from . . . merit-based selections."

Schnapper observes that conservative Supreme Court justices,

> often unable for substantive or procedural reasons to insist that the white claimant was in fact the best qualified for the position . . . explored a number of other approaches for suggesting that the white did indeed have some claim on the position—that the race-conscious practice was not only an unacceptable procedure, but also . . . led to an improper result.

Thus, in the 1977 redistricting case of *United Jewish Organizations v. Carey*, Justices William Brennan and Byron White noted that the plaintiffs—a Hasidic sect—had not contended in their brief that, as a group, they had a right to representation. Justice Warren Burger stated simply that the plaintiffs had no such constitutional right.

In *Franks v. Bowman Transportation Co.* of 1976, there was clear evidence that the black plaintiffs had been refused employment because of their race. The question was how to deal with the existing white employees whose seniority now would be adversely affected if the plaintiffs were given compensatory seniority. The majority found that the white employees had no "indefeasibly vested rights con-ferred by the employment contract." But the chief justice dissented, arguing that "in every respect an innocent employee is comparable to a 'holder-in-due-course' of negotiable paper" and thus indeed has a protectable right. This right as propounded by Justice Burger was thus, according to Schnapper, "a species of property to which whites had a vested right." The other justices rejected Burger's view, since "it would stand the statute on its head to hold that such a competitive advantage over black workers, once unlawfully accorded to whites, becomes a vested entitlement" for the white workers.

Justice Burger's position was restated ten years later in *Wygant v. Jackson Board of Education* by other justices, when they invalidated the race-based layoff plan that adversely affected white teachers: they were to be considered innocent victims whose rights, even if narrowly construed, had been trammeled by a policy of racial preference.

But Justice Brennan, in *Johnson v. Transportation Agency*, "by framing the issue in terms of rights . . . increased the burden on the male worker objecting to the affirmative action plan." Writing for the majority he asserted that the petitioner had no absolute entitlement to the road dispatcher position. Justice O'Connor, concurring and "sensing the danger in reiterating her claim of white rights," dropped that language, insisting instead on the adverse consequences to the "interests" and "employment opportunities" of whites.

Conservative justices have also used the approach that entitlements to a job derive from "legitimate expectations" of the workers. Schnapper observes that "the argument sounds dangerously close to a suggestion that those jobs are by right white jobs . . . [;] that the spoils of invidious discrimination are some form of legitimate booty." A more focused version of the expectations argument relates expectations to seniority, a line of cases that stem from the 1977 *Teamsters v. United States*, which held that "bona fide seniority systems are immune from attack under Title VII." But this has been used in such a way as to suggest that there is a "Platonic" form of seniority quite apart from actual collective bargaining agreements: "several members of the Court regard seniority—not seniority rights as embodied in an applicable collective bargaining agreement, but seniority as such—as conveying . . . entitlement to a job or promotion."

Interestingly, there is a "consistent consensus" in the Court in favor of race-conscious measures, even if there is sharp division "as to whether race can ever be treated as a form of evidence of qualification." The agreement about the use of race-specific remedies concerns wrongs specifically racial in nature. "But while there is agreement that past discrimination provides a basis for race-conscious measures in some circumstances, there is . . . considerable disagreement about what those circumstances are." For this reason constraints have been applied to limit redress. The most important constraint is the limitation of redress against what is called "societal discrimination"—that is, a harm that follows from a general or historic discrimination. But to be redressed, such harms must, according to Justice Powell in the *Bakke* case, be based upon formal "judicial, legislative, or administrative findings of constitutional or statutory violations."

Schnapper is troubled by this and by a subsequent broadening of the position. In *Wygant*, Powell, joined by three other justices, wrote that even if societal discrimination existed, and regardless of whether it had actually caused a particular harm, it "was not an injustice that could ever be remedied by race-conscious measures." The difficulty, according to Schnapper, is the breadth of the assertion. Powell's "objection is not limited to vaguely defined past problems in society at large. *Any* act of discrimination other than by 'the governmental unit involved' " fell within his definition. An even more stringent position was adopted by Justice O'Connor in *Croson*, where she wrote that "evidence and findings are irrelevant as a matter of law" in societal discrimination issues, "because the type of discrimination to which they are directed can never justify race-conscious measures."

In Schnapper's view, the position of Justices Powell and O'Connor "do more than define remedial principles; they also establish a new white right."

> If a group of whites, or an individual, has obtained some advantage because of past discrimination, a state or city can use race-conscious measures to undo that special advantage only if the discrimination took place within the jurisdiction involved. . . . Race-based advantages obtained by whites outside a jurisdiction become absolute rights within that jurisdiction.

Schnapper concludes that the abandonment of a merit-based approach to affirmative action "does not necessarily reflect any hostility, or even indifference. . . . The central problem and impetus may be institutional and procedural. . . . Nonetheless, the Court would be more faithful to its responsibility to the country, and to the development of the law, if it were to restore comparative merit as a central issue in affirmative action litigation. . . . The greater the importance the courts attach to comparative merit, the more important that factor will be in decisions regarding . . . race-conscious measures. A more merit-based approach . . . would encourage employers and schools to take seriously the questions of . . . why the introduction of racial considerations will in fact result in a more accurate evaluation of qualifications."

Leon R. Kass, M.D., on Whether There Is a Right to Die. We come finally to a right whose troubling novelty not even Henry Shue disputes: the so-called right to die. Shue contends that it is reasonable to recognize such a right because medical technology "has created undreamed of possibilities for the cruel and gratuitous infliction of pain and suffering by doctors." But Leon Kass understands that this claim derives from one of the great achievements of modernity itself: "the power of medicine to preserve and prolong life." A consequence of this, however, is the possibility that many of us will "end our . . . lives in years of debility, dependence, and disgrace." Many patients remain "alive only because of sustained mechanical intervention," and more than 1.5 million deaths annually in the United States are "preceded by some explicit decision about stopping or not starting medical treatment."

The language of rights is ill-suited to either "sound personal decision making or to sensible public policy." Moreover, possibly the very notion of a "right to die" is "groundless and perhaps even logically incoherent." Nevertheless, because of the increasing support for a right to die in the courts and legislatures, "our society's willingness and ability to protect vulnerable life against the partisans of death hangs in the balance."

A philosophic reflection on the right to die "reveals the dangers and the limits of the . . . rights-based . . . political philosophy and jurisprudence to which we Americans are wedded." Moreover, "as the ultimate new right, grounded neither in nature nor in reason, it demonstrates the nihilistic implication of the new postliberal doctrine of rights, rooted in the self-creating will." A right to die is a "profoundly strange claim" in a society "founded on the primacy of the right to life."

Just what does a "right to life" mean? In contemporary usage, a right is a "species of liberty." Hobbes taught that a right is a *blameless liberty*—that is, we do not have a right to everything we might claim as such. Thus the freedom to take my life does not establish the right to do so. Rights are, "to begin with, political creatures," meant to protect "by deeming . . . blameless or rightful certain liberties that others are denying," as, for example, the "safety . . . of the individual against . . . the tyrant, king, or prelate."

To the classic negative rights, "modern thought has sought to add certain so-called welfare rights," or a rightful claim to goods that others, or government, must provide. But even this rights claim has its limitations, and "there are many good things that I may rightfully possess and enjoy, but to which I have no claim if they are lacking . . . ; making a claim and actually having a rightful claim to make are not identical." A "right to die," therefore, must be "a *justifiable* liberty or claim." Because rights also seem to entail obligations, it will become important "to consider what obligations on others" a right to die entails.

"What, then, might be meant by a right to die? . . . Why claim a right to what is not only unavoidable but is even . . . an evil?" The questions point to "our growing disenchantment with the biomedical project, which seeks, in principle, to prolong life indefinitely." The right to die often refers to a right to refuse life-sustaining medical interventions. But there is also a blurring of the distinction between the well-established right to refuse medical treatment and a right to

30

die. The former is based on avoiding an increased risk of death, while "the latter permits the refusal of therapy . . . *so that* death *will* occur."

Moreover, the claimed right to die often requires "positive assistance in bringing about" death. Thus it would better be called "a right *to become dead*, by *assistance* if necessary." Since this "looks a lot like a claim to a right to commit suicide," it has been argued that euthanasia "or medically assisted suicide" is derived from an alleged positive right to commit suicide. The proponents of a right to die indeed presuppose the permissibility of suicide, but go further: "They claim not only a right to attempt suicide but a right to succeed, and this means, in practice, a right to the deadly assistance of others." Thus, in its radical sense, a "right to die" is properly understood as "a right to become or to be made dead, by whatever means."

This formulation does not sit well with those who believe that the right to die is a matter of autonomy or moral dignity. For them "the right to die means either the right to self-command or the right to death with dignity." But in the end these claims also turn out to embrace a right "to *become dead*, with *assistance* if necessary."

But *who* has such a right? "Only those who are 'certifiably' terminally ill"? Or "those who are incurably ill . . . although definitely not dying"? Or "everyone, mentally competent or not"? Does a senile person have this right "if he is incapable of claiming it for himself?"

And "against whom or what is" the right asserted?

> The most radical formulations . . . are . . . the complaint of human pride against what our tyrannical tendencies lead us to experience as "cosmic injustice, directed against me." Here the ill-fated demand a right not to be ill-fated. . . . It thus becomes the business of the well-fated to correct nature's mistreatment of the ill-fated *by making them dead*.

There are of course a variety of reasons why such a right is being claimed: fear of living too long; fear of losing control; fear of becoming a burden on others. But there is also "much dishonesty and mischief afoot" on the part of the advocates of the right to die. The language of individual rights is being used "in order to shift the national attitudes regarding life and death . . . to make easier the practice of terminating 'useless' lives." There are those—children of the dying, hospital administrators—who have economic interests in decreasing the cost of caring for the dying, as well as those with "eugenic and aesthetic interests who are repelled by the prospect of a society in which the young and vigorous expend enormous energy to keep alive the virtually dead." It is better to "trumpet a right to die" rather than reveal true motives. Not all reasons are suspect, "but it might be dangerous folly to circumvent the grave need for prudence . . . by substituting . . . the confused yet absolutized" right to die. "Truth to tell, public discourse about moral matters in the United States is much impoverished by our eagerness to transform questions of the right and good into questions about individual rights."

Is there, then, a right to die? From the vantage point of the beginning of the teachings about natural right, of Thomas Hobbes and of John Locke, "the very notion of a *right* to die would be nonsensical." "Because death . . . is the evil whose avoidance is the condition of the possibility of my having any and all of my goods[,] . . . my rightful liberty to self-preservation . . . is the bedrock of all other rights and of all politically relevant morality." Although these thinkers were aware "that men might tire of life," it did not lead them "to nullify the right to life." Even Locke's notion that *"every man has a property in his own person,"* when properly understood as meaning that no man can be owned by another, does not provide a ground for a right "to become dead or to be made dead."

When we turn to the later thinkers, neither Jean-Jacques Rousseau nor, ironically, the great teacher of autonomy Immanuel Kant provided a basis for a right to die. For the latter, autonomy requires "acting in accordance . . . with one's rational will . . . , doing as one ought, as a rational being." But autonomy "has now come to mean 'doing as you please.' " It is "the triumph of the Nietzschean self, who finds reason just as enslaving as blind instinct."

Even within the bounds of the modern understanding of willful autonomy there is no ground for a right to die. On the basis of autonomy it is not possible to ground the right to someone else's assistance, nor that other person's right to kill me. And as regards "a liberty right (against interference) to an assisted death," this must be restricted to the mentally competent, and even this is not clear if it depends on instructions given years before the event. "Can my fifty-three-year-old self truly prescribe today the best interests for my seventy-five-year-old and senile self?"

It is, in the end, paradoxical "to say that our autonomy licenses an act that puts our autonomy permanently out of business." But it is this paradox that appeals to the Nietzschean creative selves, insofar as they "are not bound by normality or good sense." Such an individual "does not flinch before self-contradiction . . . most especially in self-negation . . . [;] who are we to deny him this form of self-expression?" "Here . . . is the only possible philosphical ground for a right to die: arbitrary will, backed by moral relativism. Which is to say, no ground at all."

Turning to American law, where "rights are still largely defined," it would be surprising to find a constitutional basis for a right to die, given the influence of Locke on the framers. "But the notorious due process clause of the Fourteenth Amendment, under the . . . oxymoronic 'substantive due process' interpretation, has provided such a possible peg." The Supreme Court took the Nancy Cruzan case *(Cruzan by Cruzan v. Director, Missouri Department of Health)* to consider "whether Cruzan has the *right* under the . . . Constitution" to require the hospital to withdraw life-sustaining equipment.

The Court held that the state of Missouri's "interest in safeguarding life allowed it to demand clear and convincing evidence that" an incompetent person "truly wished to withdraw from treatment." Chief Justice William Rehnquist, following Fourteenth Amendment precedent and relying on the doctrine of informed consent as required for medical invasion of the body, held that a competent person has a constitutionally protected liberty interest in refusing unwanted medical treatment. "But on the crucial question of whether the protected liberty interest . . . embraces also refusing *life-sustaining* food and water, Rehnquist waffled." The Justice wrote that "for the purposes of this case, we assume that the United States Constitution would grant a competent person a constitutionally protected right to refuse lifesaving hydration and nutrition." Kass argues that the justice "was willing to stipulate for the purposes of this case . . . a constitutionally protected right-to-refuse-treatment-so-that-death-will-occur." It was this stipulation, without the qualification "for the purposes of this case," that was heralded in the news media as establishing a constitutional right to die for competent persons.

It is clear from Justice O'Connor's opinion that, had the case involved a competent patient, she would have agreed with the four-person minority who were ready to grant it even to incompetents. Only Justice Antonin Scalia "seems to have gotten it right," Kass argues, "insisting that the Constitution has absolutely nothing to say in this matter." But paradoxically, Justice Scalia's argument, "which identifies the refusal of food and water as suicide, may come back to haunt us. . . . Should Justice O'Connor's view prevail"—that the right to refuse medical intervention *is* constitutionally protected—then "Justice Scalia's powerful intellect will have provided the reasons for regarding the newly protected right as indeed a right to die." The "painful irony" in this case is that the Fourteenth Amendment "prohibits the states from depriving persons not only of liberty but also of life and property."

There is a tragic meaning to the right to die. "Drunk on its political and scientific successes, modern thought and practice have abandoned the modest and moderate beginnings of political modernity." The "new rights" that are now asserted "have no connection to nature or to reason." But medical science "has found nature unwilling to roll over and play dead," and "the welcome triumphs against disease have been purchased at the price of the medicalized dehumanization of the end of life. . . . Fear of the very medical power we engaged to do battle against death now leads us to demand that it give us poison." The more natural human associations that we have always depended on in the face of our unavoidable decline, especially the family, have been weakened. "Vulnerable life will no longer be protected by the state, medicine will become a death-dealing profession."

The right to die exposes us to three specific dangers:

• The right to die as "assisted suicide," or euthanasia, "will translate into an obligation on the part of others to kill or help kill."

• "There can be no way to confine the practice to those who knowingly and freely request death."

• "The medical profession's devotion to heal and refusal to kill . . . will be permanently destroyed, and with it, patient trust and physicianly self-restraint."

But there is also a general danger from the abuse of the rhetoric of rights, which, after all, has a legitimate function of protecting individual life and liberty. The "extension of this rhetoric . . . beyond the limited area of life in which rights claims are clearly appropriate" distorts our understanding of these claims and "weaken[s] their respectability in their proper sphere. . . . We subvert the primacy and necessity of prudence by pretending that the assertion of rights will produce the best—and most moral—results."

Summary

Harvey Mansfield, reflecting on the evolution of opinions about rights, remarks that

> The new rights have been formulated more by philosophy professors than by political scientists. The philosophers forgot that liberalism was originally a doctrine of political science, concerned as much or more with the conditions under which rights are surrendered as with the establishment of rights—and concerned not at all with the elaboration of rights. Liberalism was originally a doctrine of constitutionalism; it was about the making of a government to control and to be controlled by the people . . . . [The Constitution's] form or structure secures rights by governing under law so

that the rule of the majority is the rule of a constitutional majority as opposed to a factious majority.

How might a political scientist regard some of the dictums of the moral philosophers and jurisprudents concerning rights? What is the constitutional—in the political, not the legal sense—significance of, say, Rawls's principle of justice as fairness, or the "difference principle"? Or of Dworkin's fundamental right to equal respect and concern?

He might begin by observing that the moral philosophers, curiously, do not seem to be much interested in or to see the connection between the form of an argument and an inquiry into human nature. Henry Shue rightly reminds us that arguments proceed dialectically in two directions—inductively up toward principles, and inferentially down toward conclusions—and that this procedure is Socratic. What he does not say is that Socrates' questioning—for example, What is justice?—was not conducted merely for the sake of generating arguments so that their form may be examined, or for the sake of a systematic moral theory, but as a way into the labyrinth of human nature, for the sake of exploring the best kind of life.

Similarly, Hobbes or Locke might observe that Rawls's "original position," precisely because of its analytic scruples in avoiding the epistemologically freighted term "nature," misses the point. The eighteenth-century political thinkers began their inquiry into human nature, as William Galston reminds us, from the political and historical facts of the post-Reformation wars of religion:

> Leading humanists . . . reacted (in Judith Shklar's formulation) by "putting cruelty first" . . . as the prime vice, by focusing on the fear cruelty engendered as the core evil, and by attempting to shape new political understandings.

In the "original position" the passions count for nothing; that seems to me why, as Susan Shell writes, Rawls can argue that individuals in that hypothetical and imaginary state

> would choose to maximize the lot of the least fortunate. Such attributes as talent or the willingness to work hard [are] construed as 'common assets' whose actual distribution is 'morally arbitrary' and conveys no implication as to the right of individuals to their fruit.

But in "the state of nature" the passions are decisive; all claims of right are equal and justice is accidental. The state of nature may be hypothetical for the sake of an inquiry, but it is assuredly not imaginary, as every American knows. It is, rather, a permanent

35

possibility existing *within* civil society, whenever a common judge with authority is lacking. In this condition of insecurity an individual above all wishes to be preserved in his good fortune and to be secured from ill fortune. The distribution of talent and the other goods of fortune may be morally arbitrary, but as regards the right to the fruits thereof, the political scientist would think it obtuse to ignore the impassioned difference between "mine" and "thine."

And then there is the view that *the* fundamental right is to "equal concern and respect"—that is, to human dignity. This is a most curious notion. Although the claim is made in the name of Kant's moral autonomy, or rational self-legislation, on its face it would seem to be a right founded upon psychological insecurity, upon a need to have one's identity confirmed. As such, it is curiously reminiscent of Rousseau's definition of the *bourgeois*, who is enslaved to the good opinion of others.[2] But this is also ironic, since Rousseau taught that only in a truly egalitarian democracy—no doubt also Dworkin's aspiration—can we be free of this false need. That is, for Rousseau, the dignity of a free man cannot be dependent upon the recognition by others of his need to be recognized—his shaky identity. Kant sought to solve this problem by the rigorous identification of reason and morality: again, the political scientist must ask where the passions are. The morally autonomous man does not seem to be a political being.

But beyond the problem of identity, this notion of human dignity as a right presents problems for the older right of the liberty of conscience. Can I recognize the dignity of another—his right to equal concern and respect—apart from his actions? In my conscience, I am free to reject certain actions as simply wrong. The person whose willful actions are to me repugnant forfeits his claim to my respect, and my concern for this person may be to see him punished. My right of liberty of conscience is in conflict with the right to equal concern and respect. I might agree in principle that all men have an intrinsic dignity, might believe the person redeemable, and on that basis might freely forgive the abhorrent actions. But I cannot be compelled to this in the name of the other's right to equal concern and respect.

This brings the political scientist finally to the constitutional question. Although a person cannot be compelled in his conscience, he most certainly can be compelled to pay a price by the law. The law is made by legislatures elected by constitutional majorities, and it is interpreted, at the highest level, by the antimajoritarian Supreme Court. The effect of the new rights is felt in both venues.

Constitutional majorities are composed of a multiplicity of overlapping interests and of sects. The former above all wish to be preserved in their good fortune and to be secured from ill fortune. The latter choose to live in the ways that their consciences approve. To the extent that right and justice are divorced from the fruit of one's talents and labor—that is, that one's interests cannot find a basis in justice, or that one's unearned good fortune may be justly treated as an ill-gotten gain (as Eric Schnapper argues), forfeitable to another idea of right—to that extent one pillar of the legitimacy of constitutional majorities, or interests, is undermined. And if religious sectarianism consists in placing conditions on the recognition of human dignity, and if those conditions are found by the judiciary to be illegitimate in the name of a new, unconditioned right to human dignity, then to this extent are the moral foundations of constitutional majorities undermined by the rule of a factional minority composed of an academic and legal aristocracy. As I have indicated, these foundations, by the very principles of the constitutional system, are the most dependent upon fortune and therefore the most fragile.

And to the extent that the new moral rights are imposed through national legislation, preempting the states, then majority faction replaces constitutional majorities.

The constitutional effects of these new rights therefore are twofold: they distort the function and exaggerate the strength of the judiciary at the expense of representative self-government. And they undermine the legitimacy of constitutional majorities.

2

How Present Conceptions of Human Rights Shape the Protection of Rights in the United States

Daniel J. Elazar

One of the most prominent features of American civil society is its recognition of individual rights as the basis for political organization and its protection of those rights as perhaps the major task of government. This idea, which is uncritically accepted by conventional opinion, represents only one conception of rights and must be understood as such. Moreover, even American conceptions of rights have changed since the time of the Revolution and the writing of the U.S. Constitution.

The conceptions discussed in this chapter refer to the views prevailing among those who reflect enlightened opinion in a particular civil society. Their conceptions usually come to be embodied in the predominant legal doctrine. They reflect the public standards of the time. I use the term "enlightened opinion" to refer to the self-perception of the opinion molders in the polity. In premodern times, enlightened opinion was usually concentrated in a distinctly separable elite that could be identified as the ruling class. In more democratic, modern, and postmodern times, it is less easy to distinguish such a ruling class in many countries. Nevertheless, it is possible to identify a political class consisting of those who are involved in political life and set its tone within broad guidelines.

Looking back at the development of the contemporary conception of rights, the transitions seem clear-cut and decisive. Philosophically they may have been, but politically matters were more complex. Moreover, ever since the apogee of the natural rights doctrine, the idea of individual rights has undergone further changes, both in what constitutes rights and in the understanding of how rights protect the individual against all corporate entities—not only the government or the state. The changes that have taken place may have made late twentieth-century American civil society as different in its conception of rights from the founding generation's conceptions as the latter's were from the late medieval expressions of obligations and liberties. That possible reality and the processes that have changed our understanding of individual rights are the subjects of our investigation.

The American Tradition of Rights

The American tradition of rights goes back to the first colonial foundings. From the beginning, those who came to American shores sought to protect their individuality and their liberties. One of the ways they chose to do so was to put those liberties in writing—to embody them in constitutional documents and to proclaim them publicly. Although the colonists did not believe that governing bodies could be formally bound by those constitutional documents in specific ways, they did believe that their governors were bound to make every effort to preserve those liberties. They believed also that the people should select or reject their governors on the basis of their willingness and ability to protect those liberties.

What we today refer to as the protection of rights was during the colonial period principally the acknowledgment and protection of liberties. In the United States this practice goes back at least as far as the Puritan settlement of New England in the 1630s. In 1641 the Massachusetts General Court adopted the "Body of Liberties," which defined what we today would refer to as the rights of the citizens and residents of the Commonwealth of Massachusetts. The issue was sharpened in the Glorious Revolution in England of 1688–1689 and in the Whig tradition that emerged from it. The English Bill of Rights (1688 old calendar, 1689 current calendar) was entitled "An Act for Declaring the Rights and Liberties of the Subject and Settling the Succession of the Crown." The Whigs, influenced by John Locke, changed the terms of the debate from liberties to rights.[1]

Here we encounter the roots of the struggle between federal and natural liberty. Elsewhere I have discussed these two forms of liberty as follows.[2] Natural liberty is unrestricted, the freedom of the state of nature, whether understood in terms of Thomas Hobbes or in Lockean terms. In the end it is the liberty that leads to anarchy, or the war of all against all. According to federal principles, proper liberty is federal liberty, that is, liberty to act according to the terms of the covenant *(foedus)* that calls the body politic into existence. Every proper polity is established by a pact among its constituents that is covenantal, insofar as it rests upon a shared moral sensibility and understanding, and it is legitimate insofar as it embodies the fundamental principles of human liberty and equality. Behavior that does not fit within those terms is, in effect, a violation of the covenant and a manifestation of anarchy. Hence it can be stopped and its perpetrators punished by the appropriate institutions of government.

In sum, federal liberty is liberty established by agreement. The content of any particular agreement may and will vary. Thus John Winthrop could understand true liberty as that flowing from the covenant between God and man, in which God dictated the terms of the agreement and man pledged to accept them. Conversely, James Wilson of Pennsylvania, one of the authors of the Constitution of 1787, could understand federal liberty as a strictly secular expression of the compact establishing civil society. When the Supreme Court of the United States today holds the state and federal governments to standards of behavior based upon the United States Constitution— even when the implementation of those standards places heavy restrictions on individual behavior—in effect it does so on the grounds that the Constitution is a compact entered into by the people of the United States. This compact, *inter alia*, delineates what constitutes federal liberty within the American system.

This discussion would not be complete if we did not recall that one of the basic tensions informing American civilization is the tension between natural and federal liberty. Admiration for the former has been expressed in various ways in American history, from the eighteenth-century ideal of the "noble savage," to the "natural man" of the nineteenth century, to "doin' what comes naturally" in the first half of the twentieth, to the "letting it all hang out" of our times. Indeed, natural liberty was clearly dominant in the land from the mid-1960s through the 1970s.

Federal liberty found its first expression in the theopolitical stance of the Puritans and has retained favor among those applying religious standards and moral expectations to the American people and their polity. These have included the eighteenth-century revolutionaries, the antislavery forces of the antebellum years, the Populists and Progressives of the late nineteenth century, and those who fought the civil rights battles of the 1950s and 1960s. All of the foregoing believed that people were not naturally free to commit certain wrongs, and that as citizens or residents of the United States, living under its Constitution, they could be required to act or refrain from acting in ways that violated the terms of that Constitution.

Federal liberty bridges the premodern and modern conceptions of rights and recognizes the relationship between obligation and right. In its original form, it grew out of the premodern notion of obligations that make liberties possible. In its modern form it is an effort to balance rights and obligations.[3] It has yet to acquire a postmodern form, although elements for defining a postmodern form of federal liberty can be discerned in current debates on the subject. When Abraham Lincoln declared in the Lincoln-Douglas debates that there is no right to do wrong, he was arguing from a position of federal liberty that seems to have been the basis of his position on the subject throughout his life. He may be said to have added the dimension of prudence to the formula—that is to say, that there are many things that should be prohibited or limited in terms of federal liberty. But prudence prevents government from undertaking to limit or to prohibit.

The Whigs changed the terminology but not the means of enforcement. Indeed, as Donald Lutz has demonstrated, the first American state constitutions, written during the Revolution, adopted declarations of rights in the Whig style, using the term rights instead of liberties. But they were declarations of eternal principles rather than specifically binding constitutional law.[4] At first the United Colonies, later the United States, followed the same pattern, beginning with the Declaration of Rights of the Stamp Act Congress in 1765. The Bill of Rights marked a new departure. No longer content with declarations of eternal principles, from the first it was considered to be binding constitutional law.

The original state bills or declarations of rights of the Revolutionary period reflected the hidden or open assumption that every individual was part of a community and as such was bound by certain communitarian obligations. Separately, the community was obligated to secure that individual's life, liberty, property, and the rights that flowed from them. They reflected the sense that natural law and rights meant a natural order. Not only did individuals have inalienable rights qua individuals, but nature itself required people to form civil societies properly, through covenant or compact, and to participate in communities of which they were an inalienable part.

41

Although it would be hard to say that these ideas were developed in a philosophically rigorous manner, they pervaded Whig thought and to that extent reflected the differences between Whig thought and the natural-rights, contractarian philosophers. Whatever sense of rights as including obligations has survived in the United States, has survived within the states. In the nineteenth century this view still had considerable power and was even recognized by the U.S. Supreme Court in the license cases that enabled the states to build up their police powers vis-à-vis the federal commerce power, primarily for the purpose of maintaining community and a common moral order.[5]

By 1791, then, two great transitions had taken place with regard to rights in American history: the first substantive, from the late medieval conception of liberties to a modern conception of rights; and the second procedural, from the idea that rights can at best be protected through hortatory declarations to the idea that they can be protected through binding constitutional law.

Protecting Rights through Proper Institutions

Part and parcel of the conception of the protection of rights in the writing of the U.S. Constitution was the principle embodied in the Constitution as originally written, before the Bill of Rights was added—namely, that the best way to protect rights was through proper institutions. The Bill of Rights went beyond that principle and even changed the terms of the debate. But from the adoption of the Constitution to the Civil War, the view that individual rights were constitutional rights, to be protected through proper employment of proper institutions, dominated American rights thinking. This was true in terms of Acts of Congress, as reflected in the Judiciary Act of 1789; in U.S. Supreme Court decisions; and in the efforts of the Southern states to use states' rights to preserve slavery and of the Northern states to interpose state law to nullify the application of the federal fugitive slave laws on the eve of the Civil War.

In general this was a period when the idea of natural rights gave way in prevailing opinion to that of constitutional rights, the task of institutions being the protection of the latter. Only those who doubted that American institutions could do so appealed beyond the Constitution to eternal rights, natural or divine.

In this respect, Hamilton and Madison's argument in *The Federalist* against a federal bill of rights had a life long beyond its rejection in the debate over the ratification of the 1787 Constitution. Like most Federalist ideas, it was rapidly diffused among the states, especially but not exclusively the new ones. Ironically, from the Federalists' perspective, the states became the principal arena for the use of institutions to secure rights. Through legal and eleemosynary reforms, the law as an institution was reformulated to allow the free incorporation of private associations, including private corporations and labor unions. This represented a radical change from common law and colonial practice, where every significant association had to receive a special charter from the legislature (an extension of the granting of a liberty); all corporations were quasi-public as a result, and labor unions were considered combinations in restraint of liberty. Eleemosynary reforms, such as reforms in the care of the insane, the poor, and the aged, were also designed to secure rights in a positive way.[6]

Legislatures did more for the protection of rights than courts, and these were mostly state legislatures. Reformers were active in their states to achieve these reforms through legislation, and even before that to expand the franchise to give ordinary people access to lawmaking and legislation, to protect the helpless when voting was not enough. Later this protection of rights was embodied in antimonopoly legislation. Monopoly was defined not as total control of a market but as holding back resources from development. It was considered a violation of rights, as in the Charles River Bridge case, and was attacked by both legislatures and courts. These attacks were embodied in the antimonopoly provisions of early American state constitutions, which were the first expressions of substantive due process in the United States. Federal involvement was principally confined to certain regulatory matters affecting interstate commerce.

This period culminated in the adoption of the Thirteenth, Fourteenth, and Fifteenth Amendments. They further clarified and concretized the constitutional basis of individual rights and of what constituted individual rights within the body politic. They provided new means for the enforcement of those rights through the courts as well as legislatures.

Property as the Principal Right

It was then that private property was raised in status to become the principal institution for maintaining rights in the minds of many. In a sense this can be understood as the reification of property rights. "Property" should be understood as a bundle of powers and opportunities. The ability to own and control the use of property was always considered very important, at least as an auxiliary means or precaution, and it was so recognized throughout the colonial and early national periods of American history.

Here, too, there were two dimensions. Property rights were defined to be the most important of all constitutional rights, and the protection of those rights was defined as the principal means of protecting all individual rights. In many respects this was a response to the needs of an advancing capitalist system, made possible by the elimination of slavery from the property rights argument. In other words, the Southerners had raised the property rights argument in defense of slavery prior to the Civil War, but to Northerners, so many of whom had opposed slavery, unrestricted support of property rights was unpalatable. After the war period, they could look at property rights without that burden.

The other point of emphasis was that of due process, which has a long history in the Anglo-American world—at least as far back as Chief Justice Sir Edward Coke. As developed in the late nineteenth-century United States, it was based on the idea of "taking"—the improper removal of the bundle of powers and opportunities that constituted property from some individual. Thus taxation, when duly enacted, could be considered constitutional; but if it was considered a "taking" it was subject to further tests. In those tests was some idea of productive use, although less than there had been in early nineteenth-century doctrine.

Substantive due process survives today in relation to property, equal protection, and privacy. With regard to property, the older form of substantive due process, it survives particularly in the states. With regard to equal protection, the U.S. Supreme Court has applied substantive due process to the criminal law to establish nationwide standards. Substantive due process in the field of privacy is connected with the postmodern conception of rights. Privacy is one of the new triad. It falls foursquare within the framework of substantive due process. In other words, privacy in certain matters cannot be abridged, no matter how nominally proper the procedures used to abridge it might be. This is certainly the argument of the pro-choice forces on the abortion issue.

Going hand in hand with the special status of property rights was the elevation of the right of contract to the same status. The U.S. Supreme Court invoked the Fourteenth Amendment to extend right-of-contract protection to new areas. In the years before World Wars I and II, the first generation of the twentieth century challenged the post–Civil War definition of individual rights as property rights because of the social problems which the application of that doctrine left in its wake for workers and farmers, for the urban middle classes and poor, and for blacks. To meet their needs a new sense of individual rights as civil rights began to develop, drawing on the Civil War amendments.

A leader in this change was the U.S. Supreme Court. It began to limit state interference with the civil rights of blacks under the terms of the Civil War amendments, and government interference with what are now known as First Amendment freedoms. By the end of that generation the principle of civil rights was well established in jurisprudence and in the public mind, with strong organizations promoting and lobbying for specific civil rights measures.

The Triumph of Civil Rights and the Shift to Human Rights

The idea of individual rights as civil rights triumphed in the 1950s and 1960s, reaching its apogee in the congressional legislation of the latter decade and in the court decisions positively interpreting that legislation, which carried over into the early 1970s. At the same time, civil rights increasingly came to mean individual rights in the starkest sense the right of every individual to be free of all but the most minimal external constraints, and certainly of all group constraints as distinct from governmental ones, deemed absolutely necessary for the maintenance of law and order.

Moreover, governments were forced to redefine and restrict their definition of what restraints were necessary to maintain law and order. In the colonial period the idea that the fabric of society had to be kept intact, even at the expense of individual liberties and rights, was all powerful; but even in the national period, from 1789 to the late 1940s, the maintenance of the social fabric was given equal billing with individual rights. After 1948 or thereabouts, maintaining the social fabric became distinctly secondary if not incidental in the face of individual rights challenges. As the idea of civil rights was winning its greatest victories, conceptually it was being replaced by a new idea gaining currency in the world—that of human rights.

The idea of human rights also had two dimensions. One was the elimination of external restraints on individual behavior to the maximum possible extent, and the second was the obligation of the state, government, and public institutions to provide for the individual's welfare to the maximum possible extent. In a sense this brought matters full circle. The idea of human rights was a return to the idea of natural rights but without "nature" or "nature's God." Moreover, human rights became the measure of the constitutionality serving as the measure of rights.[7] The question of rights was settled in favor of the individual human being, without regard to race, gender, ideology, creed, or increasingly, sexual orientation. But the idea of obligations and liberties was revived and applied to government and to these public institutions, which were defined as existing by virtue of their obligations to the individual and which were occasionally granted liberties to protect themselves and society. In other words, institutions had no rights. They were obligated to serve the individuals who constituted them or who came under their protection through some version of the individual rights doctrine. Few rights flowed from those obligations, just as few obligations flowed from the rights of individuals involved. That is where matters stand today.

The Postmodern Conception of Rights

The United States was born into the modern conception of rights. Although the first British colonists in North America did bring something of the premodern conception, their view was rapidly replaced or transformed by the modern conception. In one variant or another it dominated the United States until our time. Americans older than fifty represent the last generation to be raised in the modern conception of rights. Those younger than fifty have been raised in the postmodern conception. Hence we are at a turning point.

The postmodern conception of rights can be defined as including liberties and entitlements. Simply by virtue of being living persons, people are at liberty to do what they will, provided that what they do does not seriously infringe upon the rights of others to do the same. I emphasize "seriously." To take a relatively simple issue, divorce was once no more than tolerated out of necessity; it has now become a right. Everyone is now free to divorce as easily as possible. Yet it cannot be said that divorce does not infringe upon the rights of others. The rights of children to be raised in a family environment are clearly damaged by divorce, but this is not deemed an infringement serious enough to limit the right of divorce.

The second dimension is that of entitlements. Individuals are free to do almost anything, but the civil society, usually in its institutions of government, is expected to guarantee individuals their basic needs and more—in essence, entitlements. The so-called new rights, including the right to employment and to certain social benefits, are of this nature.[8]

Accompanying this shift is the loss of the general consensus that there is an Author of Nature. Belief in God is still the predominant popular belief in the world, reaching extraordinary proportions in some countries, including the United States. But the new image of God is one of a benign crutch who makes almost no demands other

46

than that we love one another. This God is no longer seen as the bestower or definer of rights and obligations, or even as the Author of Nature, from whose moral order rights and obligations flow. This causes matters to be much more fluid and easily fosters the new understanding of rights as liberties and entitlements.

One good example of this development is the shift from freedom of speech to freedom of expression as a right. Freedom of speech was developed as a social norm to realize a free and just society. It was concluded that in order for a free and just society to develop, individuals had to be free to express their opinions on public matters; *ergo*, freedom of speech became a norm. Freedom of expression, on the other hand, is an individual norm that has no social dimensions. It is simply assumed that every individual has a right to express himself or herself in any way he or she deems fit, not only through speech. No public purposes are required or necessarily involved.

Operationally, there was an equally great contrast. Postmodern constitutional thought looks to the guaranteeing of rights through judicial fiat, almost without regard to other institutional arrangements and relationships. Modern constitutional thought looks first to securing rights through institutions and only then to court intervention.

To further sharpen and clarify the contrast between modern and postmodern conceptions of rights, let me suggest that the principal modern rights—life, liberty, property, and the pursuit of happiness—were Aristotelian in nature. That is to say, they had some view of civil society as a comprehensive whole. The triad of postmodern rights—welfare, expression, and privacy as liberties and entitlements—are Epicurean in nature; they have to do with the individual, not with civil society. No social dimension is necessarily involved here. Indeed, the isolated individual takes precedence over any social dimension that might be introduced.

Antecedents and Deviations

In a sense, every conception of human rights must rest on the notion of a common humanity. Even as the idea of human rights differs from that of individual rights in that the former steps outside of the law, it emphasizes the common humanity of human beings in doing so. The prevailing premodern conception was one of obligations and liberties, either a covenental (biblical) or organic (classical) order that existed in the nature (or way) of things.[9] The modern conception began with individual natural rights, with nature in the empirical rather than the normative sense being the basis of universal order.

47

Natural order in this sense includes obligations but either does not link them with rights or gives rights precedence. The modern view was that natural rights were self-evident, but had to be discovered if they were to be transformed into political realities. Once discovered, they could then be extended by interpretation. In that system nature or nature's God was present as the justification.

A distinction was made between human and other forms of life. One of the characteristics of postmodern conceptions of rights is that all life is held sacred. Indeed, we are moving to the point where all life is held to be equally sacred—the right to life of the snail darter as important as that of the starving Ethiopian child or, more directly, of the unemployed Appalachian family.

The moderns discovered that natural law alone is not enough. Rights that are universal by natural law serve nobody, since they are unenforceable. The moderns therefore transformed the principle of natural rights into positive law through covenants, compacts, constitutions, and consent to overcome the difficulties of agreement as to their sources. Some still sought a divine source, others a source in nature with divine sanction, and still others a source in a self-propelled nature.

Regardless of the differences of opinion as to source, it was possible in the real world to obtain agreement about what was desired in the way of rights. Through consent, these agreements were embodied in positive law. Hence consent became the critical dimension in transforming natural rights into enforceable measures. In a sense the minimum consent response for human survival was to the Hobbesian covenants of peace that Hobbes proposed almost precisely in that spirit, as the rallying point around which all men could agree as necessary for their survival. It is important to note the relationship between rights and consent. Rights may be authoritative, but in practice they have authority only when accepted by the consent of the governed. Thus consent is the bridge between abstract rights and concrete behavior of civil society.

Modern natural rights had three dimensions: rights as justice, rights as liberties, and rights as exceptions. The first had to do with the social order as a whole, with how it became a just order, and with how individuals received justice within it. The second had more to do with individuals and what they were free or not free to do in civil society. The third represented civil society's release of individuals from obligations. The postmodern idea of rights was to add the idea of rights as entitlements as its contribution to all this.

Contemporary theories of rights are results-oriented. They are justified by the way they justify the cases they like. In other words, the theories first pick the result they want, then find a theory that will justify it. It is like shooting first and then drawing the target around the spot where the bullet hit. Among other things this has led to the revival of property rights in the form of entitlements, which represent a new property. The thrust of court cases in the United States and the European Community is toward securing entitlements from arbitrary withdrawal, including such items as drivers' licenses, previously considered a privilege and now increasingly considered an entitlement.

The new doctrine of rights treats the moral autonomy of the individual as an absolute. Ronald Dworkin, a leading postmodern theorist of rights, puts it this way: individual rights are trumps over the public good. This is the total reversal of the earlier understanding of rights as growing out of civil society.

The matter is carried further in that the effort to find the moral truth or the correct moral theory is replaced by relativism.[10] Whatever the moral beliefs of the people happen to be will determine what rights the people have. Under such circumstances, constitutionalism itself is challenged. Under the original theory, although constitutions could be interpreted often with great liberality and flexibility, still they had a veto over actions that went beyond a certain point—that is, were unconstitutional. That, indeed, was the whole purpose of a constitution. Under the relativistic conditions of the postmodern understanding of rights, the most that a constitution will have is a vote. This eliminates the whole purpose of constitutionalism and opens up unlimited possibilities for a relativistic system of rights and actions.

Individual and Group Rights

On the other side of the coin is an emergent balancing of individual and group rights. This is a result of the resurgence of primordial groups in the postmodern world. The modern epoch was devoted almost single-mindedly to replacing primordial group ties with asso-ciational ties, or transforming the former into the latter. The cosmo-politans of society, those who formed the enlightened opinion that set its tone by eliminating *gemeinshaft*, deemed the primordial group to be hopelessly reactionary and primitive.

Suddenly, in the postmodern world, primordial groups have reasserted themselves. Many people led by many intellectuals, appar-ently feeling alienated and cut loose as individuals, have sought the comfort of such links—as long as they are not too demanding, of course, and do not interfere with the triad of postmodern liberties and entitlements. Thus both the United Nations Declaration of Rights and the even more avant-garde European Declaration of Rights simultaneously emphasize the new individual rights of welfare, expression, and privacy, and then try to balance them with some provision for group rights as well.

The world has yet to find enduring institutional forms for balancing individual and group rights. It is clear to many that this is one of the most important constitutional tasks of our time. Perhaps federalism, both in the sense of federal liberty and in its institutional forms, will offer us a grounding from which to develop such constitutional and institutional relationships. To date it has shown some promise for doing so and some limitations as well, as in Yugoslavia.

The question is not only to recognize how modern liberal theories of rights have strengthened human freedom, particularly vis-à-vis the state but also vis-à-vis other humans; it is also to discover how, in extending these modern liberal ideas, their postmodern expressions have challenged the very assumption that civil society exists as an actor in its own right. One need not reify civil society any more than one should reify the state—one of the problems confronted by moderns in their development of the rights doctrine. But at this time, individuals must be able to have a collective expression through civil society or they will become isolated and alienated, the trust that maintains the sound social fabric will disappear, and law and order will break down. The result is likely to be totalitarianism, a particularly virulent form of reified statism, which is likely to emerge in response to the human desire for order as well as freedom.

The modern experience should have taught us postmoderns that individual human beings need some form of community, either benign and liberating or, failing that, harsh and oppressive. In any case, when the chips are down, people will prefer life in community to life in isolation and alienation. Community can exist only on the basis of mutual trust; without mutual trust laws are ineffective and social order breaks down. This lesson has been learned by anthropologists studying primitive societies, sociologists studying social pathology, and political scientists studying how different formal constitutions succeed or fail in different social environments. It has been a lesson notably unlearned by many rights extremists, who believe that every alleged violation of someone's rights is malicious and should be treated formalistically as such by law.

It is no accident that the renewed interest in civil society is being spearheaded by the leaders of the revolt against communism in Eastern Europe as part of the fight against their totalitarian, Communist past. We in the West would do well to learn from their experience, to confront our own excesses in the other direction.

3

Between Philosophy and History—
The Evolution of Rights in
American Thought

William A. Galston

It has been observed that political theory is situated between philosophy and history, partaking of both, congruent with neither. The temptation will always exist to reduce this tense duality to unity: to theorize about politics either as an unchanging structure of atemporal truths or as a realm of pure and manipulable contingency.

This duality and the resistance to it are clearly visible in that portion of political theory that concerns itself with rights. At the one extreme stand efforts to derive rights, content fixed for all time, from features of human nature and the human condition said to be permanent. At the other extreme stand the partisans of rights *du jour*, posited in response to intellectual fads and evanescent circumstances.

Preferable to either of these monisms is the effort to hold enduring structures and shifting contingencies in steady conjunction. Much can be learned about rights from philosophic inquiry into fundamental human interests and liberties. But rights must also (and equally) be viewed as historical achievements, as protections—devised and tested through time and practice—against many of the worst evils that can befall human beings, and especially those they can inflict upon one another. From this standpoint, a key task of practical philosophy is to reflect on these products of history: to search for underlying commonalities; to explore ambiguities of (and contradictions between) existing rights; to inquire whether, given added experience and changed circumstances, the purposes that initially guided the construction of particular rights might now warrant their extension or alteration.

This, at any rate, is the line I shall pursue. I begin by exploring the impact of history, politics, and moral philosophy on the contemporary understanding of rights. I then turn to recent controversies concerning the function, content, and bearers of rights, concluding with a brief exploration of the arenas within which the conflict between "old" and "new" rights has been most acute.

In the course of these reflections, two unifying functions of rights emerge: protecting certain interests deemed to be central to our conception of minimally decent human lives; and securing adequate scope for the exercise of individual agency. What also emerges (indeed, as a leitmotif of this essay) is the *incompleteness* of the language of rights. There is a gap between "I have a right to do X" and "X is the right thing to do," which can only be filled by a moral vocabulary broader than the language of rights. Equally important is the question of how we become agents capable of exercising rights responsibly; this is the point at which the discourse of rights gives way to issues of civic education and to the inquiry into the full range of influences on the formation of character in liberal societies.

One final introductory thought, which points again to the complex interplay of philosophy and history in framing our rights. Moral and political theory can help illuminate the rights that inhere in our existence qua human beings. But theory, however acute, cannot by itself specify the rights validly subject to institutional protection within specific political contexts. At least in a constitutional democracy, only those rights that are recognized and authorized by the people, directly or through the political processes they have previously authorized, can claim institutional protection.

I offer this crashingly obvious point only because many contemporary scholars seem to believe that if they can construct a compelling philosophical argument for right X, it follows that this right must somehow be present in the penumbras and emanations of the U.S. Constitution. This *may* be so for particular cases in which the philosophical argument comes to be seen as a compelling interpretation of existing constitutional provisions. But in many other cases, philosophy should be seen as offering an agenda, not of constitutional interpretation, but of constitutional reform. For example, those who want enforceable institutional protections for broadly construed "welfare rights" would do far better to work for explicit constitutional change than to maintain that John Rawls's difference principle can somehow be located within the four corners of the Fourteenth Amendment.

History

Contemporary discussions of rights are shaped by a complex historical inheritance. In this opening section I want to sketch what I take to be the most important historical tributaries flowing into today's sea of rights.

The post-Reformation wars of religion serve as a useful point of departure. Three different responses to this turbulent period have helped constitute our understanding of rights. To begin with, doctrinal clashes had helped spark an outburst of cruelty that shocked Europe. Leading humanists, chief among them Montaigne, reacted (in Judith Shklar's formulation) by "putting cruelty first"—that is, by identifying cruelty as the prime vice, by focusing on the fear cruelty engendered as the core evil, and by attempting to shape new political understandings and institutions that would reduce the amount of cruelty and fear in the world. As Shklar puts it,

> When one puts [cruelty] first one responds, as Montaigne did, to the acknowledgment that one fears nothing more than fear. The fear of fear does not require any further justification, because it is irreducible. It can be both the beginning and an end of political institutions such as rights. The first right is to be protected against the fear of cruelty. People have rights against this greatest of public vices.[1]

This focus on cruelty is echoed in the Eighth Amendment's prohibition against cruel and unusual punishment, and it makes a dramatic reappearance as one of the Atlantic Charter's "four freedoms"— freedom from fear—in response to the twentieth-century renewal of doctrinally-driven brutality.

A second response to religious warfare was an enhanced focus on the value of human life and the formulation of rights of self-preservation. The locus classicus is of course Hobbes, but life is first among the Lockean triad as well, and it figures prominently in both the Declaration of Independence and the Fifth Amendment. In our time, H. L. A. Hart has restated this thesis as the "minimum content of natural law."[2]

A third response to the wars of religion was the development of doctrines of toleration, rights of religious conscience, and the conception of a sphere of privacy, free from government interference, of which religion was the first (and is arguably still the most important) occupant. Locke's various letters on toleration constitute the fullest, if by no means the unique, statement of this thesis, the impact of which on the First Amendment—indeed, on American constitutionalism generally—can hardly be overestimated.[3]

The impact of Protestantism on the development of rights theories extended far beyond these responses to religious conflict. In its more radical forms, Protestantism preached the fundamental equality of human beings and translated this principle into a consensual theory of legitimacy. Perhaps the classic formulation of this relation appears in the 1647 Putney debates, when Colonel Rainboro, a leader of the radicals within the Parliamentary Army, declared,

> Really I think that the poorest he that is in England has a life to live as the richest he; and therefore truly, Sir, I think it's clear, that every man that is to live under a Government ought first by his own consent to put himself under that Government.[4]

In our time Gregory Vlastos has defended a secularized version of this argument, in the form of a distinction between the intrinsic equality of human worth and the various inequalities of individual merit and accomplishment.[5]

I have focused thus far on the consequences for rights of religious conflict. Parallel but equally consequential developments were of course occurring in the society and economy of early modern Europe: in particular, the breakdown of feudal and aristocratic systems under various pressures and their gradual replacement by conceptions of property as fungible individual holdings. The causal relation between historical and doctrinal change in this area has been subject to endless debate, as have the roles of (*inter alia*) Hobbes and the Harringtonian civic republicans. I do not intend to, and indeed cannot, usefully extend this debate here. Suffice it to say that by no later than Locke's *Second Treatise*, an enormously powerful revision of medieval property theory had made its appearance, in which full-blown property rights were grounded in self-ownership and labor and were limited only modestly by the rightful claims of others and by the valid acts of consent-based representative governments. Although the Declaration of Independence famously replaces the property leg of Locke's tripod with the more general pursuit of happiness, property rights binding on the national government reappear strongly in the Fifth Amendment, in language to be repeated and ultimately applied to the states through the Fourteenth.[6]

The encounter between systems of property rights and the dynamics of market economies, which roughly spanned the century between the 1830s and the 1930s, engendered important codicils to

Locke's initial bequest. In England, liberal thought after John Stuart Mill developed ideas of what we would now call welfare rights and reconceptualized the relation between individual holdings and the common good.[7] In the United States, the Progressive movement espoused a more collectivist and Hamiltonian doctrine of government economic policy, a move that laid the intellectual foundation for the New Deal.[8] As a broad generalization, it may be said that these developments had the effect of highlighting elements of the Lockean argument largely suppressed during the late eighteenth and early nineteenth centuries: the requirements of at least limited other-regardingness and the residual economic power of popular governments. The ensuing tension between the moral logic of individual holdings and of the general welfare has continued to characterize American politics and jurisprudence down to the present day.[9]

The sea of rights has been nourished by two other tributaries in the two centuries since the American Revolution. One is Immanuel Kant's understanding of individual autonomy and dignity, which in our time has influenced conceptions of rights from Robert Nozick on the libertarian right to Jurgen Habermas on the participatory left. John Rawls, surely the most influential liberal theorist of our time, has moved decisively in the past decade toward a more Kantian understanding of moral personality. One might speculate that Kant's renewed appeal is directly related to the interpretation (I would say misinterpretation) of pre-Kantian liberalism as rooted in self-interest and therefore as lacking in moral depth.[10]

The final source of the rights tradition is a conception of liberal individuality, shaped in response to the rise of liberal societies. One element of this is the line, running from von Humboldt to Mill and Tocqueville, that focuses on the social conditions for the preservation of human distinctiveness against the weight of egalitarian "mass society." Another is the more distinctively American heroic-Romantic tradition of Emerson, Thoreau, and Whitman, which (not without ambiguity) sees a rights-based democratic society as the arena within which various dramas of individuality may be enacted.[11] A third, developed most fully by Bernard Williams, sees personal character and integrity in tension with both utilitarian consequentialism and Kantian abstraction. The point of one's life, Williams argues, is to lead it as a distinct person with commitments to which one must hold fast, on pain of sacrificing what gives identity and meaning to life. From this standpoint, the purpose of moral theory and political institutions is to safeguard, so far as possible, the space within which these concrete individual life-projects can be adopted and carried out.[12]

In sum, I suggest that intellectual and institutional responses to three great historical events—religious conflict, the attenuation of feudal-aristocratic economies, and the rise of liberal societies—have engendered the categories within which contemporary discussion of rights is by and large carried out. Not that these events remain static and separate. On the contrary, what is most characteristic of the current discussion is the extent to which they intermingle in novel ways. For example, the much-disputed constitutional "right of privacy" would, if stabilized and solidified, lend to all manner of sexual relations the kind of protected sanctity once most characteristic of religious conscience. My point is only that a modest attention to history will help us understand why members of liberal societies today characteristically invoke certain concepts in response to the felt difficulties of our common life.

Politics

World events of the late 1980s have fundamentally transformed the rights discussion. Classic Marxist animadversions against "bourgeois rights" have all but disappeared, as have the moral equivalence arguments ("you stress political rights, we ensure economic rights") characteristic of Leninist regimes in the postwar era. Throughout the former Eastern bloc, traditional liberal rights are the focus of attention—in part because they were so systematically repressed for so long, in part because they are so crucial for the intellectuals who form the vanguard of the reform movements.

In one key respect, however, the debate has not changed. Rights are constitutive of liberalism as they are of no other political philosophy or practice. Doubts about rights tend strongly to reflect broader reservations about liberalism itself.

These reservations may take, and have taken, two forms. External reservations criticize liberalism and rights in the name of competing conceptions of politics and human life. Fascism, which upended the classic liberal preference for peace over war, was one such conception; today's Islamic fundamentalism is another. Internal reservations, by contrast, criticize liberal rights as inadequately realizing, or even thwarting, core principles that liberalism itself embraces (or at least does not wish to repudiate).

One such principle is democracy. In contemporary discussions, rights are seen as hostile to democracy in several respects. Democracy requires public and public-spirited action; rights sustain privacy and egoism. Democracy requires the capacity of the people to carry out their decisions; rights thwart even overwhelming majorities. Democracy requires popular sovereignty; rights imply sources of moral authority beyond popular will and tend to empower unrepresentative and unresponsive institutions, such as the judiciary.[13]

Supporters of liberal rights must and cheerfully will plead guilty to portions of this indictment: rights do thwart majorities and do restrict popular sovereignty. These supporters will go on to insist, with Jefferson and Lincoln, that democracy degenerates into the rule of force unless it is limited in this fashion; or to put the same point differently, that the moral force of democratic self-rule rests on a foundation of respect for individuals that limits the permissible scope of self-rule. I shall discuss these arguments further below.

Nor will liberals be much troubled, at least in one important sense, by the "privacy" count of the indictment. An important purpose of rights is to establish a zone of noninterference protected from invasion, or redefinition, by even the most popularly based government. Liberals must therefore reject the democratic thesis of Benjamin Barber that the public has "the responsibility to legislate not only its own common destiny but also the standards by which what is common and what is individual (what is public and what is private) are determined."[14]

There is, however, another sense of the privacy critique that is more fundamentally troubling. Liberals will not admit that the prime function of rights is to safeguard privacy. They will point out that rights also protect opportunities for participation: the right to vote, to assemble, to petition for redress, and many others. And clearly, freedom of speech and of the press are public- as well as (some would argue, far more than) private-regarding rights.

Nor, finally, will the charge of egoism be accepted; at least not as it stands. That the exercise of rights is consistent with a measure of self-interested behavior can hardly be denied. But rights do more than empower and protect individuals one by one. They form a system of conduct and constitute a regime. They ask each member of that regime to honor the rights of every other member and to respect all members as fellow rights-bearers. In a system of rights, then, permissible self-interest is constrained by prior moral commitments.[15]

An important and cautionary practical point, however, lies at the heart of the democratic critique of rights. As the zone of individual rights expands, the space for popular determination of policy contracts. Fred Siegel has summarized this argument:

> Democratic politics ideally revolves around the compromises needed to secure widespread consent for government actions. Representative government, which encourages citizen participation, leaves the losers in a political contest with part

of what they asked for or at least a feeling that their interests were considered. A judicialized politics, in contrast, by-passes public consent. Profoundly anti-democratic when it goes beyond vindicating the fundamental rights of citizen-ship, judicial politics alienates voters by placing public policy in the private hands of lawyers and litigants. And since rights are absolute, it polarizes by producing winner-take-all outcomes, in which the losers are likely to feel embittered. . . . [Moreover,] the assertion of rights fences off the propo-nents of policies from the social costs those policies impose on the public at large. . . . What is lost, then, if rights are interpreted so expansively as to define policy, is a concern for the cumulative consequences of individually rendered rights-based decisions.[16]

Siegel's argument reminds or should remind proponents of rights that their hyperexpansion is questionable as a matter of theory, and that in practice it may well lead to an erosion of support for the regime of basic rights and for their judicial protection. Clearly this debate cannot be fully joined until we have in hand a specification of rights that marks off the arena of rights from the realm of policy. But any conception of rights that leads to interminable incursions into the public's democratic authority will end by undermining itself.[17]

The critique of rights as insufficiently democratic is frequently accompanied by the charge that they are insufficiently egalitarian. This charge assumes a number of related but distinct guises: that rights protect unacceptably unequal outcomes; that social and eco-nomic inequalities dilute the meaning of rights for the least fortunate members of the community; and relatedly, that as formal legal powers they cannot be meaningful without collective efforts to provide every-one with the means to exercise them.

To some extent this is a debate not about the concept of rights, but about their substance. Much of it can be rephrased in the familiar dichotomy of liberty rights and welfare rights and can be placed in the context of the historic debate between classical liberalism and social democracy.[18] If there are enforceable rights to a "social mini-mum" or, alternatively, to a fair share of the social product as defined by generally accepted principles of justice, then the egalitarian cri-tique, which dines off the classic Marxist distinction between "merely formal" political freedom and "real" economic position, loses much of its force. Of course, this is not to say that the existence of such economic rights is obvious or incontestable.[19]

On the practical level, this argument may even be turned on its head. A. K. Sen, whose concern for the well-being of the least advantaged is both personal and passionate, has concluded on the basis of detailed empirical-historical inquiry that extreme welfare deprivations such as famines typically stem from the absence of classic liberal-democratic political rights and can be prevented by the exercise of such rights:

> The diverse political freedoms that are available in a democratic state, including regular elections, free newspapers, and freedom of speech (without government prohibition or censorship), must be seen as the real force behind the elimination of famines. . . . The negative freedoms of newspapers and opposition parties to criticize, publish and agitate can be powerful in safeguarding the elementary positive freedoms of the vulnerable population.[20]

Another line of argument erodes the distinction between liberty and welfare rights—and more broadly between negative rights of protection against others and positive rights of claims against others—by observing that the social enforcement of protective rights always involves a positive claim on or cost to the community as a whole. If, for example, every accused person has the right to a "speedy trial" and to "compulsory process for obtaining witnesses in his favor," then the community has an obligation to furnish the wherewithal to make these rights effective and real. And more generally, if individuals in society surrender a portion of their right of self-protection in return for civil protection of their right to life, then the community undertakes what may prove to be a very costly obligation to guard all its members against violence.[21]

When all is said and done, however, proponents of rights must acknowledge the persistence of significant inequalities. Even if all (normal) human beings are equal in their possession of rights and in the means needed to exercise them, a system of rights will allow a wide range of individual choice within which variations of preference, ambition, and talent are bound to manifest themselves in every sphere of endeavor. To give rights a central political position is to draw a line between required equality and permissible inequality. Partisans of a more comprehensive equality may object to the location of this line. If so, they must undertake to show that their own proposed boundary (which will require either the reduction or the redefinition of rights) is on balance more eligible.

Finally, we may briefly inspect the critique of rights from the standpoint of community. The core of this charge is that healthy political association requires a kind of sharing—not only agreement on common purposes, but also a network of affective ties. But while politics should connect us, rights divide us. They replace substantive purposes with formal procedures and, worse, the warmth and intimacy of fellow-feeling with the chilly distance of opposing claims. This does not mean that rights should be jettisoned altogether. It does at least require a fuller recognition of the extent to which a regime of rights is incomplete without, and depends upon, a sense of mutual connection and shared fate among all members of the community.[22]

Proponents of rights need not resist the claim that an effective system of rights requires some sense of identification among individual bearers of rights. They will observe that in the United States, a shared conception of individual rights goes some distance toward providing the common ground that makes such mutual identification possible—a phenomenon highlighted by U.S. naturalization procedures and by the typical sentiments of newly minted citizens. But while acknowledging the essential role of community in realizing the human good, defenders of rights will insist that a more basic role of political association lies in preventing disaster. As Jeremy Waldron has argued, we need rights most when affection fails. We need rights to reconsider damaged ties, to forge new ones, and to protect ourselves from the indifference or hostility of others.[23] Rights, then, are a kind of social safety net that secures our minimal expectations and wards off the worst case.

To summarize, within the sphere of political discourse, three main lines of rights-critique may be discerned. The first lies squarely within the liberal tradition. It accepts for the most part the liberal definition of rights and condemns the incompleteness or hypocrisy of liberal regimes that fail to extend these rights to all their members. This effort to generalize rights is frequently accompanied by an emphasis on the material conditions needed for the meaningful exercise of rights—for example, the public provision of qualified defense attorneys for the indigent accused. The argument, though, is not that rights need to be reconceived, but rather realized.

A second, more radical line of critique accepts the general concept of rights-discourse but takes issue with standard conceptions of rights. One strand of this critique, discussed above, focuses on economic welfare rights rather than on rights of social protection and political participation. A more far-reaching version, advanced by Roberto Unger, speaks of "destabilization rights" as empowering citizens to challenge all concentrations of capital and power.[24]

The third, most radical critique questions the entire category of rights as a way of describing and justifying political life. As we have seen, rights may be queried on the basis of (allegedly) competing

60

substantive values such as equality, democracy, community, affective ties, and gender-specificity. They may also be subjected to an internal critique designed to demonstrate their futility. For example, Mark Tushnet has argued that rights are inherently unstable and vulnerable to changes in social setting, are in principle indeterminate, and are empty, abstract reifications of meaningful human experiences.[25]

Clearly, defenders of rights must reject the most radical critique, although they can cheerfully concede that rights form only a part of a comprehensive political morality and do not function well if applied in abstraction from the other aspects of that morality. Conversely, defenders of rights must accept a substantial portion of the realization-of-rights thesis. Controversy is likely, however, along two dimensions: whether X is truly necessary as a means to the exercise of rights, and whether on balance it promotes or undermines the regime of rights. Debates over affirmative action revolve to some extent around these issues.

The intermediate critique, centering on the content of rights, may well prove the most perplexing, especially when proposed new rights come into practical conflict with older ones. For example, welfare rights can clash with established property rights, and the right of women and minorities not to be degraded may run afoul of the expansive definition of free speech characteristic of postwar constitutional jurisprudence. The extent to which these and other innovations are welcomed or resisted will be strongly influenced by one's stance on broader issues, such as the limits of liberal politics and the nature of a choiceworthy human life.

Moral Theory

Many of the political disagreements over rights find reflection and a measure of illumination within the debates characteristic of modern moral philosophy. Perhaps the best known of these is the conflict, real or alleged, between individual rights and collective ends. From the classic Benthamite standpoint, of course, all talk of natural rights is "nonsense upon stilts."[26] John Stuart Mill believed that personal liberty properly understood was compatible with general utility (again, properly understood)—a claim that has been exposed ever since to vast quantities of abuse and defense.[27] Today many sophisticated utilitarians argue that their theory supports and allows adequate scope for rights as now understood, while others contend with equal fervor that a choice between rights and utility cannot be indefinitely avoided.[28] Ronald Dworkin and Robert Nozick, two theorists with very different substantive conceptions of rights, have converged on the claim that the point of individual rights as a general concept is to block certain appeals to collective goals.[29] John Rawls, of course, has criticized utilitarianism for not taking seriously the separateness of persons. His own theory, as Dworkin suggests, accordingly (if tacitly) appeals to the very general right of each individual to equal concern and respect.[30]

I cannot hope to advance, let alone resolve, the debate on a topic of such scope and complexity. But two summary remarks may prove useful. First, it is most unlikely that there is nothing of substance at issue in this debate. Rather, what we have is mutually independent and normatively weighty considerations that frequently tug in opposing directions and that, in the absence of a common denominator of value, must be balanced against one another through intuition and common sense in specific cases.[31]

Rights-theorists are on strong ground when they appeal to sentiments of personal inviolability and to what G. A. Cohen has called "self-ownership"—the thought that "each person is the morally rightful owner of himself." As Cohen candidly acknowledges, many critics of rights

> lose confidence in their unqualified denial of the thesis of self-ownership when they are asked to consider who has the right to decide what should happen to, for example, their own eyes. They do not immediately agree that, were eye transplants easy to achieve, it would then be acceptable for the state to conscript potential eye donors into a lottery whose losers must yield an eye to beneficiaries who would otherwise be not one-eyed but blind.[32]

Conversely, utilitarians are on strong ground when they insist that at some point numbers matter—that is, that the consequences (for others affected) of honoring an individual's right will come at some level of scope and severity to appear intolerable. This position is only strengthened by the tendency of many theorists to trace the importance of rights to the importance of the interests they help to defend: at some point it will come to seem unreasonable to protect A's interest in X at the expense of the equivalent interests of B, C, . . . N.

The second remark is that precisely this tension between the perspectives of the individual and the collectivity is reflected in the charter documents of the United States. The Preamble to the Constitution depicts the purposes of the institutions it creates in decidedly collective terms: ensuring domestic tranquillity, providing for the common defense, and promoting the general welfare. Yet it also speaks of establishing justice and securing liberty, terms susceptible to a far more individualistic reading.

This tension is further heightened by the Bill of Rights. Many of its opponents held the Bill of Rights to be unnecessary because, as Alexander Hamilton said, the Constitution is itself a bill of rights.[33] Some even considered it potentially harmful because, as James Madison feared, any incomplete enumeration of the people's rights might warrant the mistaken conclusion that the others had been forfeited to the new government.[34] But to the best of my knowledge, none argued that a bill of rights would be inconsistent with the Constitution's principles and purposes. A tension between individual rights and collective purposes is thus built into the basic structure of American political institutions.

Indeed, the language in which some rights are expressed may be interpreted as bearing witness to this tension. Consider, for example, the Fourth Amendment, which protects individuals against "unreasonable" searches. The language of the amendment provides no standard of reasonableness, but it seems fair to suggest that one possible test is the balance between the extent of the contemplated violation of personal security and the weight of the public tranquillity, welfare, or defense interests at stake. That governments will constantly be tempted to justify intrusions by exaggerating or trumping up threats is true enough, but the task of weighing public against personal claims cannot be avoided. That task must, then, have an institutional locus, which Madison found in the judiciary:

> If a [bill of rights is] incorporated into the constitution, independent tribunals of justice will consider themselves in a peculiar manner the guardians of those rights; they will be an impenetrable bulwark against assumption of power in the legislative and executive; they will be naturally led to resist every encroachment upon rights. . . .[35]

It is not infrequently alleged that a rights-based regime is inherently defective in that it lacks shared purposes and a guiding conception of the common good. In at least one respect this charge is flatly mistaken: rights *are* shared ends, and they can be understood as constituting or promoting the common good. A claim of this sort is clear in the logic of the Declaration of Independence, along these lines: the two greatest human aspirations are said to be "safety" and "happiness." Our safety is best promoted by a government that secures the rights to life and liberty, while our happiness is best served by a regime that allows us to pursue our own understanding of happiness rather than seeking to provide it directly, by establishing a general public definition and furnishing the means for its attainment.

63

While this interpretation of rights as ends resolves the problem of the common good on one level, it reconstitutes it on another. Government secures rights by creating a general system of rights, but no guarantee ensures that in practice the rights of each individual will be compatible with those of all the rest. Robert Nozick has distinguished two ways of understanding public rights. In the first, rights are viewed as absolute and inviolable side constraints, and no individual may be deprived of rights in order to satisfy other claims and considerations. In the second, rights are viewed as goals to be achieved, and public policy is therefore understood as a "utilitarianism of rights" in which the goal is to maximize the exercise of rights over the community as a whole.[36] From this perspective, some individuals' rights may have to be modified or even abrogated to create the most extensive possible security for the rights, taken as a total system, of the community.

This originary ambiguity has roiled our politics and our jurisprudence ever since. One historical example is President Lincoln's controversial selective suspension of habeas corpus during the Civil War. A contemporary example is the Supreme Court's acceptance of police barricades on highways, at which all motorists are stopped and administered sobriety tests. For one plausible reading of the Fourth Amendment this procedure fails to satisfy the requirement of "probable cause," and the security of persons against "unreasonable searches" is therefore breached. But because drunken driving is among the most significant modern threats to the right to life announced in the Declaration, the Court was willing to accept, as the best defense of rights with all things considered, a procedure that in other contexts it might well have struck down as violating a basic right.

A very different range of issues is raised by the charge that the emphasis on rights must give short shrift to, or inappropriately subordinate, the claims of duty. Leo Strauss has observed that "premodern natural law doctrines taught the duties of man; if they paid any attention at all to his rights, they conceived of them as essentially derivative from his duties. . . . In the course of the seventeenth and eighteenth centuries a much greater emphasis was put on rights than had ever been done before."[37] Ronald Dworkin's influential trichotomy of goal-based, rights-based, and duty-based theories has lent the color of plausibility to the suspicion that taking rights seriously may entail treating duties less than seriously.[38]

Much may be said against this suspicion. To begin, without venturing into the endless technical discussions of the "correlativity of rights and duties," it is clear that many rights entail duties.[39] If I have a right to do X, then you have (at least) a duty not to prevent me from doing X. A system of permissions is simultaneously a system of exacting prohibitions.

Second, political philosophies emphasizing rights can coexist with moral philosophies that give pride of place to duty. It would be hard, for example, to accuse Kant of being unserious about duties, but in his political writings he tries to show how this focus might be combined with strict and extensive limits on the capacity of public authority to interfere with individuals.[40]

Third, some rights are simultaneously and equally duties. In the Declaration of Independence, for example, popular resistance to tyrannical oppression is characterized as both a right and a duty.

Finally, rights are not always proffered as a complete and comprehensive moral vocabulary. John Rawls, for example, proposes a theory of justice that includes—indeed, gives pride of place to— philosophical justification for a wide range of traditional constitutional rights. At the same time he speaks of the natural duty to uphold just institutions, and he proposes the "capacity for a sense of justice" as the aspect of individual moral personality needed to sustain that duty.[41]

This point—the incompleteness of rights—may be defended from another perspective as well. As Jeremy Waldron observes, the proposition that I have a right to do X hardly exhausts what we may say about X, morally speaking. There may be compelling moral reasons why I should not do X, and indeed my right to do it is in no sense a reason to do it. The right is addressed, in the first instance, to those other than myself, and it indicates the wrongness of interfering with me. To the extent that a right is a sufficient reason for action, it is such a reason for others, not for the rights-bearer.[42]

The moral incompleteness of rights extends far beyond duties. Joseph Raz has argued that rights-based theories cannot do justice to supererogation, the virtues, or morally significant reasons for action that transcend narrow duty. Such theories, he points out, have a hard time coming to grips with the social pursuit of intrinsically valuable goods that are collective rather than individual.[43] Raz's compelling argument is directed against the proposition that only rights are to be taken as fundamental, and that other moral categories are to be regarded as derivative from them. As he makes clear, however, it is not intended as a case against rights as such, but rather in favor of a "pluralistic understanding of the foundation of morality" in which rights, duties, and intrinsic values are equally fundamental.[44]

What Do Rights Do?

Many contemporary thinkers have focused on the functions rights perform in our moral and political life. This functional analysis frequently, and not unjustly, constitutes the point of departure for broader arguments about the foundation and content of rights.

Among these thinkers, the most common theme is that of *protection*. The details differ, of course. As we have seen, Judith Shklar emphasizes the fear individuals feel in the face of potentially cruel concentrations of power. Rights, then, represent the standpoint of the potential victims and, when adequately institutionalized, serve to protect these individuals against the various horrors that powerful, cruel forces can inflict upon them.[45]

Jeremy Waldron has made a similar, if more general point: a human right is "a moral position in relation to a particularly important type of individual interest" and helps secure that interest against dangerous invasion by others, especially (but not only) the state. In Waldron's view rights emerge as crucial, and they are most likely to come into play, when bonds of affection and identification become frayed. Rights are "fallbacks"—guarantees that individuals will continue to enjoy opportunities to make their own way, even when the content of their choices renders them highly unpopular, and even outcasts, in the eyes of their community.[46]

Ronald Dworkin has translated this concern for individual protection into the language of moral philosophy. The idea of individual rights, he argues, is

> parasitic on the dominant idea of utilitarianism, which is the idea of a collective goal of the community as a whole. Individual rights are political trumps held by individuals. Individuals have rights when, for some reason, a collective goal is not a sufficient justification for denying them what they wish, as individuals, to have or to do, or not a sufficient justification for imposing some loss or injury upon them.[47]

Dworkin goes on to argue, as do other theorists, that when we say someone has a right to do something we imply that it would be wrong (for the government as well as other individuals) to interfere with his doing it, or at least that some special grounds would be needed to justify interference in this arena. Rights protect individuals from the moral as well as physical force of collectivities.

The broad thesis that rights function as protections does not by itself specify what it is that rights protect. Further specifications may usefully be divided into two general categories. *Interest* theories suggest that rights protect goods and activities that benefit individuals. Such theories usually go on to argue that the goods and activities so protected are "high-order," essential for individual well-being. Without some ranking of goods and activities, it becomes

difficult to explain why some enjoy the special protection characteristic of rights while others are left to the vagaries of individual effort
or public policy.

Will theories, by contrast, assert that the prime function of rights
is to protect individual "authority, discretion, or control" in certain
areas of life. In this view, it is the individual's own decision-making
capacity that is protected against external intervention, even when
others believe that this capacity is being exercised in a manner that
contradicts the interests of the rights-bearing agent. Will theories,
then, readily can and typically do serve as fulcra for arguments
against paternalism.

Of course, will and interest theories need not be viewed as
antithetical. It might be argued, on the one hand, that specific rights
would not have been embraced unless they were somehow linked to
interests with which most individuals can identify; on the other hand,
this general linkage is compatible with specific choices—exercises of
rights—that work against the interests of the agents.[48]

Joel Feinberg offers a functional analysis of rights that is compatible with, but goes beyond, individual protection. Rights, he argues,
are intrinsically connected to the activity of claiming—that is, of
protesting against being wronged and of demanding one's due.
Claiming, in turn, is essential to the full expression of our humanity:
"Having rights enables us to 'stand up like men,' to look others in
the eye, and to feel in some fundamental way the equal of anyone.
To think of oneself as the holder of rights is not to be unduly but
properly proud, to have that minimal self respect that is necessary to
be worthy of the love and esteem of others."[49] Conversely, as Thomas
Hill goes on to argue, to undervalue one's rights is to manifest the
vice of "servility." Within this context, then, rights may be seen as
serving the quasi-Aristotelian moral function of enabling us to hit the
mean between servility and the opposing vice of arrogance (overval-
uing one's own claims vis-à-vis others).[50]

What Rights Do We Have?

I turn now from the function of rights to their content. Here the
discussion may usefully be divided into general (philosophical) rights
and particular rights, such as those found in the Bill of Rights.

I will not tarry long at the first category. For present purposes it
must suffice to observe that several influential but mutually incompatible proposals have surfaced in the past generation. As we have
seen, H. L. A. Hart argued that there is an *ur*-right: the equal right of
all to be free. Ronald Dworkin responded with a critique of any

general right to liberty and proposed instead a fundamental right possessed by all individuals to equal concern and respect, from which particular rights, including specific kinds of liberties, may be inferred.[51] Joel Feinberg has suggested a triad of fundamental rights: the right to fair treatment, the right not to be treated cruelly or inhumanely, and the right not to be subjected to degradation and exploitation—even when such treatment is both painless and acceptable to the victim.[52] Taking as his point of departure the clash of human interests, the great variety of human conceptions of the good, and the *libido dominandi* that inclines some to impose their interests and conceptions on others, Stuart Hampshire argues that society most requires a form of procedural justice that substitutes rule-guided discussion and negotiation for conquest and terror. From this standpoint, the core human right is that of participating (or at least being fairly represented) in the procedures by which deep conflicts are adjudicated.[53]

Under the rubric of particular rights, the area of agreement among contemporary thinkers is more substantial:

1. A right to life is generally acknowledged, although according to the Fifth Amendment life may be forfeit (as may liberty and property) under certain conditions. Contemporary controversy over the right to life revolves around its scope and reach. Pro-choice and pro-life advocates disagree whether fetuses are "persons" within the meaning of the right. Those who favor the death penalty for criminals point to the language of the Bill of Rights, while those who oppose it argue that the right to life cannot be reconciled with the state-sanctioned taking of life.

2. Also subject to general agreement is a range of rights of personal protection: against slavery and personal servitude; against cruel and unusual punishment and torture; against arbitrary searches, arrest, imprisonment, and seizure or confiscation; and against invasions of religious, intellectual, and expressive freedom. To be sure, there is debate at the margin of some of these protections. For example, what does the right of free religious exercise require in certain complex cases, and how is it related to valid secular goals the state may wish to promote? Does the freedom of expression in all instances protect pornographic, racist, or abusive communications?

3. These rights of personal protection are bolstered by the right of all persons to the equal protection of the laws and by the various rights that define and help ensure fair trials. It is worth recalling that fully half the amendments in the Bill of Rights deal with the rights of accused persons.

4. Even if there is no general right to or presumption in favor of liberty, rights secure a wide range of particular liberties: among them, the freedoms to travel, to marry or not marry, to choose and follow a profession, to associate with others, to own and freely dispose of personal property. Taken together, these rights not only secure areas of liberty but also provide concrete opportunities for the "pursuit of happiness" invoked in the Declaration of Independence. Many liberty-rights, of course, engender problems of application. Is the right to travel infringed by foreign policy limitations on access to terrorist nations? Is the right to marry infringed by particular state definitions of marriageable partners?

5. Finally, rights of participation help both to secure and protect all other rights and to ensure that government remains rooted in the consent of the people, as the principles of liberal legitimacy require. These rights include: fair access to citizenship for all residents within a political jurisdiction; the equal treatment of all citizens; free political speech and assembly and the meaningful ability to bring grievances before public authority for redress; the receipt of all information needed to carry out the activities of citizenship; and a fair opportunity to gain offices of public trust and responsibility.[54]

Throughout this enumeration, I have indicated that even well-established rights give rise to controversies over their application. Other rights are more controversial still; their very existence is in dispute:

1. Above and beyond particular liberties and immunities, is there a "right of privacy" that protects individuals against public interference in, for example, matters of sexual orientation, practice, and expression? Within U.S. constitutional adjudication, this question has arisen in areas such as contraception and homosexuality and has frequently revolved around interpretations of the Ninth Amendment. But the issue is much broader and older than the public conflicts of the past quarter-century. It found classic expression in John Stuart Mill's famous "harm principle" and in the much-discussed distinction between public- and private-regarding action. It resurfaced in the Hart-Devlin debate, which reverberated across the Atlantic. And it continues to roil the waters of American politics today. Partisans of privacy rights appeal to equal respect for (and dignity of) each individual and to mistrust of government intrusion; opponents insist not only that local majorities have rights to defend their own moral conceptions, but also that liberal society cannot safely be as latitudinarian in matters of sexual conduct as the partisans believe.[55]

2. A second contested right is that of property. As I suggested earlier, the modern form of this contest is rooted in the European conflict between classical liberalism and social democracy, and in the parallel American conflict between laissez-faire and Progressive nationalism. Today some philosophers affirm a far-reaching right of property, while others either deny such a right or place it on the shifting sands of social utility.[56] Questions of "personal" property (housing, transportation, clothing, and the like) are uncontroversial. The issue is debated along two other dimensions. Some affirm, while others deny, that there is a right to private ownership of the means of production—a dispute detachable from the question of whether socialized production is prudent and efficient.[57] And some advance, while others resist, the proposition that the typical activities of the modern regulatory state amount to public "taking" of private property without just compensation, and thus to practical nullification of a core moral entitlement.[58]

3. A third area of contestation is that of "welfare rights"—guaranteed entitlements to basic levels of material provision and opportunity. As I suggested earlier,[59] this category of proposed rights emerged in the European struggle to address some of the unwanted consequences of market economies. It was crystallized in Articles 23 through 26 of the postwar Universal Declaration of Human Rights, which enumerated guarantees of employment, material decency, adequate leisure, and education. It surfaced in the United States in the 1960s and 1970s in the effort to read John Rawls's "difference principle" into the Fourteenth Amendment.

Amidst what has become a rather murky debate, three points seem evident. First, unlike other kinds of interests protected by rights, the ability of governments to secure individual material welfare is dependent to a considerable degree on each country's level of material well-being and on the specific circumstances in which it finds itself.

Second, whatever their standing may be in liberal theory (and views differ sharply), minimum welfare guarantees cannot easily be located in (or crammed into) the Bill of Rights, or indeed in any other provisions of the U.S. Constitution as it now stands.

Third, while welfare is not a free-standing and independent claim within the U.S. constitutional framework, specific welfare provisions may enjoy a kind of derivative status as the means needed to carry into practice the rights that are guaranteed explicitly or by clear implication. The right to public provision of legal counsel for indigent defendants is one clear case. More broadly, it might well be argued that citizenship guarantees are devalued unless all persons are given the opportunity to equip themselves to exercise the privileges and responsibilities of citizenship. From this perspective, access to education verges on an implied derivative right for all.

A final observation: liberal conceptions of citizenship stress the duty of independence—the obligation of all (unimpaired) adults to provide for themselves and their families. In modern market economies, the individual's ability to fulfill this duty is in part a function of circumstances outside each individual's control (as became painfully evident during the Great Depression). From this standpoint, entitlements to collective material provision might well be regarded as latent and contingent—that is, as activated if and when economic circumstances make it impossible for individuals to achieve full independence through their own efforts.

Who Are the Bearers of Rights?

The central, least problematic case for the analysis of rights is the normally developed adult human being. Matters become more complex when we move to what Kent Greenawalt has called "borderlines of status": children, the handicapped, fetuses, animals, and even vegetation and inanimate nature. Each of these cases has given rise to complex and emotionally charged debates. No one doubts that children and the handicapped have important rights; the chief difficulty is rather to define those rights of normal adults that members of these categories lack, and conversely those rights that are peculiar to them. The question of fetal rights is of course entangled with the intractable abortion debate. Proponents of animal rights have tended to focus on animals' capacity to feel pleasure and pain and to argue that they therefore possess much the same right to have their subjective sensations taken into account as do human beings. Not surprisingly, utilitarians have an easier time with animal rights than do Kantians. Rights-questions involving plants and inanimate objects have come to the fore with the rise of environmental concerns, though in these cases most theorists believe that moral categories other than rights are more useful and revealing.[60]

A final issue, heatedly debated in the United States in the controversy over affirmative action and increasingly salient for Canada and Europe as well, is whether groups as well as individuals may reasonably be regarded as rights-bearers. A remote antecedent of this debate is the distinction, evident in the Declaration of Independence, between the rights of individuals and of "peoples." The document's opening sentence proclaims the necessity of dissolving the political bands connecting one *people* with another. A bit later, the right of altering or abolishing forms of government is assigned to the people as a whole. For current purposes, the key point is that a "people" is not necessarily coextensive with the full citizen-body of an existing political community; communities may include several peoples, linked politically. A people, then, is an internally unified collectivity standing between individuals and the political community.

This transition from individuals to subnational peoples is critical because, to state the obvious, the Declaration is not simply invoking a Lockean right of revolution. The object is not to alter or abolish Great Britain's form of government, but rather to separate from it. There must, then, be some basis upon which a subnational community can invoke a right of separation. One need not go all the way down Garry Wills's road to agree that peoples are in part constituted by bonds of birth, affection, and memory.[61] That is why the colonists appealed to their "British brethren" on grounds of history and consanguinity as well as justice. The "necessity" of the separation of peoples announced at the beginning of the Declaration is explained at the end as the attenuation of affective ties between them. The collapse of Canada's Meech Lake accords and the recrudescence of subnational ethnic loyalties in Central Europe may well provide new arenas in our time for such acts of political self-assertion and for tests of their validity.

Although a strong case can be made that the treatment of individuals is the appropriate benchmark of liberal social justice, many dissenters have argued that liberalism cannot proceed in complete disregard of the fact of subnational group identity and the history of intergroup injustice. On the practical level, the United States has adopted a somewhat obfuscatory muddle-through policy that has left many on both sides unsatisfied. The debate over the Civil Rights Act of 1990 again raised the linkage between group rights and quotas, an issue that is sure to agitate American politics for years to come.[62]

Conclusion

Throughout this essay I have stressed the connection between rights and liberalism. Historically and down to the present day, doubts about rights have been embedded in broader reservations about the liberal enterprise. Over time, of course, the focus of these reservations has changed. Liberalism today is engaged neither in the grand seventeenth- and eighteenth-century contest with patriarchal monarchy and feudal aristocracy nor in the desperate struggle with fascism and communism that has dominated so much of the twentieth century. Most contemporary critics are inclined to argue, not that liberal rights are misguided or covertly repressive, but rather that they are one-sided and incomplete; that societies wholly preoccupied with claiming and exercising rights cannot provide scope for a fully rounded and worthy human existence.

Much must, I think, be conceded to these critics. The premise "I have a right to do X" does not remotely warrant the conclusion that "X is the right thing to do." Liberal theorists have not worked nearly hard enough to flesh out the conception of "rightness" that forms an indispensable complement to rights, and contemporary liberal education has done little to fill this gap. Neither have liberals paid enough attention to the role of responsibilities, duties, and virtues in the constitution of personal and social life. They have acknowledged grudgingly, or not at all, the essential contributions to liberalism of associations (such as religion and the family) that are not themselves structured by the concept and practice of rights. Neither, finally, have contemporary liberals focused adequately on the kinds of goals and goods that liberal societies characteristically pursue, or on the resulting balance that must be struck between goal-based and rights-based considerations. These and similar considerations, in my judgment, lie at the heart of liberalism's future agenda.

Let me translate these concerns into the language of rights. Broadly speaking, there are three kinds of obstacles to the achievement of individual purposes and the attainment of a choiceworthy life. First, other individuals may intervene to prevent us from pursuing our good. Rights are the best protection the human race has yet devised against such threats. Second, we may be thwarted by a scarcity of external goods—things available for use, or other individuals ready to cooperate. Here rights can be of considerable assistance, but other things are needed as well—principles of distributive justice, sentiments of social solidarity, and institutions that artfully link individual and collective goods. Finally, we may be thwarted by internal incapacities—deficiencies of mind or character. Here rights have relatively little to say, because the underlying issue is how we become agents capable (among other excellences) of exercising rights prudently and responsibly. This is the point at which the discourse of rights gives way to the classic questions of *paideia*, and at which we must concern ourselves with the full range of influences on the formation of character in liberal societies.

For centuries liberals have argued that coercion deprives acts of moral meaning. Unless individuals can author, and thus identify with, their deeds, their compliance with external norms is worth little. Rights protect the individual's ability to choose his acts and embrace them as his own.

The liberal emphasis on internally produced action is not misplaced, but it is incomplete. Fully worthy acts have both an internal dimension (self-origination) and an external dimension (correctness or appropriateness). Liberal practical philosophy has long excelled at the defense of individual choice; it must now learn how to provide standards for the right exercise of rights. Without such supplement, a system of rights cannot coherently distinguish between liberty and license. In the long run, prospects for societies without the inner resources to defend such a distinction cannot be regarded as bright.

4

Is There a Right to Die?

Leon R. Kass

It has been fashionable, for some time now and in many aspects of American public life, for people to demand what they want or need as a matter of rights. During the past few decades we have heard claims of a right to health or health care, a right to education or employment, a right to privacy (embracing also a right to abort or to enjoy pornography, or to commit suicide or sodomy), a right to clean air, a right to dance naked, a right to be born, and a right not to have been born. Most recently we have been presented with the ultimate new rights claim, a "right to die."

This claim has surfaced in the context of changed circumstances and burgeoning concerns regarding the end of life. Thanks in part to the power of medicine to preserve and prolong life, many of us are fated to end our once-flourishing lives in years of debility, dependence, and disgrace. Thanks to the respirator and other powerful technologies that can, all by themselves, hold comatose and other severely debilitated patients on this side of the line between life and death, many who would be dead are alive only because of sustained mechanical intervention. Of the 2.2 million annual deaths in the United States, 80 percent occur in health-care facilities; in roughly 1.5 million of these cases, death is preceded by some explicit decision about stopping or not starting medical treatment. Thus, death in America is not only medically managed, but its timing is also increasingly subject to deliberate choice. It is from this background that the claims of a right to die emerge.

I do not think that the language and approach of rights are well-

75

suited either to sound personal decision making or to sensible public policy in this very difficult and troubling matter. In most of the heart-rending end-of-life situations, it is hard enough for practical wisdom to try to figure out what is morally right and humanly good, without having to contend with intransigent and absolute demands of a legal or moral right to die. And, on both philosophical and legal grounds, I am from the start inclined to believe that there can be no such thing as a *right* to die—that the notion is groundless and perhaps even logically incoherent. Even its proponents usually put "right to die" in quotation marks, acknowledging that it is at best a misnomer.

Nevertheless, we cannot simply dismiss this claim, for it raises important and interesting practical and philosophical questions. Practically, a right to die is increasingly asserted and gaining popular strength; increasingly, we see it in print without the quotation marks. The former Euthanasia Society of America, shedding the Nazi-tainted and easily criticized "E" word, has changed its name to the more politically correct Society for the Right to Die. End-of-life cases coming before the courts, nearly always making their arguments in terms of rights, have gained support for some sort of "right to die." The one case to be decided by a conservative Supreme Court, the *Cruzan* case, has advanced the cause, as I will show later.

The voter initiatives to legalize physician-assisted suicide and euthanasia in Washington and California were narrowly defeated, in part because they were badly drafted laws; yet the proponents of such practices seem to be winning the larger social battle over principle. According to several public-opinion polls, most Americans now believe that "if life is miserable, one has the right to get out, actively and with help if necessary." Although the burden of philosophical proof for establishing new rights (especially one as bizarre as a "right to die") should always fall on the proponents, the social burden of proof has shifted to those who would oppose the voluntary choice for death through assisted suicide. Thus it has become politically necessary—and, at the same time, exceedingly difficult—to make principled arguments about why doctors must not kill, about why euthanasia is not the proper human response to human finitude, and about why there is no right to die, natural or constitutional. This is not a merely academic matter: our society's willingness and ability to protect vulnerable life hang in the balance.

An examination of "right to die" is even more interesting philosophically. It reveals the dangers and the limits of the liberal—that is, rights-based—political philosophy and jurisprudence to which we Americans are wedded. As the ultimate new right, grounded neither in nature nor in reason, it demonstrates the nihilistic implication of the new postliberal doctrine of rights, rooted in the self-creating will. And as liberal society's response to the bittersweet victories of the medical project to conquer death, it reveals in pure form the tragic meaning of the entire modern project, both scientific and political.

The claim of a right to die is made only in Western liberal societies—not surprisingly, for only in Western liberal societies do men look first to the rights of individuals. Also, only here do we find the high-tech medicine capable of keeping people from dying when they might wish. Yet the claim of a right to die is also a profoundly strange claim, especially in liberal society, which is founded on the primacy of the right to life. We Americans hold as a self-evident truth that governments exist to secure inalienable rights, first of all, to self-preservation; now we are being encouraged to use government to secure a putative right of self-destruction. A "right to die" is surely strange and unprecedented, and hardly innocent. Accordingly, we need to consider carefully (1) what it could possibly mean; (2) why it is being asserted; and (3) whether it really exists—that is, whether it can be given a principled grounding or defense.

Right to Die: What Does It Mean?

Though the major ambiguity concerns the substance of the right—namely, to die—we begin by reminding ourselves of what it means, in general, to say that someone has a *right* to something. I depart for now from the original notion of *natural* rights, and indeed abstract altogether from the question of the source of rights. I focus instead on our contemporary usage, for it is only in contemporary usage that this current claim of a right to die can be understood.

A right—whether legal or moral—is not identical to a need or a desire or an interest or a capacity. I may have both a need and a desire for, and also an interest in, the possessions of another, and the capacity or power to take them by force or stealth—yet I can hardly be said to have a right to them. A right, to begin with, is a species of liberty. Thomas Hobbes, the first teacher of rights, held a right to be a *blameless* liberty. Not everything we are free to do—morally or legally—do we have a right to do: I may be at *liberty* to wear offensive perfumes or to sass my parents or to engage in unnatural sex, but it does not follow that I have a right to do so. Even the decriminalization of a once-forbidden act does not yet establish a legal right, not even if I can give reasons for doing it. Thus, the freedom to take my life—"I have inclination, means, reasons, opportunity, and you cannot stop me, and it is not against the law"—does not suffice to establish the *right* to take my life. A true right would be at least a blameless or permitted liberty, at best a praiseworthy or even rightful liberty, to do or not to do, without anyone else's interference or opposition.

Historically, the likelihood of outside interference and opposition was in fact the necessary condition for the assertion of rights. Rights were and are, to begin with, political creatures, the first principles of liberal politics. The rhetoric of claiming rights, which are in principle always absolute and unconditional, performs an important function of defense, but only because the sphere of life in which they are asserted is limited. Rights are asserted to protect, by deeming them blameless or rightful, certain liberties that others are denying or threatening to curtail. Rights are claimed to defend the safety and dignity of the individual against the dominion of tyrant, king, or prelate and against those high-minded moralizers and zealous meddlers who seek to save man's soul or to preserve his honor at the cost of his life and liberty.

To these more classical, negative rights against interference with our liberties, modern thought has sought to add certain so-called welfare rights—rights that entitle us to certain opportunities or goods to which, it is argued, we have a rightful claim on others, usually government, to provide. The rhetoric of welfare rights extends the power of absolute and unqualified claims beyond the goals of defense against tyranny and beyond the limited sphere of endangered liberties; for these reasons their legitimacy *as rights* is often questioned. Yet even these ever-expanding lists of rights are not unlimited. I cannot be said to have a right to be loved by those whom I hope will love me, or a right to become wise. There are many good things that I may rightfully possess and enjoy, but to which I have no claim if they are lacking. Most generally, then, having a right means having a *justified* claim against others that they act in a fitting manner, either that they refrain from interfering or that they deliver what is justly owed. It goes without saying that the mere assertion of a claim or demand, or the stipulation of a right, is insufficient to establish it: making a claim and actually having a rightful claim to make are not identical. In considering an alleged right to die, we must be careful to look for a *justifiable* liberty or claim, and not merely a desire, interest, power, or demand.

Rights seem to entail obligations: one person's right, whether to noninterference or to some entitled good or service, necessarily implies another person's obligation. It will be important later to consider what obligations on others might be entailed by enshrining a right to die.

What, then, might be meant by a right *to die*? Taken literally, it would denote merely a right to the inevitable; the certainty of death for all that lives is the touchstone of fated inevitability. Why claim a right to what is not only unavoidable but is even, generally speaking, an evil? Is death in danger of losing its inevitability? Are we in danger of bodily immortality? Has death, for us, become a good to be claimed rather than an evil to be shunned or conquered?

Not exactly and not yet, though these questions posed by the literal reading of "right to die" are surely germane. They hint at our growing disenchantment with the biomedical project, which seeks, in principle, to prolong life indefinitely. It is the already available means to sustain life for prolonged periods—not indefinitely, but far longer than is in many cases reasonable or desirable—that has made death so untimely late as to seem less than inevitable, that has made death, when it finally does occur, appear to be a blessing.

For we now have medical "treatments" (that is, interventions) that do not treat (that is, cure or ameliorate) specific diseases, but do nothing more than keep alive, by sustaining vital functions. The most notorious such device is the respirator. Others include simple yet still artificial devices for supplying food and water and the kidney dialysis machine for removing wastes. And, in the future, we shall have the artificial heart. These devices, backed by aggressive institutional policies favoring their use, are capable of keeping people alive, even when comatose, often for decades. The "right to die," in today's discourse, often refers to—and certainly is meant to embrace—a right to refuse such life-sustaining medical treatment.

But the "right to die" usually embraces something more. The ambiguity of the term blurs over the difference between the already well-established common-law right to refuse surgery or other un-wanted medical treatments and hospitalization, and the newly al-leged "right to die." The former permits the refusal of therapy—even a respirator—even if it means accepting an increased risk of death. The latter permits the refusal of therapy—such as renal dialysis or the feeding tube—*so that* death *will* occur. The former seems more concerned with choosing how to live while dying; the latter seems mainly concerned with a choice *for death*. In this sense the claimed "right to die" is not a misnomer.

Still less is it a misnomer when we consider that some people who are claiming it demand not merely the discontinuance of treat-ment but positive assistance in bringing about their deaths. Here the right to die embraces the (welfare!) right to a lethal injection or an overdose of pills administered by oneself, by one's physician, or by someone else. This "right to die" would better be called a right to assisted suicide or a right to be mercifully killed—in short, a right *to become dead*, by *assistance* if necessary.

This, of course, looks a lot like a claim to a right to commit suicide, which need not have any connection to the problems of dying or medical technology. Some people in fact argue that the right to die through euthanasia or medically assisted suicide grows not from a right to refuse medical treatment but rather from this putative right to commit suicide (suicide is now decriminalized in most states). There does seem to be a world of moral difference between submitting to death (when the time has come) and killing yourself (in or out of season), or between permitting to die and causing death. But the boundary becomes fuzzy with the alleged right to refuse food and water, artificially delivered. Though few proponents of right to die want the taint of a general defense of suicide—which though decriminalized remains in bad odor—they in fact presuppose its permissibility and go well beyond it. They claim not only a right to attempt suicide but a right to succeed, and this means, in practice, a right to the deadly assistance of others. It is thus certainly proper to understand the "right to die" in its most radical sense—namely, as a right to become or to be made dead, by whatever means.

This way of putting the matter will not sit well with those who see the right to die less as a matter of life and death, more as a matter of autonomy or dignity. For them the right to die means the right to continue, despite disability, to exercise control over one's own destiny. It means, in one formulation, not the right to become dead, but the right to choose the manner, the timing, and the circumstances of one's death, or the right to choose what one regards as the most humane or dignified way to finish out one's life. Here the right to die means either the right to self-command or the right to death with dignity—claims that would oblige others, at a minimum, to stop interfering, but also, quite commonly, to "assist self-command" (!) or to "provide dignity" (!) by participating in bringing one's life to an end, according to plan. In the end, these proper and high-minded demands for autonomy and dignity turn out in most cases to embrace also a right to *become dead*, with *assistance* if necessary.

This analysis of current usage shows why one might be properly confused about the meaning of the term "right to die." In public discourse today it merges all the aforementioned meanings: right to refuse treatment, even if or so that death may occur; right to be killed or to become dead; right to control one's own dying; right to die with dignity; right to assistance in death. Some of this confusion inheres in the term; some of it is deliberately perpetrated by proponents of all these "rights," hoping thereby to gain assent to the more extreme claims by merging them with the more modest ones. Partly for this reason, however, we do well to regard "right to die" at its most radical—and I will do so in this essay—as a right to become dead, by active means and if necessary with the assistance of others. In this way we take seriously and do justice to the novelty and boldness of the claim, a claim that intends to go beyond both the existing common-law right to refuse unwanted medical treatment and the so-called right to commit suicide all by oneself. (The first right is indisputable; the second, while debatable, will not be contested in this essay. What concerns us here is those aspects of the "right to die" that go beyond a right to attempt suicide and a right to refuse treatment.)

Having sought to clarify the meaning of "right to die," we face next the even greater confusion about who it is that allegedly has such a right. Is it only those who are "certifiably" terminally ill and irreversibly dying, with or without medical treatment? Also those who are incurably ill and severely incapacitated, although definitely not dying? Everyone who is competent to act on such a right? Everyone, mentally competent or not? Does a senile person have a "right to die" if he is incapable of claiming it for himself? Do I need to be able to claim *and act* on such a right in order to have it? Or can proxies be designated to exercise my right to die on my behalf? If the right to die is essentially an expression of my autonomy, how can anyone else exercise it for me?

Equally puzzling is the question: Against whom or what is a right to die being asserted? Is it a liberty right mainly against those officious meddlers who keep me from dying—against those doctors, nurses, hospitals, right-to-life groups, and district attorneys who interfere either with my ability to die (by machinery and hospitalization) or with my ability to gain help in ending my life (by criminal sanctions against assisting suicide)? If it is a right to become dead, is it not also a welfare right claimed against those who do not yet assist—a right demanding also the provision of the poison that I have permission to take? (Compare the liberty right to seek an abortion with the welfare right to obtain one.) Or is it, at bottom, a demand asserted also *against nature*, which has dealt me a bad hand by keeping me alive, beyond my wishes and beneath my dignity, and alas without terminal illness, too senile or enfeebled to make matters right?

The most radical formulations—whether in the form of "a right to become dead" or "a right to control my destiny" or "a right to dignity"—are, I am convinced, the complaint of human pride against what our tyrannical tendencies lead us to experience as "cosmic injustice, directed against me." Here the ill-fated demand a right not to be ill-fated; those who want to die but cannot claim a right to die, which becomes, as Harvey Mansfield puts it in chapter 5, a tort claim against nature. It thus becomes the business of the well-fated to correct nature's mistreatment of the ill-fated *by making them dead.* Thus would the same act that was only yesterday declared a crime against humanity become a mandated act, not only of compassionate charity but of compensatory justice!

Why Assert a Right to Die?

Before proceeding to the more challenging question of the existence and ground of a "right to die," it would be useful briefly to consider why such a right is being asserted, and by whom. Some of the reasons have already been noted, in passing:

• fear of prolongation of dying due to medical intervention; hence, a right to refuse treatment or hospitalization, even if death occurs as a result
• fear of living too long, without fatal illness to carry one off; hence, a right to assisted suicide
• fear of the degradations of senility and dependence; hence, a right to death with dignity
• fear of loss of control; hence, a right to choose the time and manner of one's death

Equally important for many people is the fear of becoming a burden to others—financial, psychic, social. Few parents, however eager or willing they might be to stay alive, are pleased by the prospect that they might thereby destroy their children's and grand-children's opportunities for happiness. Indeed, my own greatest weakening on the subject of euthanasia is precisely this: I would confess a strong temptation to remove myself from life to spare my children the anguish of years of attending my demented self and the horrible likelihood that they will come, hatefully to themselves, to resent my continued existence. Such reasons in favor of death might even lead me to think I had a *duty* to die—though (to repeat) such reasons, indeed any reasons, to die do not as such establish my *right* to die, understood as a right to become dead. (I would, of course, have to commit suicide without assistance and without anyone's discovering it—that is, well before I were demented. I would not want my children to believe that I suspected them of being incapable of loving me through my inevitable decline.)[1]

But the advocates of a "right to die" are not always so generous.

On the contrary, much dishonesty and mischief are afoot. Many people have seen the advantage of using the language of individual rights, implying voluntary action, in order to shift the national attitudes regarding life and death, in turn to make easier the practice of terminating "useless" lives.[2] Many who argue for a right to die mean for people not merely to have it but to exercise it with dispatch, so as to decrease the mounting socioeconomic costs of caring for the irreversibly ill and dying. In fact, most of the people now agitating for a "right to die" are themselves neither ill nor dying. Children looking at parents who are not dying fast enough, hospital administrators and health economists concerned about cost-cutting and waste, doctors disgusted with caring for incurables, people with eugenic or aesthetic interests who are repelled by the prospect of a society in which the young and vigorous expend enormous energy to keep alive the virtually dead—all these want to change our hard-won ethic in favor of life.

But they are either too ashamed or too shrewd to state their true motives. Much better to trumpet a right to die, and to encourage people to exercise it. They understand all too well that the present American climate requires one to talk of rights if one wishes to have one's way in such moral matters. (Consider, in this connection, the use of arguments for abortion rights by organizations hoping thereby to get women—especially the poor, the unmarried, and the non-white—to do their supposed duty toward limiting population growth and the size of the underclass.)

This is not to say that all reasons for promoting a "right to die" are suspect. Nor do I mean to suggest that it would never be right or good for someone to elect to die. But it might be dangerous folly to circumvent the grave need for prudence in these matters by substituting instead the confused yet absolutized principle of a "right to die," especially given the mixed motives and dangerous purposes of some of its proponents.

Truth to tell, public discourse about moral matters in the United States is much impoverished by our eagerness to transform questions of the right and the good into questions about individual rights. Partly this is a legacy of modern liberalism, the political philosophy on which the genius of the American founding mainly rests. It is augmented by American self-assertion and individualism, increasingly so in an age when family and other mediating institutions are in decline, and the naked individual is left face to face with the bureaucratic state.

But the language of rights gained a tremendous boost from the moral absolutism of the 1960s, with the discovery that the non-negotiable and absolutized character of all rights claims provides the most durable battering ram against the status quo. Never mind that it fuels resentments and breeds hatreds, that it ignores the consequences to society, or that it short-circuits a political process that is more amenable to working out a balanced view of the common good. Never mind all that: go to court and demand your rights. And the courts have been all too willing to oblige, finding or inventing new rights in the process.

These sociocultural changes, having nothing to do with death and dying, surely are part of the reason why we are now confronted with vociferous claims of a right to die. These changes are also part of the reason why, despite its notorious difficulties, a right to die is the leading moral concept advanced to address these most complicated and delicate human matters at the end of life. Yet the reasons for the assertion—even if suspect—do not settle the question of truth, to which, at long last, we finally turn.

Is There a Right to Die?

Let us examine the question from the perspectives of philosophy and of law.

Philosophy. Philosophically speaking, it makes sense to take our bearings from those great thinkers of modernity who are the originators and most thoughtful exponents of our rights-based thinking. They above all are likely to have understood the purpose, character, grounds, and limits for the assertion of rights. If a newly asserted right, such as the right to die, cannot be established on the natural or rational ground for rights offered by these thinkers, the burden of proof must fall to the proponents of novel rights, to provide a new yet equally solid ground in support of their novel claims.

If we start at the beginning, with the great philosophical teachers of *natural* rights, the very notion of a *right* to die would be nonsensical. As we learn from Hobbes and from John Locke, all the rights of man, given by nature, presuppose our self-interested attachment to our own lives. All natural rights trace home to the primary right to life, or better, the right to self-preservation—itself rooted in the powerful, self-loving impulses and passions that seek our own continuance, and asserted first against deadly, oppressive polities or against those who might insist that morality requires me to turn the other cheek when my life is threatened. Harvey Mansfield summarizes the classical position elegantly:

> Rights are given to men by nature, but they are needed because men are also subject to nature's improvidence. Since

life is in danger, men's equal rights would be to life, to the liberty that protects life, and to the pursuit of the happiness with which life, or a tenuous life, is occupied.

In practice, the pursuit of happiness will be the pursuit of property, for even though property is less valuable than life or liberty, it serves as guard for them. Quite apart from the pleasures of being rich, having secure property shows that one has liberty secure from invasion either by the government or by others; and secure liberty is the best sign of a secure life.[3]

Because death, my extinction, is the evil whose avoidance is the condition of the possibility of my having any and all of my goods, my right to secure my life against death—that is, my rightful liberty to self-preservation—is the bedrock of all other rights and of all politically relevant morality. Even Hans Jonas, writing to defend the right to die, acknowledges that it stands alone, and concedes that "every other right ever argued, claimed, granted, or denied can be viewed as an extension of this primary right [to life], since every particular right concerns the exercise of some faculty of life, the access to some necessity of life, the satisfaction of some aspiration of life."[4] It is obvious that one cannot found on this rock any right to die or right to become dead. Life loves to live, and it needs all the help it can get.

This is not to say that these early modern thinkers were unaware that men might tire of life or might come to find existence burdensome. But the decline in the will to live did not for them drive out or nullify the right to life, much less lead to a trumping new right, a right to die. For the right to life is a matter of nature, not will. Locke addresses and rejects a natural right to suicide, in his discussion of the state of nature:

> But though this be a state of liberty, yet it is not a state of license; though man in that state has an uncontrollable liberty to dispose of his person or possessions, yet he has not liberty to destroy himself, or so much as any creature in his possession, but where some nobler use than its bare preservation calls for it. The state of nature has a law of nature to govern it, which obliges everyone; and reason, which is that law, teaches all mankind who will but consult it, that, being all equal and independent, no one ought to harm another in his life, health, liberty, or possessions.[5]

Admittedly, the argument here turns explicitly theological—we are said to be our wise Maker's property. But the argument against a man's willful "quitting of his station" seems, for Locke, to be a corollary of the natural inclination and right of self-preservation.

Some try to argue, wrongly in my view, that Locke's teaching on property rests on a principle of self-ownership, which can then be used to justify self-destruction: Since I own my body and my life, I may do with them as I please. As this argument has much currency, it is worth examining in greater detail. Locke does indeed say something that seems at first glance to suggest self-ownership:

> Though the earth and all inferior creatures be common to all men, *yet every man has a property in his own person*; this nobody has a right to but himself. The labor of his body and the work of his hands we may say are properly his.[6]

But the context defines and constricts the claim. Unlike the property rights in the fruits of his labor, the property a man has in his own person is inalienable: a man cannot transfer title to himself by selling himself into slavery. The "property in his own person" is less a metaphysical statement declaring self-ownership, more a political statement *denying* ownership by *another*. This right excludes each and every human being from the commons available to all human beings for appropriation and use. My body and my life are my property *only in the limited sense* that they are *not yours*. They are different from my alienable property—my house, my car, my shoes. My body and my life, while mine to use, are not mine to dispose of. In the deepest sense, my body is nobody's body, not even mine.[7]

Even if one continues, against reason, to hold to strict self-ownership and self-disposability, there is a further argument, one that is decisive. Self-ownership might enable one at most to justify *attempting* suicide; it cannot justify a right to succeed or, more important, a right to the assistance of others. The designated potential assistant-in-death has neither a natural duty nor a natural right to become an actual assistant-in-death, and the liberal state, instituted above all to protect life, can never countenance such a right to kill, even on request. A right to become dead or to be made dead cannot be sustained on classical liberal grounds.

Later thinkers in the liberal tradition, including those who prized freedom above preservation, also make no room for a "right to die." Jean-Jacques Rousseau's complaints about the ills of civil society centered especially and most powerfully on the threats to life and limb from a social order whose main purpose should have been to protect them.[8] And Immanuel Kant, for whom rights are founded not in nature but in reason, holds that the self-willed act of self-destruction is simply self-contradictory.

It seems absurd that a man can injure himself (*volenti non fit injuria* [Injury cannot happen to one who is willing]). The Stoic therefore considered it a prerogative of his personality as a wise man to walk out of his life with an undisturbed mind whenever he liked (as out of a smoke-filled room), not because he was afflicted by actual or anticipated ills, but simply because he could make use of nothing more in this life. And yet this very courage, this strength of mind—of not fearing death and of knowing of something which man can prize more highly than his life—ought to have been an ever so much greater motive for him not to destroy himself, a being having such authoritative superiority over the strongest sensible incentives; consequently, it ought to have been a motive for him not to deprive himself of life.

Man cannot deprive himself of his personhood so long as one speaks of duties, thus so long as he lives. That man ought to have the authorization to withdraw himself from all obligation, i.e. to be free to act as if no authorization at all were required for this withdrawal, involves a contradiction. To destroy the subject of morality in his own person is tantamount to obliterating from the world, as far as he can, the very existence of morality itself; but morality is, nevertheless, an end in itself. Accordingly, to dispose of oneself as a mere means to some end of one's own liking is to degrade the humanity in one's person (*homo noumenon*), which, after all, was entrusted to man (*homo phaenomenon*) to preserve.[9]

It is a heavy irony that it should be autonomy, the moral notion that the world owes mainly to Kant, that is now invoked as the justifying ground of a right to die. For Kant, autonomy, which literally means self-legislation, requires acting in accordance with one's true self—that is, with one's rational will determined by a universalizable, that is, rational, maxim. Being autonomous means not being a slave to instinct, impulse, or whim, but rather doing as one ought, as a rational being. But autonomy has now come to mean "doing as you please," compatible no less with self-indulgence than with self-control. Herewith one sees clearly the triumph of the Nietzschean self, who finds reason just as enslaving as blind instinct and who finds his true "self" rather in unconditioned acts of pure creative will.

Yet even in its willful modern meaning, "autonomy" cannot ground a right to die. First, one cannot establish on this basis a right to have *someone else's* assistance in committing suicide—a right, by the way, that would impose an obligation on someone else and

87

thereby restrict *his* autonomy. Second, even if my choice for death were "reasonable" and my chosen agent freely willing, my autonomy cannot ground *his right* to kill me, and hence, it cannot ground my right to become dead. Third, a liberty right (against interference) to an assisted death can at most approve assisted suicide or euthanasia for the mentally competent and alert—a restriction that would prohibit effecting the deaths of the mentally incompetent or comatose patients who have not left explicit instructions regarding their treatment. It is, by the way, a long philosophical question whether all such instructions must be obeyed, for the person who gave them long ago may no longer be "the same person" when they become relevant. Can my fifty-four-year-old self truly prescribe today the best interests for my seventy-five-year-old and senile self?

In contrast to arguments presented in recent court cases, it is self-contradictory to assert that a proxy not chosen by the patient can exercise the latter's rights of autonomy. Can a citizen have a right to vote that would be irrevocably exercised "on his behalf," and *in the name of his autonomy*, by the government?[10] Finally, if autonomy and dignity lie in the free exercise of will and choice, it is at least paradoxical to say that our autonomy licenses an act that puts our autonomy permanently out of business.

It is precisely this paradox that appeals to the Nietzschean creative self, the bearer of so many of this century's "new rights." As Mansfield brilliantly shows, the creative ones are not bound by normality or good sense:

> Creative beings are open-ended. They are open-ended in fact and not merely in their formal potentialities. Such beings do not have interests; for who can say what is in the interest of a being that is becoming something unknown? Thus the society of new rights is characterized by a loss of predictability and normality: no one knows what to expect, even from his closest companions.[11]

The most authentic self-creative self revels in the unpredictable, the extreme, the perverse. He does not even flinch before self-contradiction; indeed, he can display the triumph of his will most especially in self-negation. And though it may revolt us, who are we to deny him this form of self-expression? Supremely tolerant of the rights of others to their own eccentricities, we avert our glance and turn the other moral cheek. Here at last is the only possible philosophical ground for a right to die: arbitrary will, backed by moral relativism. Which is to say, no ground at all.

Law. Such foreign philosophic doctrines, prominent among the elite, are slowly working their relativistic way through the broader culture.

But in America, rights are still largely defined by law. Turning, then, from political and moral philosophy to American law, we should be surprised to discover any constitutional basis for a legal right to die, given that the framers understood rights and the role of government more or less as did Locke. Perusal of the original Constitution of 1787 or of the Bill of Rights finds absolutely nothing on which even the most creative of jurists could try to hang such a right.

But the notorious due process clause of the Fourteenth Amendment, under the ruling but still oxymoronic "substantive due process" interpretation, has provided such a possible peg, as it has for so many other new rights—notwithstanding the fact that the majority of states at the time the Fourteenth Amendment was ratified had laws that prohibited assisting suicide. The one "right-to-die" case to reach the Supreme Court, *Cruzan by Cruzan v. Director, Missouri Department of Health* (decided by a five-to-four vote in June 1990) explored the Fourteenth Amendment in connection with such a right.[12] This case may well have prepared the way for finding constitutional protection, at least for a right-to-refuse-lifesustaining-treatment-in-order-that-death-may-occur.

The parents of Nancy Cruzan, a comatose young woman living for seven years in a persistent vegetative state, petitioned to remove the gastrostomy feeding and hydration tube in order that Nancy be allowed to die. The trial court found for the parents, but the Missouri supreme court reversed; when the Cruzans appealed, the United States Supreme Court took the case in order to consider "whether Cruzan has a *right* under the United States Constitution which would require the hospital to withdraw life-sustaining treatment from her under the circumstances" (emphasis added).

At first glance, the Court's decision in *Cruzan* disappointed proponents of a right to die, because it upheld the decision of the Missouri supreme court: it held that Missouri's interest in safeguarding life allowed it to demand clear and convincing evidence that the incompetent person truly wished to withdraw from treatment, evidence that in Nancy Cruzan's case was lacking. Nevertheless, the reasoning of the majority decision was widely interpreted as conceding such a right to die for a *competent* person—a misinterpretation, to be sure, but not without some ground.

Chief Justice William Rehnquist, writing for the majority, scrupulously avoided any mention of a "right to die," and he wisely eschewed taking up the question under the so-called right of privacy. Instead, following precedent in Fourteenth Amendment jurisprudence and relying on the doctrine that informed consent is required for medical invasion of the body, he reasoned that "the principle that a competent person has a constitutionally protected *liberty interest* in refusing unwanted medical treatment may be inferred from our previous decisions." (A "liberty interest" is a technical term denoting a liberty less firmly protected by the due process clause than is a "fundamental right"; generally speaking, restrictions on the latter may be justified only by a compelling state interest, but restraints on the former may be upheld if they do not unduly burden its exercise.) But on the crucial question of whether the protected liberty interest to refuse medical treatment embraces also refusing *life-sustaining* food and water, Rehnquist waffled skillfully:

> Petitioners insist that under the general holdings of our cases, the forced administration of life-sustaining medical treatment, and even of artificially-delivered food and water essential to life, would implicate a competent person's liberty interest. Although we think the logic of the cases discussed above would embrace such a liberty interest, the dramatic consequences involved in refusal of such treatment [i.e., death] would inform the inquiry whether the deprivation of that interest is constitutionally permissible. But *for purposes of this case*, we *assume* that the United States *Constitution would* grant a *competent* person a *constitutionally protected right* to refuse *lifesaving* hydration and nutrition [emphasis added].[13]

Because the decision in *Cruzan* concerned an incompetent person incapable of exercising "a hypothetical right to refuse treatment or any other right," the right that Rehnquist was willing to assume had no bearing on the decision. But the chief justice could have put the matter differently. He might have said, "Whether or not a competent person has such a right, Nancy Cruzan, being incompetent, does not." True, he drew back from accepting in his own name the petitioner's claim, indicating instead that an inquiry would still be needed to determine whether a state may constitutionally deprive a competent person of his "liberty interest" to elect death by refusing artificial hydration and nutrition. But he was willing to stipulate for the purposes of this case—one suspects that he really means for the purpose of getting a majority on his side in this case—a constitutionally protected right-to-refuse-treatment-so-that-death-will-occur. This stipulation, missing the qualification "for the purposes of this case," was heralded in many newspapers and magazines around the country as establishing a constitutional right to die for competent persons.

Justice Sandra Day O'Connor, apparently the swing vote in the case, wrote a concurring opinion solely to indicate why the stipulated right was a right indeed. It is clear from her opinion that, if the case had in fact involved a competent patient, then a "right-to-elect-death-by-refusing-food-and-water" would have been judicially established, for she would have sided with the four-member minority who were ready to grant it even to incompetents:

> I agree that a [constitutionally] protected liberty interest in refusing unwanted medical treatment may be inferred from our prior decisions . . . and that the refusal of artificially delivered food and water *is encompassed* within that liberty interest. I write separately to clarify why I believe this to be so [emphasis added].[14]

What Chief Justice Rehnquist treats as hypothetical, Justice O'Connor treats as actual, and she presents her argument for its establishment. In the end she even speaks about the need to safeguard similar liberty interests *for incompetents*, giving shockingly little attention to the duty of the state to protect the life of incompetent people against those who would exercise on their behalf their putative right to die.[15]

Only Justice Antonin Scalia, writing a separate concurring opinion, seems to have gotten it right, insisting that the Constitution has absolutely nothing to say in this matter. He argues, first, that the liberty protected by the Fourteenth Amendment could not and does not include a "right to suicide," and second, that arguments attempting to separate the withdrawal of the feeding tube from Nancy Cruzan from ordinary suicide all fail. He reasons, to me convincingly, that a right to refuse treatment here means necessarily a right to put an end to her life.

> What I have said above is not meant to suggest that I would think it desirable, if we were sure that Nancy Cruzan wanted to die, to keep her alive by the means at issue here. I only assert that the Constitution has nothing to say about the subject. To raise up a constitutional right here we would have to create out of nothing (for it exists neither in text nor tradition) some constitutional principle whereby, although the State may insist that an individual come in out of the cold and eat food, it may not insist that he take medicine; and although it may pump his stomach empty of poison he has ingested, it may not fill his stomach with food he has failed to ingest.[16]

Yet paradoxically, Justice Scalia's powerful argument, which identifies the refusal of food and water as suicide, may come back to haunt us—especially when conjoined with Justice O'Connor's insistence that such right of refusal is already constitutionally protected. For should Justice O'Connor's view prevail, Justice Scalia's powerful intellect will have provided the reasons for regarding the newly protected right as indeed a right to die. The elements are all in place for inventing a constitutional right to suicide and, in the case of competents, for assistance with suicide, that is, a right to die. Justice Scalia's worry is not misplaced:

> I am concerned, from the tenor of today's opinions, that we are poised to confuse [this] enterprise [of legislating regarding end-of-life decisions] as successfully as we have confused the enterprise of legislating concerning abortion.[17]

Almost no one seems to have noticed a painful irony in this proceeding.[18] The Fourteenth Amendment prohibits the states from depriving persons not only of liberty but also of life and property, without due process of law. A so-called vitalist state, like Missouri, has at least for now been vindicated in its efforts to protect an incompetent person's life against those who assert the superiority of his "liberty interest" to elect death by starvation. But no thought seems to have been given to the conduct of the so-called nonvitalist states, like New Jersey, that go the other way and give the benefit of incompetency to death—all in the name of liberty! In abandoning those vulnerable persons whom others insist have lives no longer worth living, these states come much closer to violating the strict letter of the Fourteenth Amendment's insistence that the state not take life than does Missouri, in allegedly thwarting Cruzan's liberty to elect death.

The Tragic Meaning of "Right to Die"

The claim of a "right to die," asserted especially against physicians bent on prolonging life, clearly exposes certain deep difficulties in the foundations of modern liberal, technological society. Modern liberal, technological society rests especially upon two philosophical pillars raised first in the seventeenth century, at the beginning of the modern era: the preeminence of the human individual, embodied in the doctrine of natural rights, as espoused first by Hobbes and Locke; and the idea of mastery of nature, attained through a radically new science of nature, as proposed by Francis Bacon and René Descartes.

Both ideas were responses to the perceived partial inhospitality of nature to human need. Both encouraged man's opposition to nature, the first through the flight from the state of nature into civil society, in order to safeguard the precarious rights to life and liberty; the second through the subduing of nature in order to make life longer, healthier, and more commodious. One might even say that it is especially an opposition to death which grounds these twin responses. Politically, the fear of violent death at the hands of warring men requires law and legitimate authority to secure natural rights, especially life. Technologically, the fear of death-as-such at the hands of unfriendly nature inspires a bolder approach—namely, a scientific medicine to wage war against disease and even against death itself, ultimately with a promise of bodily immortality.

Drunk on its political and scientific successes, modern thought and practice have abandoned the modest and moderate beginnings of political modernity. In civil society, the natural rights of self-preservation, secured through active but moderate self-assertion, have given way to the nonnatural rights of self-creation and self-expression; the new rights have no connection to nature or to reason, but appear as the rights of the untrammeled will. The "self" that here asserts itself is not a natural self, with the predictable interests given it by a universal human nature with its bodily needs, but a uniquely individuated and self-made self. Its authentic selfhood is demonstrated by its ability to say no to the needs of the body, the rules of society, and the dictates of reason. For such a self, self-negation through suicide and the right to die can be the ultimate form of self-assertion.

In medical science, the unlimited battle against death has found nature unwilling to roll over and play dead. The successes of medicine so far are partial at best and the victory incomplete, to say the least. The welcome triumphs against disease have been purchased at the price of the medicalized dehumanization of the end of life: to put it starkly, once we lick cancer and stroke, we can all live long enough to get Alzheimer's disease. And if the insurance holds out, we can die in the intensive care unit, suitably intubated. Fear of the very medical power we engaged to do battle against death now leads us to demand that it give us poison.

Finally, both the triumph of individualism and our reliance on technology (not only in medicine) and on government to satisfy our new wants-demanded-as-rights have weakened our more natural human associations—especially the family, on which we all need to rely when our pretense to autonomy and mastery are eventually exposed by unavoidable decline. Old age and death have been taken out of the bosom of family life and turned over to state-supported nursing homes and hospitals. Not the clergyman but the doctor—in truth, the nurse—presides over the end of life, in sterile surroundings that make no concessions to our finitude. Both the autonomous will and the will's partner-in-pride, the death-denying doctor, ignore the unavoidable limits on will and technique that nature insists on. Failure to recognize these limits now threatens the entire venture, for

93

rebellion against the project through a "right to die" will only radicalize its difficulties. Vulnerable life will no longer be protected by the state, medicine will become a death-dealing profession, and isolated individuals will be technically dispatched to avoid the troubles of finding human ways to keep company with them in their time of ultimate need.

That the right to die should today be asserted to win release from a hyperpowerful medical futility is thus more than tragic irony: it is also very dangerous. Three dangers especially stand out.

First, the right to die, especially as it comes to embrace a right to "aid in dying," or assisted suicide, or euthanasia, will translate into an obligation on the part of others to kill or help kill. Even if we refuse to impose such a duty but merely allow those others who are freely willing to practice it, our society would be drastically altered. For unless the state accepts the job of euthanizer, which God forbid that it should, it would thus surrender its monopoly on the legal use of lethal force: a monopoly it holds and needs in order to protect innocent life, its first responsibility.

Second, there can be no way to confine the practice to those who knowingly and freely request death. The vast majority of persons who are candidates for assisted death are, and will increasingly be, incapable of choosing and effecting such a course of action for themselves. No one with an expensive or troublesome infirmity will be safe from the pressure to have his right to die exercised.

Third, the medical profession's devotion to heal and refusal to kill—its ethical center—will be permanently destroyed, and with it, patient trust and physicianly self-restraint. Here is yet another case where acceding to a putative personal right would wreak havoc on the common good.

Nothing I have said should be taken to mean that I believe life should be extended under all circumstances and at all costs. Far from it. I continue, with fear and trembling, to defend the practice of allowing to die while opposing the practice of deliberately killing— despite the blurring of this morally bright line implicit in the artificial food and water cases, and despite the slippery slide toward the retailing of death that continues on the sled of a right to refuse treatment. I welcome efforts to give patients as much choice as possible in how they are to live out the end of their lives. I continue to applaud those courageous patients and family members and those conscientious physicians who try prudently to discern, in each case, just what form of treatment or non-treatment is truly good for the patient, even if it embraces an increased likelihood of death. But I continue to insist that we cannot serve the patient's good by deliberately eliminating the patient. And if we have no right to do this to another, we have no right to have others do this to ourselves. There is, when all is said and done, no defensible right to die.

A Coda: About Rights

The rhetoric of rights still performs today the noble, time-honored function of protecting individual life and liberty, a function now perhaps even more necessary than the originators of such rhetoric could have imagined, given the tyrannical possibilities of the modern bureaucratic and technologically competent state. But with the claim of a "right to die," as with so many of the novel rights being asserted in recent years, we face an extension of this rhetoric into areas where it no longer relates to that protective function, and beyond the limited area of life in which rights claims are clearly appropriate and, indeed, crucial. As a result, we face a number of serious and potentially dangerous distortions, in our thought and in our practice. We distort our understanding of rights, and weaken their respectability in their proper sphere, by allowing them to be invented—without ground in nature or in reason—for dealing with moral questions outside their limited domain. We distort our understanding of moral deliberation and the moral life by reducing all complicated questions of right and good to questions of individual rights. We subvert the primacy and necessity of prudence by pretending that the assertion of rights will produce the best—and most moral—results. In trying to batter our way through the human condition with the bludgeon of personal rights, we allow ourselves to be deceived about the most fundamental matters—about death and dying, about our unavoidable finitude, and about the sustaining interdependencies of our lives.

Let us, by all means, continue to deliberate about whether and when and why it might make sense for someone to give up on his life, or even actively to choose death. But let us call a halt to all this dangerous thoughtlessness about rights. Let us refuse to talk any longer about a "right to die."

5

Responsibility versus Self-Expression

Harvey C. Mansfield, Jr.

"Be all that you can be in the a-a-rmy." Before the Gulf War this was a recruitment slogan, crooned by a female voice, for the U.S. Army. It represents quite a change from the stern face of Uncle Sam with a beckoning finger in the World War I poster. Of course the circumstances were different—peace versus war. But the change in moral climate, from responsibility to self-expression, is much more impressive.

The example is politically neutral, chosen so as not to discourage inquiry from any side into the reasons for the contrast. Indeed, the patriotic slogan "I want you!" dates from the Wilson administration, and the military "be-in" was contrived under Ronald Reagan. But I cannot conceal my sympathy for Uncle Sam and for the conception of rights on which his confident appeal was based. From the beginning America has been a society whose government is devoted to the protection of rights, but fairly recently—perhaps in the New Deal, perhaps in the 1960s—a new conception of rights has taken hold.

For the new rights, "protection" by government is not enough. A more active furtherance of some kind is required, so that government helps us to "be," even while we are serving in the military (which seems to have a special kinship with nonexistence). A society based on the rights of life, liberty, and the pursuit of happiness faces a special test when it must justify placing its citizens in harm's way.

Let us then focus the contrast between the new rights and the old on that justification. I shall begin with the argument for Uncle Sam.

Responsibility and the Old Rights

The argument I present is not taken from one source, though clearly John Locke and the American founders are its principal authors. The old rights are the rights of man—meaning human beings, one is obliged to say today. They are the rights of certain beings with a fixed nature and with alterable laws and customs. Since men have from nature the power to alter laws and customs, one can also say that their nature is partly fixed, partly alterable. The rights pertain to the fixed part, so they are inalienable. Rights cannot be taken away by bad laws and customs, because they are not granted by good ones. If there were no fixed human nature, there could be no inalienable rights.

Before considering what these rights may be we must know what a right is. A right is permission to do a range of things that an individual is able to do. He may exercise the right in company with others; indeed, as in the right to consent, there are occasions when he *must* act with others. But a right belongs to the individual to exercise at his discretion and at his initiative on his own behalf.

A right to do something is also a right *not* to do it. So although the right is granted by nature, it is actuated by self-permission. Such a right presupposes the competence of an individual to judge for himself whether to exercise the right, as well as a certain assertiveness in making his right respected. It also presumes that the thing to which one has a right is possible to do. One cannot have a right to an impossible condition, such as immortality, for rights are about actions, not wishes. Rights are rights against the interference of other human beings, not against the motions of nature. There is no right not to have rain on the Fourth of July.

What are the rights of man? By imagining how men would be in a state of nature prior to the establishment of laws and customs, one can see what one's rights are. One uses a hypothesis to establish a nonhypothetical truth. Having individual bodies and sharing a specifically human faculty of reason, men would have equal rights at least to the extent—and this is sufficient—that no one or group of them would have a clear title to rule other men. And since prior to laws and customs men would live in penury and mutual distrust, their first concern would be for their lives. Rights are given to men by nature, but they are needed because men are also subject to nature's improvidence. Since life is in danger, men's equal rights would be to

97

life, to the liberty that protects life, and to the pursuit of the happiness with which life, or a tenuous life, is occupied.

Natural and Civil Rights. In practice, the pursuit of happiness will be the pursuit of property, for even though property is less valuable than life or liberty, it serves as guard for them. Quite apart from the pleasures of being rich, having secure property shows that one has liberty secure from invasion either by the government or by others; and secure liberty is the best sign of a secure life. Secure property is security in general. And this is all the more true because an invasion of property does not immediately endanger one's life and liberty, whereas a direct test obviously puts them at risk. Property is an early warning system, an alarm protecting life and liberty.

Secure property requires laws and customs; to get it men must leave the state of nature and form civil society. When they do this, they exchange natural rights for civil rights. Natural rights are the rights on which civil society is founded; civil rights are the ones it secures. Natural rights belong to natural man—that is, man in the state of nature. They are the rights to life, liberty, and the pursuit of happiness in the Declaration of Independence. They are the rights for the sake of which Americans established a Constitution.

But the rights actually secured under the Constitution are civil rights, such as those in the Bill of Rights. They are more specific than natural rights, but they are therefore also more limited. In entering civil society we deprive ourselves of the exercise of natural rights in order to establish a Constitution that will secure civil rights. Natural rights are unlimited but useless, because there is no one except ourselves to enforce them; civil rights are effectual but limited, because they are defined by law.

The exchange of natural for civil rights is accomplished by consent and protected by the right of consent—the right of consent to a government with the power to make and enforce laws. The right of consent is both natural and civil, and it is *between* natural and civil rights: natural insofar as it is prior to civil rights, civil insofar as consent establishes civil rights under government. One such civil right is the right to vote, which is the civil version of the right of consent. The right of consent is the key right; it makes all other rights effectual by joining them to government, and at the same time it makes clear that although rights are secured by government they are not granted by government.

The people use their right of consent to establish a constitution that secures—and thereby limits—their rights. The constitution will specify certain civil rights as in our Bill of Rights, but the principal security it offers, more than the naming of those rights, is the form of government it constructs. A well-formed constitutional government gives effect to the right of consent, which would otherwise remain abstract. In such a government the majority rules, but not a factious, willful majority. With such constitutional provisions as the separation of powers and federalism, the ruling majority should be a *constitutional* majority. Though of course partisan, it should be respectful of the rights of minorities and mindful of the common good. Without a working constitutional government a list of rights is of little account, even if all agree on their desirability. Not merely the judiciary but the whole government serves to secure rights; and this means that prompt executive action is as necessary as careful legislation and wise adjudication.

Equal Rights and Unequal Exercise. Rights in the older conception have two other, opposite qualities. They are formal, and they are connected to interests. The formality of rights refers to the difference between the formal possession of a right and its actual exercise. The difference is necessary because it is the business of government to secure only the former and not the latter. If the government exercises our rights for us—for example, our right of free speech by telling us what to read or our right of private property by commanding us how to live—then we no longer have the right.

But the formality of rights leads to a difficulty. Though rights are equal formally, they are in practice necessarily unequal. Natural differences in human nature, combined with the variance of luck, will cause some to exercise the right of free speech or the right of acquiring property more successfully than others. A gap between the ideal of equal rights and the reality of unequal exercise will appear.

How to deal with this gap cannot, perhaps, be prescribed in theory, except to say that it is an inevitable feature of any society based on rights. Any attempt to close it completely would require so much force and regulation that the rights intended to be secured would in fact be suffocated. Any such attempt would inevitably contravene the right of consent or the right to vote. For this right is quintessentially formal; it allows the people to vote in accordance with their prejudice as much as with their enlightened judgment. To close the gap between the ideal and the reality, a government would have to deny the right of consent to prejudiced voters. But that, we have seen, is the key right.

Some help for this difficulty can be obtained from the notion of interests, an eighteenth-century feature added to the Lockean conception of rights. Interests are opposite to the formality of rights, since they describe how one can expect rights actually to be exercised. Because of interests, one can have a certain confidence that the formal establishment of rights will not encourage whimsicality, weirdness, insobriety, nastiness, criminality, or crazy behavior in general.

Although rights are formally open-ended, their actual exercise is disciplined by the consideration of what it is in our interest to do. Our interest derives from our human nature, but it is not confined, like natural rights, to the state of nature; it continues with equal or heightened alertness into civil society. Just as the natural right to life is sustained by the natural desire for self-preservation, so the civil right to acquire property is activated by our interest in an improved standard of living; and the right to free speech is used to satisfy our interest in reputation or celebrity.

Through the connection to interests, rights gain not only sobriety but also many supporters, whose interest lies in the maintenance of the rights by which they profit. Since interests derive from human nature, they are active in all human societies. Even a traditional economy obeys economic "incentives," as interests are sometimes called, to some extent. But giving greater freedom to the play—or the work—of interests can transform a society from benightedness to enlightenment. The appeal of interests is independent of "values," although values—that is, opinions—favorable to the pursuit of interests can allow interests greater scope.

Did I forget to say what interests consist of? Not really. They are an average reason joined—and confined—to an impersonal self. But you already knew that.

Responsibility and Rights. We have now come a certain distance, but we are not yet in sight of Uncle Sam, who relies on a sense of responsibility. Responsibility is the rights-based transformation of what used to be called duty or virtue. Duty implies devotion to something higher than oneself, and virtue implies a concern with the perfection of one's soul. Both can be found in a society of rights, but they are not truly consistent with its emphasis on the self-preservation of individuals.

Rights seem to say that human beings are sovereign and that devotion to a higher being or a larger whole is a matter of choice, not duty. Virtue is self-assumed, as one cannot be fully virtuous without an awareness of the worth of virtue. But virtue, in calling for perfection, seems to be confined in its full extent to a few, and it seems to require us to admire, perhaps obey, those few. Virtue does not seem consistent with the equality of rights.

Responsibility is of human origin and democratic. Let us define

100

responsibility as the act of voluntarily taking charge of a situation in order to improve it. Responsibility is exercised in the context of rights and interests, the two beacons of our moral life, but it is not identical to them. My right is wider than my responsibility, and my interest is narrower. My right of free speech includes, some (wrongly) say culminates in, a right to speak irresponsibly. And it is not clear that my interest is best served by a responsible action that may involve some risk to myself.

But although responsibility is not identical to rights and interests, it is not antithetical either. My right includes, if it does not require, responsibility; so the responsible person has, compared with the irresponsible, at least equal justification, if no more. This equality may sound like a joke, and it is; yet it is a genuine advantage to the responsible to have a basis for intervention that the irresponsible cannot easily deny.

Similarly, although one's interest may counsel abstractly against exposing oneself to risk, one's concrete interest may be attached to a position in which he is made responsible for certain actions, because enough people will believe that reputation or fame are in their interest. They may then believe that responsibility is their duty, in a sense not requiring devotion to something higher.

In this way responsibility is linked to interest even if it is not the same. We are reminded of the "interest of the office"; Publius, the author of *The Federalist*, argued that it would encourage responsible behavior in officers of the American Constitution. It is interesting that our notion of responsibility does not occur in Locke, the founder of liberalism, who speaks ambiguously of duties, either to God or to one's interest. Our notion seems to begin in *The Federalist*, in which one sees liberalism no longer merely in theory but at work in the framing of a new constitution. Liberalism at work is in need of responsibility; rights and interests are too theoretical to suffice by themselves. Many people have to be willing to take actions for which, in rights theory at least, they lack sufficient reason.

As we have seen, however, the old rights are grounded in the human nature that gives men certain abilities. Thus one does not truly have a right without at least the ability to claim it, and the best evidence for the ability is the actual claiming of one's rights. One must, as we say, "stand up for" one's rights. When one stands up for his own rights, he also stands up for others in a like situation. He renounces inactivity; he refuses to "take this sitting down." Perhaps a certain aristocratic sense of honor and generosity is at the origin of the democratic notion of responsibility. Through the notion of responsibility liberal democracies recapture the love of the noble and

101

the concern for the whole that seem so foreign to them and yet so ineradicably human. That achievement is the basis for Uncle Sam.

To summarize the old rights, then: they are derived from a fixed human nature; they belong to competent individuals; they are equal; they are protected by private property; they are divided into natural and civil rights; their key is the right of consent; they are constitutional; they are formal; they are connected to interests; and they are responsible. Every one of these qualities is denied or radically modified in the new rights that are claimed today.

Self-Expression and the New Rights

Let us begin with the irresponsibility of the new rights. My examples now will not appear to be politically neutral, though in a sense they are. I remark that the present budget crisis is due in great part to new rights, known as entitlements, that generate expenditures described as "uncontrollable." They have been granted in a way that deliberately avoids responsible control, including actuarial calculation, so as to make them firm commitments.

The idea is that rights are not secure unless they are entitlements, protected *from* the common good. Judges have expanded the rights of defendants without regard to the effect on crime. The women's movement has gained equal rights for women without considering, or in some cases caring, for the consequences to the family. In particular, the right of abortion releases fathers from responsibility for children because it necessarily implies that every child is born through the sole decision of the mother not to abort.

Whether these new rights actually have bad consequences I do not inquire here. Most fathers may overlook the implication of a right of abortion. Thus the examples do not require conservative fears; it is enough to observe that the rights were conceived and established without regard for, and even in defiance of, their effect on responsibility. The new rights are irresponsible not so much because they are careless of the cost-benefit equation, or because they are insufficiently utilitarian, as because they make people irresponsible: "I have my right; it's up to you to adjust."

Origins of the New Rights. Authorities differ as to when the new rights first came upon the American moral landscape. Obviously the 1960s saw a vociferous attack from the New Left on Uncle Sam's patriotism. Patriotism understood as "My country right or wrong" was replaced by the moralism of "My country only when it's right." The responsible questions of how to make a wrong country right and how far any country can be right were ignored or shouted down.

In the 1960s the irresponsible self paraded—"demonstrated"—in broad daylight. But some say that the new rights had their origin in the New Deal, when government took over responsibility to secure "freedom from want," as Franklin Roosevelt put it. That such a course might prove harmful to individual responsibility was denied or ridiculed, perhaps wrongly. But government's new responsibility was not *intended* to liberate the individual from his responsibilities. The New Deal is part of the prehistory of the irresponsible self that appeared thirty years later.

As theory the new rights were born in Friedrich Nietzsche's doctrine of the creative self. How that doctrine came from Nietzsche's books of the late 1880s to American politics in the 1960s is a story that has not yet been fully told.[1] One essential in the course of events is the historicism taken from German philosophy that was decisive in American pragmatism, for the pragmatists influenced the progressives and the progressives were predecessors of the New Deal. Pragmatism is not as American as apple pie. It denies the fixity of human nature and thus subjects rights to the contingency of circumstances. That historical circumstances could be harnessed under democratic control was the reformist faith of the pragmatists, the progressives, and the New Dealers. But with the abandonment of human nature, they lost the rational ground of rights and launched themselves, to some extent unwittingly, toward Nietzsche's unfixed self, the self that has to create itself.

The Equalizing Self. This new self, lacking any natural definition, is obliged to define itself by self-expression. It is obliged, that is, only to the extent of its energy. Those selves who are content with convention—or too weak to oppose it—will allow themselves to be defined, passively and inauthentically. The creative ones will lead them, not by seeking their counsel but by pushing them aside. The creatives are not obliged to respect the rights of other selves that lack a natural definition requiring respect, that are inchoate, malleable, or conformist. Equal respect goes to those equal in nature; if there are no natures, men are equal only at their unformed origins. As they "find their identities" and acquire qualities, they become unequal.

Nonetheless, for no better reason than an inconsistent regard for fellow humans or because they have read Karl Marx as well as Nietzsche, the creatives may decide to devote themselves to equal rights. They become *equalizers* of those whose rights are *equalized*. Instead of the strong and the weak we have the equalizers and the equalized—called by John Rawls the "least advantaged." Since no natural basis for equality exists, all equality depends on public rec-ognition and comes to mean "equal in public esteem."

This development greatly affects the lives of women. Heretofore women were largely excluded from "responsible positions"—that is, jobs from which one gains public reputation. But they took quiet satisfaction and pride instead from doing family tasks that are usually taken for granted. Women understood, or had an inkling, that the highest responsibility is perhaps to be found in taking charge of problems so ordinary that no one notices them. Someone must be responsible for what responsible people overlook—for what is private and nonpolitical. Now women may still feel drawn to the woman's job that is never done, but because their identities must be created by public esteem, they have no justification for doing what they very well see still needs doing. Their new rights of equality do not put supper on the table. They only make women who do cook feel like fools.

Creative beings are open-ended. They are open-ended in fact and not merely in their formal potentialities. Such beings do not have interests; for who can say what is in the interest of a being that is becoming something unknown? Thus the society of new rights is characterized by a loss of predictability and normality: no one knows what to expect, even from his closest companions.

Under the old rights the notion of interest was used as a lever to pry individuals and groups out of the fates destined for them by tradition: it was in one's interest to get ahead. But now those interests are seen as confining; instead of liberating they imprison their victims in stultifying "roles." A role is where one has been put by a malignant oppressor, anxious to take away in fact every formal promise of liberty. In the case of women, the system of new rights does not permit one to consult women's interests to see whether they are likely to benefit from equalized rights. Nor are women given any guide except the trend of fashion, which is ambivalent between work and home. What remains is choice, unguided and untended by society, as if it did not matter whether women like to have children and whether society needs them. To put it mildly, the element of sobriety supplied by the notion of interest to a rights-based society is forgone.

Spurious Beneficiaries. Competence is no longer a requirement for rights, as we see in the new rights accorded to the disabled not despite but because of their disabilities. Instead of having a right to do something with one's own abilities one has a right to have something done by others about one's disabilities. The disabled acquire a right not to be disabled, not merely when the disability results from the irresponsible human action of others but also, and especially, when it is just bad luck. The rights of the disabled are a kind of tort against nature, and it becomes the business of the equalizers to make them whole.

The disabled are induced to dwell on their disabilities rather than encouraged to make do with their abilities, for no one who is not comatose is completely disabled. At the same time, no one has all the abilities he would like; so all of us are in a sense disabled and might seem eligible for a new right of imperfect creatures to have perfection—in the sense of perfect health—here on earth. To make sure that no one is excluded, the ranks of the disabled can be expanded to include criminals and drug addicts, as in recent legislation, on the ground that their behavior is not their fault but rather is due to natural causes.

With the old rights nature's improvidence is a sort of bounty, because it leaves us free; under the new dispensation we become nature's victims and lose sight of our freedom. The shift from competence to disability transforms a right from a permission requiring other people's respect into a duty to be fulfilled by others. It mandates charity and thus overrides the true charity that comes freely from the heart.

Other beneficiaries of the new rights are animals and trees. Promoters of the new rights take umbrage at the despoiling of nature justified by the old rights. The old rights were rights of *man*, giving him sovereignty over the rest of nature because of the superiority of human nature. The consequences have been depletion, pollution, and the potentiality of nuclear catastrophe. To meet these perils, the new rights' promoters maintain, man must surrender his sovereignty over nature and the rights of animals must be recognized. In their view it is not enough to appeal to the rights of future generations of human beings, because they too might despoil the environment.

The rights of animals, implying the perfection of nature when left intact, might seem inconsistent with the rights of the handicapped as nature's victims. Is nature to be respected or corrected by human beings? How to reconcile the integrity of nature's species with the superiority of the human species is a question as old as Aristotle and never better understood than by him.

The philosophy of the rights of man does homogenize nature and leave it utterly subject to human technology as mere undifferentiated material. But environmentalism does not succeed in establishing, or reestablishing, human responsibility for nature. Environmentalism is rather the same, strange patronizing we have already seen, in which the patrons confess themselves to be no better than the patronized. Animals and even trees are awarded rights that they have no earthly possibility of claiming on their own, yet cannot be denied by humans. These humans have lost the confidence to claim their rights, but they retain the authority to proclaim the rights of other species. Here is equality gone mad among Nietzsche's last men, who have lost the will to assert their own humanity.

Yet of course the very term "environment" is anthropocentric, and one infers that nature's rights are intended mainly, or entirely, for human benefit. But human benefit is understood as whatever advances human creativity. The idea of hierarchy in nature and the human virtue of moderation, both of which are necessary to responsibility in this matter, are not consistent with untrammeled creativity. So environmentalism descends to extremism. Instead of enlarging responsibility, its advocates issue proposals and undertake demonstrations so outlandish as to depend for any good effects on the responsibility of those whom they insult.

Private Property under the New Rights. Environmental rights are often asserted against holders of private property. So, in general, are the other new rights, which do not include the right of private property. Under the old rights, private property is the guardian of a self whose individuality is already secure. But in the new view the acquisition of property appears to give identity to the self, and the new identity is rapacity. That identity is not so new in theory; it goes back to the discovery of the bourgeois by Rousseau. But only recently has holding property in America provided the owner with less and less security, and exposed him to more and more litigation.

One main target of the attack on property has been the corporation and its basis in the concept of limited liability. Limited liability permits cooperation in an enterprise without engaging one's whole self or all of one's resources. Proponents of the new rights, concerned to equalize the selves they are creating, denounce the arrangement as an evasion of responsibility. The shareholder and the corporate officer should not be allowed to hide behind the corporate shell but should be held fully responsible for the corporation's misdeeds.

Here again, an expansive responsibility is the enemy of a prudent responsibility that is tied to one's interest rather than expressive of one's whole self. One's interest is an objective self, imposed as it were by the necessities of the situation and of human nature. To the extent that interest is objective—that is, represents what any normal person would do in the situation—one can have interests in the plural, none of them constituting a full commitment. Limited liability protects this possibility, on the one hand; on the other, the replacement of interests by created "values" expressing the whole self attacks it.

The Attack on Formality. The right of private property depends on the formality of rights. When Marx sought to oppose bourgeois property, he first took aim at the formality of rights. A right is only as good as one's capacity to exercise it, he argued; so the equal right to acquire property is a mere formality, of which the effectual truth is the endorsement of very unequal properties actually gained through this right. Thus the rights of man are in fact rights of the bourgeoisie.

Promoters of the new rights generalize the objection to denounce any discrepancy between the formal right and its actual exercise. Only if the exercise is equal are the rights equal; if not, then we are not really serious about rights. Affirmative action is a program to make formally equal rights equal in their exercise, thus *guaranteeing* equality. Under affirmative action it is the legally imposed responsibility of an employer, public or private, not merely not to discriminate unjustly but to take positive or affirmative action to see that potential beneficiaries of nondiscrimination become actual, equally paid employees.

That responsibility overrides the responsibility of the employees, and in general of citizens, to exercise their own rights. Free rights requiring action on one's own behalf become guaranteed entitlements, in principle requiring little or nothing. This result follows from intolerance of a gap between the right—protected by the government—and its exercise by citizens.

Another result of that intolerance is the loss of the distinction between natural and civil rights. We now speak of human rights, which as such have no necessary relationship to civil society. Human rights become civil or constitutional rights immediately, with no sense of having to pass through a form of government for their securing and specification. Thus they owe nothing to a free government and are indifferent to its survival. The only business of any government is to guarantee rights that are justly expressed as relentless and peremptory demands. The spirit is, Freedom now!

The "perfect freedom" that John Locke thought to be characteristic of the state of nature is carried over into civil society as a demand that has lost none of its force through the necessity of forming and obeying a government. The new rights have the security of civil rights and the amplitude of natural rights, as if we could have our cake and eat it too. All the realism of the early liberals disappears beneath a foolish confidence that war should be over with, that crime is on the lam, that sloth is cool and incivility cute. Liberal security is taken for granted in postliberal complacency.

Government and New Rights. Government is not needed to moderate natural rights in the new scheme, nor does it give effect to the right of consent standing between natural and civil rights. The spirited activity of free citizens as well as the necessity of government—in sum, the realm of politics—is lost from sight.

The new rights have been formulated more by philosophy professors than by political scientists. The philosophers forgot that liberalism was originally a doctrine of political science, concerned as much or more with the conditions under which rights are surrendered as with the establishment of rights—and concerned not at all with the elaboration of rights. Liberalism was originally a doctrine of constitutionalism; it was about the making of a government to control and to be controlled by the people. The constitution of that government is the focus of attention because all rights are secured by and from the government. Its form or structure secures rights by governing under law so that the rule of the majority is the rule of a constitutional majority as opposed to a factious majority.

The new rights, however, are postconstitutional. Since self-expression is the norm, the new rights have little to do with self-government. Self-expression can lead to "participation," especially in demonstrations of protest, but such participation shows little respect for the persuasion, deliberation, and moderation that constitutional structures encourage. Promoters of the new rights look on the Constitution as a system to be manipulated—hence, part instrument, part obstacle. They do not think that they live under the Constitution, much less that it is a fundamental law to be venerated. They believe that government is for providing services and collecting taxes, and they would be hard put to say what makes it free.

Wants Become Rights. Those with creative rather than natural selves are preoccupied with the business of self-creation. They do not know their own selves, much less others'; so they have no basis for respecting others' rights. Self-creation, if authentic, cannot be bound to respect any claim that is not self-created. Creative individuals, trying to live by their doctrine, are too busy with themselves and with their own rights to be bothered with persuading others and seeking their consent. In practice—which is usually inauthentic—creative individuals are understood as changing, historical beings rather than as natural beings with a fixed definition.

The rights of historicized beings are impossible to distinguish from wants; even "needs" come to mean "felt needs." These wants alternate in status between posited rights whose positing is not necessary but is merely asserted—the deontological view, according to contemporary philosophy—and preferences, capable of being "traded off" for one another—the utilitarian view. Their status alternates because, in practice, proponents find the first view too absolute and the second too relative. They have abandoned the distinction between natural and civil rights, by which the absoluteness and the relativity of rights are reconciled through the right of consent. They have substituted for it two partisan views that cannot be reconciled and hence must be alternated.

When rights are wants, those who have the wants are no longer required to claim their rights, to fight for them, or to defend them once gained. Elite groups can make the necessary claims on behalf of those who want, since the latter are regarded as too weak actually to enjoy the rights they have had until now in a merely formal sense. In the postconstitutional understanding one does not have a right or choice unless it is an equal right or choice. If one shows by inactivity that he is too weak to exercise his rights, then the government, prompted by elite groups, will step in to guarantee those rights, in effect exercising them better than oneself. When government intervenes, it does not by right have to seek someone's consent or the consent of his fellow-citizens, because he may feel too weak to consent and his fellow-citizens may be overlooking his wants when they consent.

Under these circumstances the new rights become "entitlements," originally a technical term for claims on a budget that must be paid out regardless of how many claim them. Entitlements are thus secure from responsibility to what the common good may require. They resemble pensions in their security, but they differ in not being funded. Entitlements also do not result from a potential or actual contribution of the entitled to the community: not requiring any prior or subsequent action, they do not reward rights responsibly exercised. We can certainly get someone else to demand our entitlements for us, and we can even get someone else to apply for them on our behalf. We do not have to answer for how we spend our entitlements, since any failure, for example, to find decent housing is accounted to society, and the remedy is to extend its responsibility to equalize.

Equalizing proceeds by denigrating past progress in rights as merely formal and lacking in seriousness, while looking forward to an equalized society in infinite approximation. Despite its dissatisfaction with itself, however, a society of entitlements is a static society

109

of defensive special interests. The new rights transform citizens into government dependents—restless, suspicious, ungrateful, passive, and incompetent.

Right of Privacy. The new right of privacy might seem to offer a refuge from government dependency, but in fact it only increases irresponsibility. The old rights were all private rights in the sense of rights belonging to private individuals, but as civil rights they were limited for the sake of others' rights and the common good. The creation of a special right of privacy attempts to define a sphere into which others' rights and the common good cannot enter—a couple's use of contraceptives, a woman's choice of abortion. The attempt has three bad effects apart from these specific matters. First, it detracts from the privacy of rights not subsumed under the right of privacy—as if voting, for example, were not private by right. Second, it misrepresents privacy as absolute, although in fact privacy is most valuable when shared with one's friends and family. After all, absolute privacy is available in solitary confinement in prison if the jailer stays away.

Third, the fact that the Supreme Court seized on the right of privacy to defend a married couple's use of contraceptives (the *Griswold* case) and then used it to deny any family interference in the individual choice of abortion (*Roe v. Wade*) should give pause. The right of privacy actually reflects the government's decision to define the private and to make it subsist by the government's definition.

Because the government defines the private, it intrudes on the private. When the government forbids contraceptives and abortion in the belief that they are contrary to the common good, it may be wrong but it is not on the wrong track. It tells citizens that private actions have public consequences, yet it does not deprive itself of their willing support. A *civil* right comes with a reminder in its very name of the public good of a free society; though its source and immediate end are private, the manner of exercise and the ultimate end promote a *civil* society. A right of privacy seals itself off from any such accompaniment and encourages citizens to forget their citizenship and to tell the government where it can stuff any notion of civility. At the same time it makes privacy an entitlement requiring free contraceptives and abortions, since these are the devices of privacy and everyone must be rendered equally private.

Dependency is the probable effect on the equalized of equalizing rights. But their patrons, the equalizers, have an attitude of mind that in the scheme of new rights is the functional equivalent of the patriotism demanded by Uncle Sam. This attitude, best seen in the

American Civil Liberties Union, is a moralizing extremism reflecting the principle that no right is safe unless it can be carried to an extreme. Rights, as we have seen, are equalized at the extreme. The least limitation on a right weakens it and invites its abolition by government at the urging of prejudiced citizens. A prohibition of child pornography, for example, immediately subtracts from free speech and will eventually undermine it as a whole.

To this extremist attitude, rights are always in peril. They are endangered by the desire to practice moderation in exercising them, for moderation makes it seem that rights are confined to the moderate and intended for routine actions. So a truly disgusting instance of self-expression, when it comes under attack, gives the equalizers a thrill comparable to a call from Uncle Sam. The extreme exercise of a right comes to be the only true exercise, because the best test of devotion to a principle is thought to occur at its furthest reach. Anyone devoted to protecting rights is held to be responsible for guaranteeing the whole range of behavior associated with a right, and without passing adverse value judgments. That is why the right to decent, "affordable" housing—which might seem to imply that being housed is a good thing—is accompanied by the right to be homeless. Thus responsibility is disjoined from moderation.

I do not claim that the old rights are perfect. They have weaknesses that invite the reproaches of proponents of the new rights. The gap between the right and its exercise, in particular, seems to be an inherent defect. Nor do I say that it is possible simply to return to the old rights. Women believe themselves to be beneficiaries of the new rights, and they are not going to be forced back into the kitchen. But we need to become aware of the discontinuity between the old rights and the new, and to beware of the package of bad consequences that comes with the seemingly innocent slogan, "Be all that you can be."

6

New White Rights—The Transformation of Affirmative Action Jurisprudence

Eric Schnapper

*You needed that job and you were the best qualified. But they had
to give it to a minority because of a racial quota. Is that really fair?
. . . Harvey Gantt says it is. Gantt supports Ted Kennedy's racial
quota law that makes the color of your skin more important than
your qualifications.*[1]

In those words, certainly the most controversial political advertise-
ment of the 1990 campaign, Senator Jesse Helms voiced the traditional
conservative argument against racial preferences for minorities.[2] In
this view, a better qualified white applicant has or ought to have a
right not to be rejected, because of his or her race, in favor of a less
qualified black applicant.

The appeal to merit principles and the criticism of race-based
affirmative action have long gone hand in hand. The Helms advertise-
ment would have been ineffective, if not downright peculiar, if it had
admonished, "You were the least qualified applicant, but the job went
to a better qualified minority applicant because of a quota"; or, "No
one knows for sure who was the best qualified applicant, but the job
went to a minority applicant because of a quota"; or even, "You were
about as qualified as a minority applicant who got the job because of
a quota."

For more than forty years, objections to affirmative action have been grounded on an argument that such measures, or at least some of them, are inconsistent with merit-based decision making. In 1950 the Supreme Court held that state courts could enjoin picketing in favor of affirmative action if the demonstrators sought to induce an employer to hire minority workers regardless of "individual qualification."[3] When Senator George Smathers argued in 1964 that Title VII would lead to quotas, he objected that the law

> would, in the final analysis, cause a man to hire someone whom he did not want to hire, not on the basis of ability, but on the basis of religion, color or creed. . . .[4]

The Minority Report of the House Judiciary Committee objected that Title VII would require an employer to maintain a "racially balanced" work force and denounced that supposed requirement as denigrating actual ability:

> Neither competence nor experience is the key for employment under this bill. Race is the principal, first criterion.[5]

Scholarly analyses made the same point. In *The Morality of Consent*, published in 1975, Professor Alexander Bickel denounced use of racial quotas on the ground that

> the cost in efficiency, as well as the injustice, ought to be deemed unacceptable. Productivity and efficiency are on the decline anyway in this country, quite seriously in some sectors of the economy. Accepting further deterioration is no help to anyone. . . . To reject an applicant to a university faculty or for a position in business or for a job as an electrician or in the civil service who has met established, realistic, and unchanged qualifications in favor of a less qualified candidate is morally wrong and in the aggregate disastrous.[6]

A claim of superior qualifications has often been central to the arguments of litigants challenging affirmative action.[7]

Since 1973 the Supreme Court has decided almost a score of cases presenting challenges to affirmative action measures, and in every instance at least one member of the Court, sometimes a majority, found the measure at issue to be either unlawful or unconstitutional. Given the legal and ideological background of these decisions, one would expect the opinions of the conservative justices to be replete with arguments that the race-conscious measures improperly elevated less qualified minority candidates over more qualified whites. Although they are the mainstay of public criticism of

113

affirmative action, however, such arguments are largely absent from these Supreme Court opinions. A few eloquent passages stress the importance of merit-based decision making, but paradoxically they were made *in defense* of the particular race-conscious measures at issue.[8] The next two sections of this chapter describe the increasing indifference on the part of conservative justices to whether disputed affirmative action programs had in fact disadvantaged better qualified nonminority candidates.

The paucity of merit-based arguments in the Supreme Court's affirmative action decisions stems in large measure from the particular facts of those cases. Scholarly and political critiques of affirmative action simply posit that the minority beneficiaries of such programs will be less qualified than whites seeking the position or the benefit at issue. But in actual litigation a judge cannot or should not hypothesize at will the facts that would best support a given ideology, but must deal instead with the contentions of the parties and with the evidence in the record. In none of the cases that came before the Supreme Court did the proponent of affirmative action stipulate that the minority beneficiaries of the program were less qualified than the nonbeneficiaries, let alone unqualified. Every case involved either a sharp disagreement about the qualifications of the affected individuals or a situation in which there manifestly were no significant differences in their abilities.

This circumstance, of course, did not lead conservative justices to acquiesce casually in race-conscious measures, but the legal arguments they advanced in criticism of those practices could not proceed—as had the arguments of politicians and theorists—on an assumption that the practices at issue disfavored the most qualified. The consequent fashioning by various justices of new objections to affirmative action has been significant because these new arguments unavoidably entail different contours for the limitations to be imposed on an affirmative action. Any protection or right thus accorded whites was necessarily different in both rationale and scope from the right, asserted in the Helms commercial, to be safeguarded against quotas favoring the less qualified.

Thus far the Court's response to this situation has not been to propound any single new rationale or right. Rather, the often divergent opinions of individual justices have suggested a variety of different arguments, protections, and consequent rights. No one of these has been embraced by any consistent bloc of votes, let alone a persistent majority. Support for the diverse approaches has ebbed and flowed from opinion to opinion, as members of the Court struggled to adapt to cases where qualifications were disputed or indistinguishable.

This chapter suggests that the standards for evaluating the legality of an affirmative action program would be more sensible and predictable if central importance were attached to whether or not there are in any given case significant, identifiable differences in the comparative merit or qualifications of the individuals affected. That is not to suggest that an affirmative action program should automatically be upheld whenever such differences are absent, or necessarily be struck down whenever they are present. But any legal analysis of a program ought to begin with an objective, fact-based inquiry into whether merit principles are significantly affected by the disputed practices. The Supreme Court decisions discussed below involved different types of affirmative action, some voluntary and some Court-ordered, and such actions are under a variety of legal standards, including the Fourteenth Amendment and several statutes. This chapter does not attempt to consider the possible importance of those distinctions.

The Declining Relevance of Merit

The Supreme Court first confronted the constitutional issues presented by race-conscious measures in 1974, in *DeFunis v. Odegaard*.[9] Eight justices limited their opinions to the question of whether the case was moot; only Justice William O. Douglas, in a dissenting opinion, reached the merits of the case, which concerned the race-conscious manner in which applicants were admitted to the University of Washington Law School. Douglas was unwilling to sanction racial preferences as a form of redress for past discrimination, despairing of the difficulty of calculating "how grievously each group has suffered from discrimination."[10] He quoted with approval the passage in the Court's 1950 decision in *Hughes v. Superior Court* insisting that employment decisions ought to be based on "fitness for the work," not "membership in a particular race."[11] In the competition for admission to a state law school, Douglas urged, "So far as race is concerned, any state-sponsored preference to one race over another . . . is in my view 'invidious' and violative of the Equal Protection Clause."[12] Marco DeFunis, like any other white, "had a constitutional right to have his application considered on its individual merits in a racially neutral manner."[13]

Yet Douglas refused to conclude that the race-conscious selection process at issue was unconstitutional. For Douglas the words "racially neutral manner" were a term of art, whose meaning was decidedly

115

different from "colorblind." Douglas, indeed, was insistent that making admissions decisions on a colorblind basis would be wrong, perhaps even unconstitutional. He maintained that it would be impossible to determine accurately the comparative qualifications of applicants without taking their race into account. First, Douglas argued, the Law School Aptitude Test involved questions connected to the cultural backgrounds of "the dominant Caucasian" race:

> Many Eskimos, native Americans, Filipinos, Chicanos, Asian Indians, Burmese, and Africans came from such disparate backgrounds that a test sensitively attuned for most applicants would be wide of the mark for many minorities.[14]

These differing cultural backgrounds, Douglas insisted, *had to* be taken into account in order to eliminate discrimination from the selection process.

Second, he maintained that an applicant's undergraduate record could not be fairly evaluated in a colorblind manner:

> A black applicant who pulled himself out of the ghetto into a junior college may thereby demonstrate a level of motivation, perseverance and ability that would lead a fairminded admissions committee to conclude that he shows more promise for law study than the son of a rich alumnus who achieved better grades at Harvard.[15]

Third, Douglas thought race might be important in determining the likelihood that a particular applicant would succeed after law school:

> Because of the weight of . . . prior handicaps, th[e] black applicant may not realize his full potential in the first year of law school, or even in the full three years, but in the long pull of a legal career his achievements may far outstrip those of his classmates whose earlier records appeared superior by conventional criteria.[16]

Such an applicant's background might bear on "the likelihood that a particular candidate will more likely employ his legal skills to service communities that are not now adequately represented than will competing candidates."[17] In short, Douglas believed it was not only permissible but also necessary to take into account the race of an applicant in order to evaluate his or her qualifications in an accurate, "racially neutral" manner.

The actual record in *DeFunis* posed for Douglas the most difficult problem. The law school had not itself questioned the reliability of LSAT scores and grades as methods of selecting law students.[18]

Unwilling to permit the fate of a generation of law students to turn on such litigation tactics, Douglas proceeded to raise on his own the difficulties of judging the abilities of minority applicants. Having no record on which to rely, Douglas turned instead to scholarly publications and his own judgment. At the end of his opinion, perhaps precisely because of the lack of a record on these issues, Douglas announced he would remand the case for a new trial.

Although it is not altogether clear which issues Douglas thought ought to be dealt with on remand, perhaps the central one would have been whether DeFunis was in fact better qualified than the minority students who had been given special treatment. If DeFunis were not better qualified, Douglas appears to suggest, he would lose, even if the particular race-conscious plan at the law school was not exactly what Douglas thought justified. For Douglas, actual merit— meaningfully measured—was to be accorded controlling importance, unrestricted by the manner in which a particular case had been tried or in which a specific program had operated.

In 1978, *University of California Regents v. Bakke*[19] presented issues and a procedural posture similar to those of *DeFunis*. Alan Bakke challenged the special admissions program for disadvantaged racial minorities at the medical school of the University of California at Davis. *Bakke* presented even less of a record than *DeFunis*, having been decided without trial on cross motions for summary judgment.

But Justice Lewis Powell, Jr., whose opinion controlled the outcome of *Bakke*, took an approach drastically different from that of Justice Douglas in *DeFunis*. The traditional admissions criteria at Davis, like those at the University of Washington, were grades and standardized tests. Powell noted that racial classifications might indeed be required for a "fair appraisal of each individual's academic promise in the light of some cultural bias in grading or testing procedures," but he flatly refused to consider the issue because in *Bakke*, as in *DeFunis*, the school had not raised it. This issue, which had dominated Douglas's earlier opinion, was relegated by Powell to a footnote:

> To the extent that race and ethnic background were considered only to the extent of curing established inaccuracies in predicting academic performance, it might be argued that there is no "preference" at all. *Nothing in this record*, however, suggests either that any of the quantitative factors considered by the Medical School were culturally biased or that the [school's] special admissions program was formulated to correct any such bias.[20]

In *DeFunis* Douglas insisted that differences in actual ability were of controlling importance, and insisted that the case could not be decided without first determining what differences existed; in *Bakke* Powell thought such differences were only arguably relevant, and proceeded to decide the case consciously ignorant of whether they in fact existed.

In the Supreme Court the medical school did argue that its special admissions program could be justified as a method of increasing the number of doctors in medically underserved minority communities. If minority doctors were in fact more willing to serve in such areas, that would certainly have provided a basis for holding they were better qualified than whites intent upon serving a lucrative, upper-class clientele. But Powell again dismissed this argument out of hand because it had not been presented below. There was, Powell observed,

> virtually no evidence in the record indicating that [such a] program is . . . needed. . . . The only evidence in the record with respect to such underservice is a newspaper article.[21]

In reality virtually every adult in the country knew there was a grave shortage of doctors in poor black communities, but Justice Powell concluded that the procedural posture of the case required him to ignore the obvious. Powell also objected that there was no evidence in the record regarding whether white doctors were less likely than black ones to choose to practice in a black community.

In sum, *Bakke*, like *DeFunis*, was a case in which the minority applicants who had received preferential treatment might indeed have been better qualified than the complaining whites. Under these circumstances Justice Douglas thought it essential to resolve the issue of comparative qualification through a retrial to supplement an inadequate record. If, as Douglas appears to have maintained, race-conscious measures are unconstitutional only where they lead to the selection of the less qualified, the validity of such measures could not be determined without first ascertaining what effect they actually had on merit considerations. Justice Powell, on the other hand, was prepared to decide *Bakke* without knowing whether the special admissions plan at issue selected medical students less able, more able, or as able as those who would otherwise have been chosen. Powell's willingness to do so was particularly striking because a news story published while *Bakke* was pending revealed that the Davis medical-school student selected as the best clinical practitioner of his class had entered the school under the disputed special admissions program.

Two other aspects of *Bakke* are noteworthy. First, although holding the Davis plan unconstitutional, Powell indicated he would sustain an admissions plan like that at Harvard, which considered an applicant's race as evidence that he or she would contribute to the diversity of the student body. The general effect of the Powell decision was thus to suggest to admissions committees that a more sensitive and penetrating evaluation of the potential of minority applicants was not only legally unfruitful, but also legally unnecessary. For the time being, at least, the Supreme Court did not care whether minority applicants had a possibly hidden potential, or were likely to put their education to particularly good use, or were less qualified. Under the Harvard plan, all that mattered was that minorities would contribute to the diversity of the student body.

Justice John Paul Stevens, in an opinion joined by Justices Warren Burger, Potter Stewart, and William Rehnquist, argued in *Bakke* that Title VI of the 1964 Civil Rights Act forbade Davis from excluding Bakke or any other white on account of race. They insisted that Title VI contained a simple absolute prohibition, not the more complex constitutional rule advanced by Powell, forbidding any racial considerations in the selection of participants for a federally funded program. Whatever the technical legal merits of this interpretation of Title VI, such a prohibition was not, like Powell's opinion, simply indifferent to merit considerations; Stevens's opinion would in some circumstances be flatly inconsistent with selecting the best qualified participant. Justice Douglas had suggested in *DeFunis* that it was never possible to pick the best qualified law school applicant without considering race. Although reasonable people could disagree about that contention, race would obviously be of controlling importance to qualification in some circumstances, such as the selection by a police department of an informant to infiltrate an all-black gang. In Justice Stevens's view, a police department receiving federal funds, and thus subject to Title VI, would be forbidden by law to consider race in picking its informants, a prohibition with potentially fatal consequences.

Three years after *Bakke*, the Court confronted a case in which the relevance of race to qualifications was evident to virtually every justice. In 1981, in *Minnick v. California Department of Corrections*, the white plaintiffs challenged the use of racial considerations in hiring, promotions, and assignments.[22] The U.S. Department of Justice had previously recommended that the proportion of minority correctional officers in a prison be at least 70 percent of the population of minority inmates.[23] In *Minnick* the state defended the use of racial consideration as part of its efforts to deal with violence in the prisons.[24] The trial court held that the Department of Corrections could make assignments on the basis of race

119

in order to serve the compelling state interest in promoting the safety of correctional officers and inmates, encouraging inmate rehabilitation, minimizing racial tensions, and furthering orderly and efficient prison management.[25]

At the same time, however, the trial court enjoined the department from considering race in its hiring and promotion decisions. The state appellate court overturned that injunction, holding that the problems of racial tension and violence justified racial considerations not only in assignments but also in hiring and promotion.

After the Supreme Court agreed to hear the case, it became apparent that there were "significant ambiguities in the record concerning . . . the justification for [the] use" of racial considerations.[26] The Court voted to follow the course of action urged by Justice Douglas in *DeFunis*, remanding the case for additional evidence and findings. Justice Stewart argued in a dissenting opinion for an absolute constitutional prohibition, like that urged on statutory grounds by Stevens in *Bakke*, of any consideration of race. Stewart would have forbidden considerations of race in any corrections department personnel decisions, regardless of whether, as the lower courts had concluded, minority-group correctional officers would at times be better able than white officers to deal with racial tensions and violence in the prisons.[27] The rest of the Court, however, seemed willing to uphold race-based decisions that were related to actual qualifications.

In 1986, *Wygant v. Jackson Board of Education* presented a similar problem in an educational setting; the result, however, was very different.[28] In 1972 the Jackson schools were experiencing "racial tensions [that] had escalated to violent levels."[29] One factor that apparently contributed to the problem was the paucity of minority teachers, most having been laid off in 1971. In response to this situation, the school board and union agreed that future layoffs, although otherwise based on seniority, would not reduce the proportion of minority teachers in the school system. As a practical matter, this meant that some more senior white teachers would be laid off while less senior blacks were retained.[30] The constitutional challenge filed by white teachers was initially dismissed at the district court level on a motion for summary judgment. Thus when the case reached the Supreme Court, the school board had never been afforded any opportunity to offer evidence to justify the disputed race-conscious layoff rule.

The school board argued in the Supreme Court that the layoff provision was justifiable because minority teachers brought an additional and important qualification to their jobs because they could serve as role models for minority children. Four justices would have sustained the disputed provision on this basis. Justice Stevens argued:

> In the context of public education, it is quite obvious that a school board may reasonably conclude that an integrated faculty will be able to provide benefits to the student body that could not be provided by an all-white, or nearly all-white, faculty. . . . It is one thing for a white child to be taught by a white teacher that color, like beauty, is only "skin deep"; it is far more convincing to experience that truth on a day-to-day basis during the routine, ongoing learning process.[31]

A plurality of the Court, however, rejected this proffered justification.

Unlike what had occurred in *Bakke*, however, in *Wygant* Justice Powell did not object that there was insufficient evidence that a faculty with a substantial number of black teachers would be more effective than a faculty with few or no minority teachers. Powell could not reject this proffered justification on evidentiary grounds, as he had in *Bakke*, because in *Wygant* there had never been a trial at which the school board could introduce any evidence. Rather, Powell insisted it was irrelevant as a matter of law whether retaining black teachers would in fact improve the quality of the teaching staff, because that sort of justification was too "amorphous" and "overexpansive" for the courts to accept.[32] Justice Stevens objected that there was "nothing in the record—not a shred of evidence" to contradict the school board's contention that retaining junior black teachers would in fact be better for the system than retaining senior white ones.[33] Justice Thurgood Marshall insisted the case should not be decided in the absence of a fully developed factual record.[34] But for Justices Powell, Burger, Rehnquist, and Sandra Day O'Connor, the evidence and state of the record simply did not matter, because in their view it was not important whether the black teachers retained under the layoff plan were better qualified than Wendy Wygant and the laid-off whites.[35] If in this instance there was a conflict between merit and colorblindness, Powell and the rest of the plurality preferred colorblindness.

In *Mississippi University for Women v. Hogan*, decided in 1982, the Court again pretermitted any evidentiary hearing regarding whether sex-based distinctions were merit-related.[36] The defendant in this instance was a state nursing school that refused to admit male students. The school argued that admitting men would have a deleterious effect on the education of the women students. All members of the Court apparently agreed that this contention, if true, would

121

justify excluding men. A brief submitted by students and alumnae of the nursing school argued:

> An institution of collegiate higher learning maintained exclusively for women is uniquely able to provide the education atmosphere in which some . . . women can best attain maximum learning potential. . . . It can free its students of the burden of playing the mating game while attending classes, thus giving academic rather than sexual emphasis.[37]

In this view, sex would be a critical indicator of qualification, because male students would seriously interfere with the education of the existing female students.

Justice O'Connor, writing for the Court, insisted that these concerns were in fact groundless:

> The uncontroverted record reveals that admitting men to nursing classes does not affect teaching style, . . . that the presence of men in the classroom would not affect the performance of female nursing students, . . . and that men in coeducational nursing schools do not dominate the classroom. . . . In sum, the record in this case is flatly inconsistent with the claim that excluding men from the School of Nursing is necessary to reach any of [the school's] educational goals.[38]

The difficulty with this disposition of the school's justification was that, as in *Wygant*, the case had never gone to trial. The record contained no support for the school's factual assertions because the district court had dismissed the case prior to trial, believing that the school was entitled to prevail without offering any evidence of its own.

Most recently, in a 1990 dissenting opinion in *Metro Broadcasting v. F.C.C.*, Justice O'Connor returned to Justice Powell's 1990 approach in *Wygant*, insisting that even if minority ownership of broadcast stations did result in program diversity—that is, if minority owners were in fact better qualified in that regard—that difference was irrelevant as a matter of law.[39] Justice Anthony M. Kennedy objected in *Metro Broadcasting* that it would be a drastic change in the law to prefer black applicants, not as a method of redressing past discrimination, but because they would be better able to "advance some 'important' governmental interest,"[40] an unequivocal rejection of the use of race to select the best qualified applicants.

There has thus been a marked change in the basis of judicial objections to affirmative action. In the early years, conservatives often asserted or assumed that race-conscious actions would always be inconsistent with merit-based decisions. Justice Stewart expressed that view when he wrote:

> Under our Constitution, the government may never act to the detriment of a person solely because of that person's race. The color of a person's skin and the country of his origin are immutable facts that bear no relation to ability. . . .[41]

Where race is in fact unrelated to ability, race-based decisions might be criticized as irrational and arbitrary. But whether race is actually unrelated to ability is a question of fact. In *Wygant*, Justice Stevens flatly disputed the factual basis of Stewart's position, insisting that there were indeed situations in which race was related to ability:

> The Equal Protection Clause absolutely prohibits the use of race in many government contexts. . . . The government may not use race to decide who may serve on juries, who may use public services, who may marry, and who may be fit parents. The use of race in these situations is "utterly irrational" because it is completely unrelated to any valid public purpose. . . . Nevertheless, in our present society, race is not always irrational to sound government decision making.[42]

The majority in *Metro Broadcasting* asserted that the contention that a black applicant would be more qualified, or would be likely to be more qualified, than a white is a " 'complex' empirical question."[43] Initially the conservative justices attempted to avoid the potential tension between merit-based and colorblind decision making by refusing to undertake any inquiry into that empirical question. More recently those justices have increasingly insisted that colorblindness is to be preferred regardless of whether color-conscious decisions might, in the case at hand, result in the selection of better qualified individuals.[44] A strict insistence on colorblindness is theoretically coherent and has an undeniable appeal, but colorblindness is not necessarily the same thing as merit selection. If the best qualified individuals cannot be identified without considering race, a rigid requirement of colorblindness would forbid selection of the best qualified and would thus confer on less qualified whites a right to protection from such merit-based selections.

The cases that have come before the Court illustrate some of the ways in which race might in practice relate to merit. First, the accurate evaluation of an applicant's record may turn on whether the applicant was earlier treated differently by others on the basis of his or her race, a problem that could not be evaluated without considering the applicant's race. Second, race, although irrelevant to most abilities, may be very relevant to the ability or willingness of an individual to deal with racial issues. In a racially tense situation, for example, students, inmates, or fellow officers may react differently to a teacher, guard, or other official depending on his or her race. Third, in seeking a desirable nonracial attribute, such as the likelihood that an individual will not engage in or tolerate discrimination or, as in *Bakke*, will choose to work in medically underserved neighborhoods, the race of an individual may in practice be the most reliable predictor of that characteristic. It is not true a priori that black teachers are less likely than whites to discriminate against black students, but it might well be true in fact. To recognize any of these possibilities is not to assert that they occur ordinarily or even occasionally, but merely to observe they *are* possibilities and thus raise factual issues that a party might seek to litigate. The principal failing of most affirmative action opinions written by conservative justices is not that they resolved those factual issues incorrectly, but that they failed to address them seriously, if at all.

The Problem of Qualification Equivalence

If a primary defect of race-conscious measures is that they disadvantage better qualified whites, it should follow as a corollary that race-conscious measures are less objectionable—perhaps not inherently desirable, but still significantly different—when those measures are utilized to make selections from among a group of individuals who are equally qualified. An "equally qualified" white might have a claim, perhaps even a right, not to be affected by such measures, but if merit is a key consideration, that claim or right ought to be different in kind and less compelling than that of a "better qualified" white.

This distinction is more than just a test of whether critics of affirmative action are genuinely concerned about merit. Every member of the Supreme Court regards the resolution of these cases as involving a balance of the circumstances of each, although the justices weigh those circumstances in different manners. If merit differences militate against the validity of such a plan, merit equivalence ought to cut in the opposite way, and that distinction should be of controlling importance in some close cases. That would be equally true for a case in which merit differences, although present, are impossible to detect or predict: some infants will grow up to be better singers than others, but no one knows how to pick a future choir from a group of one-year-olds.

A case of merit equivalence raises a special situation, as well, in light of the reasoning of *Griggs v. Duke Power Co.* in 1971.[45] *Griggs* held that Title VII of the 1964 Civil Rights Act forbids more than just intentional discrimination; it also prohibits certain employment practices that have a discriminatory *effect*. Thus, if an examination or an education requirement disproportionately eliminates minority candidates for a job (for example, if 90 percent of whites, but only 50 percent of blacks, can satisfy the requirement), that selection procedure cannot be used unless the "standard is shown to be significantly related to successful job performance."[46]

If a group of job applicants are in fact all equally able to do a job, *any* method of choosing among them will necessarily be unrelated to their comparative job performances, since all the applicants by definition can perform the job equally well. Since no selection standard *could* choose applicants who would perform more ably than the rest, the only standards that would be legal under *Griggs* would be standards that have no adverse impact. That is, an employer hiring from a group of equally qualified applicants *must*, under *Griggs*, use a selection criterion that has no adverse impact on minority candidates.

In the long term, at least in theory, an employer could find such a selection standard that was free of adverse impact. But in the short term—that is, if an employer needs to hire one hundred new workers this month—such a standard may not be available. When that situation arises, and it has arisen repeatedly in Title VII litigation, the courts have routinely ordered the defendants to hire a sufficient number of minority candidates to eliminate any adverse impact.[47] Thus if an employer's test were held unlawful because it had an adverse impact on a pool of equally qualified applicants, a court would permit continued interim use of the test only if the percentage of minority candidates in the group hired was the same as the percentage in the group of applicants.[48] In such a case, where a pool of equally qualified applicants is 25 percent black, *Griggs* requires the employer to hire a 25 percent black group, either through a selection standard with no adverse impact or through race-conscious adjustments in the results of a standard with adverse impact. The Reagan Justice Department, although passionately opposed to what it regarded as quotas, routinely sought under *Griggs* just such race-conscious adjustments to selection procedures.[49] In 1987, in *United States v. Paradise*, for example, the Justice Department proposed that the Alabama State Police be required to award 25 percent of certain promotions to blacks because blacks made up one-quarter of the labor pool affected by a promotion test found to have an unlawful adverse impact.[50]

The earliest Supreme Court case to deal with a situation of merit equivalence was *United Jewish Organizations v. Carey*, in 1977.[51] Prior to 1974 certain black and Hispanic communities in Brooklyn had been divided among a number of predominantly white Senate and assembly districts. As a result of action taken by the Department of Justice under the Voting Rights Act of 1965, the district lines were redrawn by the state to reduce the division of minority communities, with the effect and the purpose of increasing the number of Senate and assembly districts with effective black and Hispanic majorities. Despite that increase, 70 percent of the senate and assembly districts in Brooklyn were predominantly white, even though whites constituted only 65 percent of the population. In some instances, however, the redistricting divided white communities among predominantly non-white districts.

The litigation in *United Jewish Organizations* presented a case of merit equivalence: whites did not and could not claim to be better qualified to vote, or to be more entitled than blacks or Hispanics to representation in Albany. Under those circumstances the plurality opinion, joined by Justice Rehnquist, concluded that whites had no cause to complain about the results of the redistricting:

> The plan did not minimize or unfairly cancel out white voting strength. . . . Petitioners have not objected to the impact of the 1974 plan on the representation of white voters in the county or in the State as a whole. . . . The plan left white majorities in approximately 70 percent of the assembly and senate districts in [Brooklyn], which had a countywide population that was 65 percent white. Thus, even if voting in the county occurred strictly according to race, whites would not be underrepresented relative to their share of the population. . . . As long as whites in [Brooklyn], as a group, were provided with fair representation, we cannot conclude that there was a cognizable discrimination against whites. . . .[52]

The effect of the plan was itself not objectionable so long as it left whites with "fair representation," a number of predominantly white districts proportionate to the white population. That is to say, in the terminology of *Griggs*, so long as the number of minority districts was increased only to the point needed to eliminate adverse impact of the pre-1974 districting, whites were not being treated unfairly. In such circumstances Rehnquist and a majority of the Court concluded that the consideration of race in drawing the lines at issue was not, by itself, unconstitutional.

In *Bakke*, Justice Powell's opinion appears to have proceeded on the assumption that the qualifications of each medical school applicant were sufficiently distinct, and could be measured with sufficient precision, that the applicants could be placed in rank order, with each applicant significantly better than the next ranking applicant. Powell struck down the race-conscious plan utilized in that case, endorsing in its place the type of admissions plan in effect at Harvard. But Harvard's account of its own plan, in which race was one among several factors considered, explained that there were often few significant or measurable differences among a very large group of applicants capable of doing well at the school:

> The number of applicants who are deemed to be not "qualified" is comparatively small. The vast majority of applicants demonstrate through test scores, high school records and teachers' recommendations that they have the academic ability to do adequate work at Harvard, and perhaps to do it with distinction. . . . Consequently, after selecting those students whose intellectual potential will seem extraordinary to the faculty—perhaps 150 or so out of an entering class of over 1100—the Committee seeks variety. . . . When the Committee on Admissions reviews the large middle group of applicants who are "admissible" and deemed capable of doing good work in their courses, the race of an applicant may tip the balance. . . .[53]

Justice Powell's objection in *Bakke*—that whites, "No matter how strong their qualifications," could not win the seats Davis set aside for minorities—seems inconsistent with Harvard's view that most admittees are selected from a large pool whose qualifications and ability are similar.[54]

Justices Marshall, Harry Andrew Blackmun, William J. Brennan, Jr., and Byron R. White, in an opinion defending the Davis plan, argued by analogy to *Griggs* that that plan could be justified as a manner of overcoming the disparate impact of the medical school's ordinary admissions criteria. Noting that Powell conceded the plan could have been adopted to redress an earlier violation, they insisted that the defendant officials

> could simply . . . promulgat[e] a regulation prohibiting disparate treatment not justified by the need to admit only qualified students, and could . . . declar[e] Davis to have been in violation of such a regulation on the basis of the exclusionary effect of [its earlier] admissions policy.[55]

Justice Blackmun, in a separate opinion, emphasized that the Davis plan, like all medical school admissions decisions, was being used to choose among individuals all of whom were "highly qualified."[56]

In *Wygant*, a majority of the Court struck down an affirmative action plan, although the adversely affected whites had not asserted and could not plausibly have asserted any claim to being better qualified than the black beneficiaries of the plan. The school board in *Wygant*, faced with the need to reduce the teaching staff, wanted to do so with no adverse impact, so that the proportion of blacks laid off was the same as the proportion of whites. The board could have done so in a racially neutral and constitutional manner by selecting teachers to be laid off at random, through some form of lottery.[57] The teachers' union, however, preferred that layoffs be based at least in part on seniority. Whatever the merits or drawbacks of seniority systems, an employee's seniority has no necessary relationship to his or her comparative qualifications. In March 1991, for example, Minnesota's teacher of the year was laid off because she had less seniority than her fellow, less skilled teachers.[58] The union representing the Jackson teachers preferred that seniority rather than relative ability be the basis for the layoffs. Like a lottery, seniority was racially neutral; unlike a lottery, a strict seniority rule would have led to laying off a disproportionate number of minority teachers.

The only way the school board could ensure that the layoffs would have no adverse impact on minority teachers and yet still be based in part on seniority was to provide that seniority would not control where it would reduce the proportion of minorities in the school system. After extended negotiations the school board and union agreed on such a system. The collective bargaining agreement, first adopted in 1972, specified that the teachers with the least seniority could be laid off except where doing so would have an adverse impact. This meant that in some instances white teachers would be laid off who had more seniority than black teachers who were retained. When that eventually occurred, several of the white teachers involved challenged the constitutionality of the layoff rule.

The Supreme Court held that the layoff plan was unconstitutional, a result apparently prompted by the Court's antipathy to actually laying off whites, rather than merely not hiring them, as an affirmative action measure. But, more surprisingly, the Court's analysis attached no significance whatever to the fact that the white plaintiffs did not claim to be any better qualified than the blacks who were retained.[59] Justice Marshall's dissenting opinion in *Wygant* noted, but did not emphasize, that no merit differences were involved in the case.[60]

Steelworkers v. Weber in 1979 presented a similar case of qualification equivalence.[61] The race-conscious measure in that case was used for the selection of employees who would be placed in a craft training program. Apparently because a training program was involved, the employer did not require applicants to meet any merit-related requirement. The selection system was similar to that in *Wygant*; promotions went to the most senior bidders, provided that at least 50 percent of all vacancies were awarded to blacks. This meant that in some instances more senior whites, such as Brian Weber, were rejected in favor of less senior blacks. The Court upheld that race-and-seniority standard in *Weber*. None of the opinions in *Weber* referred to the fact that no differences in ability were involved.[62]

In *Johnson v. Transportation Agency* (1987), Justice O'Connor became the first of the conservative justices to announce that the force of her reservations about affirmative action was indeed less where significant merit differences were absent.[63] In *Johnson* an affirmative action program favoring the promotion of women was a factor in the employer's decision to promote Diane Joyce instead of plaintiff Paul Johnson. The qualifications of Joyce and Johnson for the position of road dispatcher was very similar. After several applicants were interviewed by a personnel board, Johnson was tied for second, with a score of 75, while Joyce was third, with a score of 73. Joyce had four years experience as a road maintenance worker, with stints as a dispatcher; Johnson had two years experience as a road maintenance worker and some experience as a dispatcher a decade earlier for another employer. Both were rated "well qualified." A second board interviewed all seven applicants rated high enough to be eligible for promotion and recommended that the position be given to Johnson. The agency director decided to award the position to Joyce. He testified that he regarded as insignificant the fact that Johnson's score was slightly higher than Joyce's, and that he did not have "any basis" for deciding one was more qualified than the other.[64]

A majority of the Court in *Johnson* held that the selection of Joyce did not violate Title VII. Justice O'Connor's separate concurring opinion attached particular significance to the similarity in the qualifications of the two applicants. She announced at the outset of her opinion that "the question posed" by the case was "whether a public employer violates Title VII by promoting a qualified woman rather than a marginally better qualified man."[65] After an analysis of the circumstances under which affirmative action would be permissible under Title VII, O'Connor concluded:

> The Director . . . was aware that [Joyce's and Johnson's] scores were rather close. . . . The Director stated that had Joyce's experience been less than that of [Johnson] by a larger margin, [Johnson] might have received the promotion. . . . While I agree with Justice Scalia's dissent that an

affirmative action program that automatically and blindly promotes those marginally qualified candidates falling within a preferred race or gender category . . . would violate Title VII, I cannot agree that this is such a case.[66]

The majority also noted, although with less emphasis, that "any differences in qualifications between Johnson and Joyce were minimal, to say the least."[67]

Justice Scalia's dissent in *Johnson* is equally noteworthy. Scalia repeatedly insisted that Johnson was in fact "more qualified than Joyce."[68] He then argued at great length that the majority opinion had held that employers could make promotions purely on the basis of race or sex as long as the individual chosen was "minimally capable." The majority, he insisted, required

no more than eliminating from the applicant pool those who are *minimally qualified* for the job. Once that has been done, once the promoting official assures himself that all the candidates are . . . minimally qualified . .. he can ignore, as the Agency Director did here, how much better than minimally qualified some of the candidates may be, and can proceed to appoint . . . solely on the basis of race or sex.[69]

This description of the majority opinion is manifestly incorrect, as is the suggestion that there were substantial differences in the qualifications of Joyce and Johnson. But Scalia tacitly conceded the distinction made by O'Connor, that affirmative action plans are far more difficult to attack when the choice to be made is among candidates with very similar or indistinguishable qualifications.

These decisions reveal another element that transcends any single case. Lawsuits in which the competing claimants had essentially identical qualifications are not aberrations: a majority of the Supreme Court's affirmative action cases involve precisely this situation. In a footnote responding to Scalia's dissent, the majority in *Johnson* accused him of ignoring

the fact that "it is a standard tenet of personnel administration that there is rarely a single 'best qualified' person for a job. An effective personnel system will bring before the selecting official several fully qualified candidates who each may possess different attributes which recommend them for selection. Especially where the job is an unexceptional, middle-level craft position, without the need for unique work experience or educational attainment and for which several well-qualified candidates are available, final determinations as to which candidate is 'best qualified' are at best subjective."[70]

Scalia in reply recognized the importance of this statement, commenting that, if true,

> It has staggering implications for future Title VII litigation, since the most common reason advanced for failing to hire a member of a protected group is the superior qualification of the hired individual.[71]

Scalia insisted he was "confident" the majority would disavow the statement when the Court recognized its implications.[72] But the factual correctness of the majority's observation obviously does not turn on whether its implications are ideologically unpalatable to Justice Scalia or anyone else.

If the Court is serious in its occasional suggestion that denigration of merit considerations is a key flaw of race-conscious measures, the Court's affirmative action jurisprudence ought—as O'Connor's opinion in *Johnson* suggests—to develop into two distinct branches. The legal standards for cases in which substantial qualification differences exist should be different from those in which such differences are absent. There would still be restrictions under the Constitution and Title VII in cases of qualification equivalence, but the legal standards in such cases would be different from and less stringent than those in cases involving competing claimants with different abilities. In cases involving qualification equivalence, it ought also to be of considerable importance whether the proportion of all positions set aside for a given group exceeds their proportion of the relevant pool. *Griggs* and its progeny provide special sanction for race-conscious measures that merely neutralize the effects of non-job-related selection criteria. Criteria that select among the equally qualified, of course, are by definition not job-related.

White "Rights" and "Expectations"

The frequent absence of any serious merit-based argument leaves somewhat hollow the original conservative objections to race-conscious measures. One could of course fashion an argument that the mere consideration of race is intolerable per se. But that would be to assert that the affected white applicant had no particular claim to a given job: that the job could fairly have been given to anyone else, that it could equitably have been filled by flipping a coin or awarded to a black for some trivial or irrational reason. The wrong would then have occurred not because that black got the job, but solely because he or she got it on account of race rather than some merit-irrelevant criterion such as zodiac sign, college connections, or dumb luck. Such an argument would be intellectually coherent but certainly less compelling than a claim that the white applicant was the best qualified.

The conservative justices soon sensed they could not concede in this manner that the black individual involved might fairly have gotten the position in question, limiting their objections to the particular procedure—that is, race-based—utilized to arrive at an otherwise unobjectionable result. Often unable for substantive or procedural reasons to insist that the white claimant was in fact the best qualified for the position, the conservatives explored a number of other approaches for suggesting that the white did indeed have some claim on the position—that the race-conscious practice was not only an unacceptable procedure, but also one that led to an improper result.

In the earliest cases, the justices defending race-conscious measures moved quickly to exploit the initial absence of any such claim. In *United Jewish Organizations v. Carey* in 1977, the plaintiffs objected that their Hasidic community had been divided among several different legislative districts as a consequence of a redistricting plan intended to create additional predominantly nonwhite districts.[73] Justice Brennan emphasized that the white plaintiffs were "denied the opportunity to vote as a group in accordance with the earlier districting configuration, but they do not press any legal claim to a group voice as Hasidim."[74] Justice White pointedly quoted a passage in the plaintiffs' brief acknowledging that they did not "contend that there is any right—constitutional or statutory—for permanent recognition of a community in legislative apportionment."[75] Even Chief Justice Burger, although maintaining that the redistricting scheme was unconstitutional, conceded that the plaintiffs "certainly have no constitutional right to remain unified within a single political district."[76]

Chief Justice Burger took a different approach in his dissenting opinion in 1976 in *Franks v. Bowman Transportation Co.*[77] The black plaintiffs in that case had proved that the defendants had refused to hire them because of their race. A majority of the Court concluded that the appropriate remedy in such a case should include giving to the victims of that discrimination the seniority date they would have had but for the violation of Title VII. Such seniority relief was important because job assignments, layoffs, and recalls all were made on the basis of seniority. Although altering the seniority dates of blacks would adversely affect some white employees, the Court emphasized that those white employees did not have any "indefeasibly vested rights conferred by the employment contract."[78] The chief justice argued in his dissenting opinion that white employees indeed had a "right" to the jobs or other benefits that might be lost to blacks with enhanced seniority:

> Competitive-type seniority relief at the expense of wholly innocent employees can rarely, if ever, be equitable. . . . More equitable would be [an increased] monetary award to the person suffering the discrimination. Such monetary relief would serve the dual purpose of deterring wrongdoing . . . as well as protecting the *rights* of innocent employees. In every respect an innocent employee is comparable to a "holder-in-due-course" of negotiable paper or a bona fide purchaser of property without notice of any defect in the seller's title. In this setting I cannot join in judicial approval of "robbing Peter to pay Paul."[79]

The employer in *Franks*, by discriminating against blacks, had conferred on some white workers an enhanced seniority status they would not have obtained had Title VII not been violated. In Chief Justice Burger's view, that enhanced seniority status once awarded was a species of property to which whites had a vested right, although it had been illicitly acquired.

Burger's position in *Franks* was rejected by every other member of the Court, and understandably so. The very purpose of Title VII in this regard is to forbid employers from giving white employees specially enhanced seniority because of their race. It would stand the statute on its head to hold that such a competitive advantage over black workers, once unlawfully accorded to whites, becomes a vested entitlement that the white workers had a right to enjoy for the rest of their careers. To assert that whites had a right to the fruits of unlawful discrimination is to suggest that preferential status for whites is a normal or at least acceptable situation to which Title VII is no more than a procedural encumbrance.

The approach taken by Justice Burger alone in *Franks*, however, was joined ten years later by several other members of the Court. In *Wygant v. Jackson Board of Education*, the school board sought to justify its race-based layoff plan, at least in part, as a remedy for past hiring discrimination against blacks.[80] A plurality opinion by Justice Powell, joined by Justice Rehnquist and Chief Justice Burger, invalidated the plan in part on the ground that the whites adversely affected had a right to the positions at issue:

> We have previously expressed concern over the burden that a preferential layoffs scheme imposes on innocent parties. . . . Though hiring goals may burden some innocent individuals, they simply do not impose the same kind of injury that layoffs impose. . . . "[T]he *rights* and expectations surround-

ing seniority make up what is probably the most valuable capital asset that the worker *'owns'*. . . ."

While hiring goals impose a diffuse burden, often foreclosing only one of several opportunities, layoffs impose the entire burden of achieving racial equality on particular individuals. . . . That burden is too intrusive.[81]

Even if, as the school board contended, Wendy Wygant or other identifiable white teachers had gotten their jobs as a result of unlawful discrimination, Justice Powell's opinion suggested that the earlier discrimination had conferred on them some sort of property right in the job, a right that could not be rescinded merely to "achiev[e] racial equality."

The right to the job described by Justice Powell was a special and limited one. A white had a right to a job only as against a less senior black; the employer evidently remained free to strip the white of that right for any nonracial purpose, however trivial, or even for no reason at all. Justice O'Connor used similar language in her separate opinion in *Wygant*, asserting that an affirmative action plan would be invalid if it "imposed disproportionate harm on the interests, or unnecessarily trammeled the *rights* of innocent individuals directly and adversely affected by a plan's racial preference."[82] Justice O'Connor did not explain under what circumstances an affirmative action plan could be said to affect the "rights" rather than merely the "interests" of whites.

In the years since *Wygant*, no member of the Court has suggested that the specific position or opportunity denied to particular whites in any actual case was their "right," but references to possible such rights persist. In *United States v. Paradise*, Justice Brennan sustained a court-ordered race-conscious promotion scheme because it did not "disproportionately harm the interests, or unnecessarily trammel the rights, of innocent individuals."[83] Justice O'Connor complained that the disputed court order in that case had been issued "without first considering the effectiveness of alternatives that would have a lesser effect on the rights of nonminority [employees]."[84] O'Connor's assertion that nonminority rights were at issue in *Paradise* was particularly significant because that case involved the sort of applications for new positions that Justice Powell had insisted in *Wygant* were different from the entitlements of workers facing loss of their positions.

In *Johnson v. Transportation Agency*, Justice Brennan perceived the tactical advantage to be gained by insisting that the conservative justices make good on their assertion that whites had a right to the benefit at issue.[85] Writing for the majority, Brennan defined a central issue in the case as whether the promotion plan, which in that instance favored women, "unnecessarily trammeled the rights of male employees."[86] By framing the issue in terms of rights, Brennan increased the burden on the male worker objecting to the affirmative action plan, for although Mr. Johnson's interests may have been injured, it was difficult to argue that he had any right to the disputed promotion. Brennan, having cast the issue in language earlier advanced by conservative justices, proceeded to make that very point:

> Petitioner had no absolute entitlement to the road dispatcher position. Seven of the applicants were classified as qualified and eligible, and the Agency Director was authorized to promote any of the seven.[87]

Justice O'Connor, sensing the danger in reiterating her claim of white rights, eschewed any reference to rights in her concurring opinion, instead urging that the value of an affirmative action plan should be weighed against its adverse impact on the "interests" and "employment opportunities" of whites.[88] Brennan pressed the point again in 1989 in *Richmond v. Croson Co.*, insisting that the minority set-aside program in that case did "not interfere with any vested right of a contractor to a particular program."[89] In *Croson*, the opinions attacking the constitutionality of the disputed program carefully avoided asserting that whites had any right to the benefit at issue.[90]

A second approach to filling the gap created by the absence of a merit claim has been to suggest that whites have some entitlement to the position or benefit at issue simply because they *expected* it would be theirs. The Supreme Court initially dismissed such expectations as irrelevant. In *Franks* the majority observed that "this Court has long held that employee expectations arising from a seniority system agreement may be modified by statutes furthering a strong public policy interest."[91] In *Fullilove v. Klutznick* in 1986, Justice Burger's plurality opinion insisted that "it is not a constitutional defect in this program that it may disappoint the expectations of nonminority firms."[92] In *Bakke* the joint opinion of Justices Brennan, White, Marshall, and Blackmun suggested that any expectations of the plaintiff in that case, like the expectations of the white workers in *Franks*, were "themselves products of discrimination and thus 'tainted.' "[93]

In 1984 in *Firefighters v. Stotts*, however, Justice O'Connor urged in her concurring opinion that a court could not "unilaterally modify a consent decree to . . . provide retroactive relief that abrogates legitimate expectations of other employees and applicants."[94] Although *Stotts* itself did not involve any constitutional issue regarding affirmative action, the Court thereafter took a different view of the significance of white expectations. In *Paradise*, Justice Brennan argued that, because seniority had traditionally played only a minor role in promotion decisions, "greater seniority did not . . . by itself create an expectation of promotion."[95] In *Johnson*, Brennan maintained that the "denial of the promotion unsettled no legitimate firmly rooted expectation on the part of the petitioner."[96] In *Croson*, Brennan cited *Wygant* for the proposition that race-conscious measures should not disrupt "the settled and legitimate expectations of innocent parties."[97] Then in 1990 in *Metro Broadcasting v. FCC* Brennan did an apparent about-face, quoting Burger's opinion in *Fullilove* that it was of no constitutional importance that an affirmative action program disappointed white expectations.[98]

The assertion that affirmative action violates the rights of whites to certain jobs, although stirringly evocative, is probably too extravagant to be effective. The argument sounds dangerously close to a suggestion that those jobs are by right white jobs or, at the least, that the spoils of invidious discrimination are some form of legitimate booty. It is difficult to explain, even by analogy to ordinary property concepts, how these positions could be the right of certain individuals, let alone what sort of right can be said to exist only when the competing claimant relies on an affirmative action plan.

The Court's references to white expectations has somewhat greater potential force. While it is peculiar and usually false to say that a person has a right to a job or to admission to medical school, it is perfectly coherent to say that the same individual has such an expectation. But to attach legal consequences to the existence of such expectations could have far-reaching consequences. Virtually all the progress that has occurred in civil rights over the past four decades has confounded white expectations. Even the most sensible and benign reforms in employment or educational practices disappoint the expectations of those who would have fared better under the previous system. The same would be true of almost any conceivable form of affirmative action. Justice Brennan has sought to limit the potential impact of white expectations by suggesting that they must be both legitimate—presumably, untainted by past discrimination— and firmly rooted. But these constraints are too nebulous to be of any efficacy.

A number of justices evidently attach particular significance to white rights or expectations related to seniority. This line of thinking undoubtedly has its roots in a series of Supreme Court decisions, beginning in 1977 with *Teamsters v. United States*, holding that bona fide seniority systems are immune from attack under Title VII.[99] In *Weber*, Justice Rehnquist emphasized that Brian Weber had more seniority than a number of the blacks awarded the promotion he had sought.[100] The argument was noteworthy precisely because the actual seniority agreement at the plant in question, as Justice Blackmun observed, provided that those blacks rather than Weber should be given the promotions.[101] It was not the seniority rules in the applicable collective bargaining agreement to which Rehnquist was appealing; rather, Rehnquist was invoking what he regarded as some sort of Platonic concept of what seniority rules ought to be.

Precisely the same situation was presented in *Wygant*, where Justice Powell's opinion emphasized the extraordinary importance of "union seniority plans" and decried the race-based layoff at issue because it interfered with "the rights and expectations surrounding seniority."[102] It was true that Wendy Wygant had more years of seniority than several black teachers who were not laid off; but the actual union seniority plan in Jackson expressly provided that Wygant's seniority did *not* entitle her to be retained in place of those junior blacks. A footnote in *Wygant* acknowledged, somewhat grudgingly, that "the Constitution does not require layoffs to be based on strict seniority," as if to suggest that minor deviations from strict seniority, but not necessarily major ones, would be constitutionally permissible.[103] These decisions suggest that several members of the Court regard seniority—not seniority rights in an applicable collective bargaining agreement, but seniority as such—as conveying some sort of entitlement to a job or promotion, an entitlement which makes a race-conscious rule to the contrary particularly suspect.

A number of opinions suggest that the magnitude of the harm to or burden on whites is an important part of the balance in determining the validity of an affirmative action plan. This makes a good deal of sense where such a plan would impose a substantial burden on whites in order to convey a comparatively smaller benefit on minority competitors. The majority opinion in *Weber* stressed that

> the plan does not require the discharge of white workers and their replacement with new black hires. . . . Nor does the plan create an absolute bar to the advancement of white employees. . . .[104]

In *Wygant*, however, Justice Powell went considerably further, attaching controlling significance to the very fact that whites were to be laid off at all:

> Even a temporary layoff may have adverse financial as well as psychological effects. A worker may invest many productive years in one job and one city with the expectation of earning . . . stability and security. . . . Layoffs disrupt these settled expectations. . . .[105]

Taken in isolation, Justice Powell's compassion for the suffering of laid-off whites is entirely laudable; but it is difficult to understand how that could lead to the conclusion that it would be more fair or less harsh to lay off blacks instead. It seems to have been of little or no consequence to Justice Powell that abolition of the disputed race-conscious rule would result in the layoff of black workers, with precisely the same financial and psychological effects on them that he thought so dreadful when suffered by whites. This lapse is all the more indefensible because the central purpose and effect of the plan in *Wygant* was to see that these burdens were shared equally, that the same proportion of blacks and whites were laid off. It may be that race-conscious methods are suspect or to be closely scrutinized; but it seems peculiar, if not racist, to say of a plan that laid off 5 percent of whites and 5 percent of blacks that the result was intolerably harsh and unfair because laid-off whites were likely to suffer financially and emotionally.

There is, finally, a disagreement within the Court as to which whites adversely affected by a race-conscious measure could properly be characterized as "innocent." The issue is important because of the consensus that such measures require a special degree of justification if those burdened are innocent. The more conservative justices generally regard as innocent those whites who were not themselves perpetrators of discrimination against the minority beneficiaries of the plan.[106] This definition, as a practical matter, includes virtually every conceivable white who could be affected by such an affirmative action plan. Employment discrimination, for example, is practiced by supervisors and union officials, not by ordinary employees, such as Brian Weber, who might be affected by remedial measures. Similarly, even if the Davis Medical School had had a history of discrimination in admissions, it would be exceedingly peculiar to find a faculty member or an official of the admissions office applying to join the incoming medical school class. The more restrictive view of innocence advanced by liberal justices suggests that it includes neither whites who benefited from past discrimination nor whites who obtained from past discrimination a competitive advantage for future benefits.[107] Somewhat surprisingly, Justice Scalia has been among those adhering to a narrower view of which whites can fairly claim to be innocent.[108]

The Court has thus considered a variety of grounds, unrelated to merit, that might give an adversely affected white some special claim to a benefit allocated to others under an affirmative action plan. The only circumstance in which a consensus favors such a claim is where the harm suffered by that white would markedly exceed the concomitant benefit conferred on the black beneficiary, as in the hypothetical case of dismissing whites in order to hire blacks. Most other alternatives seem tinged by an unseemly special solicitude for whites, an indifference to minorities, or an inclination to protect the spoils of invidious discrimination.

White "Rights" to the Spoils of "Societal Discrimination"

Although the Court is sharply divided as to whether race can ever be treated as a form or evidence of qualification, there is a consistent consensus that, at least in some circumstances, race-conscious measures can be utilized, indeed at times must be utilized, to correct past discrimination. Thus Justice Scalia, the most passionate opponent of such practices, explained in his concurring opinion in *Croson* that in certain instances "the States may act *by race* to 'undo the effects of past discrimination.' "[109] Such measures are race-specific precisely because the wrongs they seek to correct were racial in nature; to redress the practices of an employer who denied promotions on the basis of race, a court would have to know which of the employees were black. Such redress may well affect third parties adversely. If a thief steals my car and sells or gives it to my neighbor, I am entitled to get my car back, no matter how much my neighbor may rely on or have paid for it. Because racial discrimination against blacks frequently benefits competing whites, indeed because such benefits are the purpose of racial discrimination, steps to redress it will often adversely affect whites.

But while there is agreement that past discrimination provides a basis for race-conscious measures in some circumstances, there is among the justices considerable disagreement about what those circumstances are. Restrictions on such corrective action are generally characterized as constraints on the remedial authority of the entity involved. But any such constraints also limit the ability of blacks to obtain redress, and thus confer on whites concomitant rights. The most important of the constraints the Court has imposed forbids race-conscious measures to correct what the Court has come to call "societal discrimination."

In *Bakke* the medical school sought to justify its special admissions program, *inter alia*, as a method of "countering the effects of societal discrimination."[110] Justice Powell observed that this purpose might encompass several possible goals:

> For example, it is said that preferences for Negro applicants may compensate for harm done them personally, or serve to place them at economic levels they might have attained but

for discrimination against their forebears. . . . Another view
of the "compensation" goal is that it serves as a form of
reparation by the "majority" to a victimized group as a
whole.[111]

Justice Powell insisted that such purposes could not sustain the plan
at issue in *Bakke* because there had been no formal

judicial, legislative, or administrative findings of constitutional or statutory violations. . . . [Only] after such findings
have been made [is] the government interest in preferring
members of the injured groups at the expense of others . . .
substantial, since the legal rights of the victims must be
vindicated. . . . [The medical school] does not purport to
have made, and is in no position to make, such findings. . . .
Hence, the purpose of helping certain groups whom the
faculty of the Davis Medical School perceived as victims of
"societal discrimination" does not justify a classification that
imposes disadvantages upon persons like respondent.[112]

Several things about this analysis are unclear. By the 1978 decision in *Bakke* there had of course been literally thousands of judicial,
legislative, and administrative findings of racial discrimination
against blacks in the United States; many of those concerned blacks
in California. If Powell were suggesting that no such findings had
ever been made, he was obviously mistaken. Conceivably Powell
might have meant that Davis Medical School would itself have to
reiterate the same findings, or that there had to be findings of
discrimination more closely related to the admissions process. It is
also unclear whether, as used in this passage, "societal discrimination" is something that would justify affirmative action, given the
proper findings, or is a phrase used by Powell to refer to vague
suspicions of discrimination that lack the requisite formal findings.

Powell observed in a footnote "that there has been societal
discrimination in this country against various racial and ethnic
groups," but objected that there is "not one word in the record" to
support the conclusion that, in the absence of that discrimination,
Bakke "would not have been admitted even if there had been no
special admissions program."[113] This comment seemed to indicate
that societal discrimination (with or without formal findings is unclear) would justify a race-conscious program if there were in fact
evidence of the requisite causal connection.

Powell subsequently suggested that the key defect in *Bakke* had
been the lack of any relevant findings either that there had been
discrimination against blacks or that discrimination was the reason
why relatively few black applicants could qualify under Davis's regu-

lar admissions plan. Powell voted to uphold the set-aside plan in *Fullilove* because in that instance he believed the requisite findings had been made. On his view the legislative history of the federal statute at issue

> demonstrates that Congress reasonably concluded that *private and government* discrimination had contributed to the negligible percentage of public contracts awarded to minority contractors.[114]

Powell cited as an example a 1975 House report finding "that low participation by minorities in the economy was the result of 'past discrimination.' "[115] He quoted at length a 1977 House report:

> Over the years, there has developed a business system which has traditionally excluded measurable minority participation. In the past more than the present, this system of conducting business transactions overtly precluded minority input. Currently, we more often encounter a business system which is racially neutral on its face, but because of past overt social and economic discrimination is operating, in effect, to perpetuate these past inequities.[116]

Two facets of the quoted reports are particularly noteworthy. First, neither referred specifically to discrimination by either federal officials or federal prime contracts; discrimination in the economy as a whole was the identified problem. Second, the reports do not contain a focused finding that discrimination had reduced the number of minority contractors doing business with the federal government; they concluded, more generally, that discrimination had reduced the representation of minorities in business at all. In short, like Powell's opinion in *Bakke*, his opinion in *Fullilove* envisioned no limitations on the *type* of discrimination that could be redressed by race-conscious measures, including discrimination in society at large, as long as the requisite findings had been made.

In *Wygant*, however, Justice Powell and three other members of the Court took a different position. "Societal discrimination," they insisted, even though it certainly existed and regardless of whether it had actually caused a particular problem, was not an injustice that could ever be remedied by race-conscious measures. The school board in *Wygant* had argued that it needed minority teachers to "provide role models for its minority students, as an attempt to alleviate the effects of societal discrimination."[117] Powell did not challenge the board's contention that societal discrimination had injured minority students in a way that could be remedied only by

141

the presence in their schools of minority teachers. Rather, he insisted that any such conclusion, even if correct, was legally irrelevant.[118]

Part of Powell's objection was that if a generalized reference to past discrimination were sufficient to justify race-conscious measures, virtually anything would be justifiable. This argument is related to his objection in *Bakke* that there was no evidence of a causal connection between societal discrimination and black medical school admissions. But in *Wygant*, Powell went beyond merely insisting on more specific evidence; he maintained that societal discrimination could never justify race-conscious measures, no matter what the evidence or how clear the causal connection. Thus the fact that *Wygant* came to the Supreme Court prior to trial was irrelevant; it would not matter what evidence the school board might be able to offer regarding the effect of societal discrimination.

Powell's opinion in *Wygant* was significant as well because of the breadth of practices lumped together as "societal discrimination." His objection was not limited to vaguely defined past problems in society at large. *Any* act of discrimination other than by "the governmental unit involved" fell within Powell's definition of societal discrimination. Justice O'Connor in her concurring opinion insisted in similar terms that race-conscious measures could be upheld only when the government body was "attempting to remedy *its own* unlawful conduct . . . rather than attempting to alleviate the wrongs suffered through general societal discrimination."[119]

This distinction was reiterated in 1989, albeit with some modification, in *Richmond v. Croson Co.*[120] In that case Richmond sought to justify its set-aside plan, as was done in *Fullilove*, as a step to redress general discrimination against minority-owned businesses. The Fourth Circuit, relying on Powell's opinion in *Wygant*, held that Richmond could only use a set-aside to redress discrimination by the city itself. Justice O'Connor, writing for herself and three other justices, held that a city's power was broader than she and Powell had suggested in *Wygant*, and included the authority to redress either discrimination by the city or "private discrimination within its legislative jurisdiction."[121] But, she insisted, Richmond could not use race-conscious measures to redress any other forms of governmental or private discrimination.[122]

In *Fullilove*, of course, the federal set-aside plan had been sustained on the basis of a "generalized assertion" of past discrimination. O'Connor insisted in *Croson* that Congress alone could use set-asides to remedy societal discrimination.[123] She reasoned that the Fourteenth Amendment, although imposing restrictions on the states, contained a grant of affirmative power to Congress.

In *Croson* Justice O'Connor grounded her objection to state remedies for "societal discrimination" on a belief that it would never be possible to ascertain with sufficient specificity what effects such discrimination had had:

> While there is no doubt that the sorry history of both private and public discrimination in this country has contributed to a lack of opportunities for black entrepreneurs, this observation, standing alone, cannot justify a rigid racial quota in the awarding of public contracts in Richmond, Virginia. Like the claim that discrimination in primary and secondary schooling justifies rigid racial preferences in medical school admission, an amorphous claim that there has been past discrimination in a particular industry cannot justify the use of an unyielding racial quota.
>
> It is sheer speculation how many minority firms there would be in Richmond absent past societal discrimination, just as it was sheer speculation how many minority medical students would have been admitted to the medical school at Davis absent past discrimination in educational opportunities. Defining these sorts of injuries as "identified discrimination" would give local governments license to create a patchwork of racial preferences based on statistical generalizations about any particular field or endeavor.[124]

This passage highlights the difference between Justice Powell's position in *Bakke* and Justice O'Connor's position in *Croson*. Powell would have permitted Davis to base its special admissions plans on discrimination by others if there were findings that such discrimination had occurred, and that it had affected medical school applicants. He rejected this particular justification in *Bakke* because the medical school there had failed to introduce any evidence to support such findings. O'Connor, on the other hand, held in *Croson* that such evidence and findings are irrelevant as a matter of law, because the type of discrimination to which they are directed could never justify race-conscious measures.

The decisions in *Wygant* and *Croson* do more than define remedial principles; they also establish a new white right. If a group of whites, or an individual, has obtained some advantage because of past discrimination, a state or city can use race-conscious measures to undo that special advantage only if the discrimination took place within the jurisdiction involved. Such corrective measures are forbidden if the discrimination occurred outside the jurisdiction. Race-based advantages obtained by whites outside a jurisdiction thus become absolute rights within that jurisdiction. The inability of a city or state to undo such race-based advantages turns them, as a practical matter, into vested rights.

This is much like saying that it is unlawful for Ben Johnson to take muscle-building steroids in Canada, but that such illegality is irrelevant if he is running in a race in South Korea. In *Croson*, Justice Scalia insisted that if

> a state agency has a discriminatory pay scale compensating black employees in all positions at 20 percent less than their nonblack counterparts, it may assuredly promulgate an order raising the salaries of "all black employees."[125]

If, however, those employees were transferred to another agency, city, or state, to be paid "their existing salary," the new employer, not having been involved in the original discrimination, could not issue such a corrective order. The greater salaries paid white workers, a constitutional violation at one agency, become a constitutional right when those workers moved to another.

The position originally taken by Justice Powell in *Bakke* seems preferable to the subsequent approaches to this problem. If the mere and undeniable existence of societal discrimination established a conclusive justification for all affirmative action, there would in practice be few, if any, legal or constitutional constraints on such programs. Of course, there might be affirmative action, such as recruiting minorities, of such mildness that an assertion of societal discrimination ought to suffice. But the more stringent programs typically challenged in the courts might fairly require a more specific justification, one that establishes a closer, more identifiable connection between the program at issue and the referenced acts of discrimination. This approach does not suffer from the evident defects of the decisions in *Wygant* and *Croson*, which preclude the use of race-conscious measures to remedy a situation demonstrably caused by a type of discrimination that those cases hold to be legally irrelevant.

Conclusion

To observe that the conservative justices have largely abandoned any serious merit-based approach to affirmative action cases is not to suggest that the conclusions they arrived at were always incorrect, or that every litigated or hypothetical affirmative action plan is sensible, lawful, or constitutional. In a complex and imperfect world, race-conscious measures are like other social innovations, or new weapons systems: some are effective and laudable, some mediocre, and some ill-conceived and counterproductive. Still, it is important for the law to try to direct the shaping of such measures in a productive and equitable manner.

This judicial abandonment of a merit-based approach does not necessarily reflect any hostility, or even indifference, to merit-based decisions. The central problem and impetus may be institutional and procedural. In virtually all the affirmative action cases reaching the Supreme Court, the comparative qualifications of the interested parties had not been litigated below at all, let alone fully and competently. Generally the lawyers had paid little attention to the issue, in part because in recent years no one on the Court other than Justice Stevens has consistently been interested in it. Were the Court now to hold that the presence or absence of substantial differences in comparative merit is a critical threshold issue to be judged without any preconceptions about when race might in fact be relevant to qualifications, the Supreme Court itself would virtually always be unable to make final decisions in these cases. Rather, the Court would ordinarily be relegated to the sort of role advocated by Justice Douglas in *DeFunis*, emphasizing the importance of the issue and remanding the case for trial. It would be asking rather a lot of the justices to forsake in this manner the power to decide who wins and who loses particular affirmative action cases. These are exceptionally interesting disputes, especially to a Court that must deal with many far more mundane controversies. And the justices care passionately about the policies at issue.

Nonetheless, the Court would be more faithful to its responsibility to the country, and to the development of the law, if it were to restore comparative merit as a central issue in affirmative action litigation, even though that would result in a reduced role and profile for the Court itself. Whether an affirmative action plan in fact disfavors better qualified individuals ought routinely to be treated as a critical threshold issue in evaluating any particular plan. It is entirely fitting, in a nation so long dedicated to opportunity and ability, that that issue play a major role in constitutional analysis. A race-conscious measure that disfavors the more qualified should on that account be more difficult to justify as a matter of both policy and law. Just as important, a measure that has no such effect should receive a more receptive response by the public as well as in the courts.

The legitimacy of this approach requires the elimination of ideological preconceptions or bias regarding what the facts are, or are permitted to be. Whether being black actually makes an individual a better police officer or teacher is a question of fact that should have nothing to do with judicial philosophy. No one but an ideologue would pretend that race never, or always, matters. As long as judges

145

divide along ideological lines in deciding that sort of issue, the public neither can nor should have confidence in the reliability of the supposed factual finding. The Court should refuse to assume that there are always substantial merit differences among competing candidates. Justice Scalia was correct, although a bit hyperbolic, when he suggested in *Johnson* that the absence of such differences would have "staggering implications." The courts should not assume reality to be politically correct, but should find the facts in a dispassionate manner and let the implications fall where they may.

If comparative merit is to be accorded central importance, the courts ought not permit themselves to be encumbered by the way a case was litigated in earlier proceedings. The Supreme Court should generally desist from deciding any affirmative action case without a full and reliable record. If the case was never tried, if the record on the issue of comparative merit is incomplete, even if the parties failed ever to address the issue on their own, the case ought to be remanded for completion of the necessary proceedings.

For those who set policy, the course chosen by the courts will carry considerable weight. The greater the importance the courts attach to comparative merit, the more important that factor will be in decisions regarding whether to adopt, and how to shape, race-conscious measures. A more merit-based approach on the part of the courts would encourage employers and schools to take seriously the questions of whether and why the introduction of racial considerations will in fact result in a more accurate evaluation of qualifications, and to make more thoughtful judgments about what the relevant qualifications may be. It could also give rise to some reassessments of how particular affirmative action programs should be structured, and about which individuals ought to participate in them.

This approach might help to reshape as well the public debate regarding race-conscious measures. In *Fullilove*, Justice Stewart quoted Justice Louis Brandeis's observation that the "government is the potent, the omnipresent teacher. For good or ill, it teaches the whole people by its example."[126] The manner in which the Court analyzes affirmative action cases will, to a significant but unknowable degree, affect how others do so. If, as has often been the case, the Court's decisions seem determined solely by ideological preconceptions and proclivities, those decisions will encourage a similarly ideologically driven approach by others. If, however, the Court were to ground its analyses of these cases on a fair and sensitive evaluation of whether some consideration of race might yield a more accurate judgment of qualification, it would set a different and more felicitous example. Instead of the usual impassioned firefights about the horrors or wonders of affirmative action, we might have a more serious discussion about when significant merit differences do and do not exist and about whether and why the race of a police officer or teacher might (and might not) be relevant, at a given time and place, to his or her willingness and ability to do a particular job. In a community that made a serious effort to understand and resolve such issues, political appeals of the sort made famous by Senator Helms might fall on deaf ears.

7

"Kantianism" and Constitutional Rights

Susan Shell

During the past fifteen years a new attitude toward rights has made itself felt both on the bench and, especially, among more liberal students and critics of the judiciary.[1] This new approach has been convincingly explained as a response to the conservative use to which legal realism was increasingly being put by the Court.[2] In the days of the *Lochner* court, progressive politics saw itself allied with the will of the majority against an active judiciary bent on frustrating the democratic will in the name of fundamental rights.[3] In overturning laws duly enacted by popularly elected legislators, *Lochner*-era judges were not always overly scrupulous in their fidelity to constitutional language, or overly shy about appealing—over the head of the Constitution, as it were—to an allegedly more fundamental standard of justice. Franklin Delano Roosevelt and the erosion of the Old Guard of the *Lochner* era changed all that, and for some years the outlook of the new "legal realists" on the bench roughly coincided with the New Deal economic and social agenda.[4]

It was above all the civil rights movement, with its implicit attack on majoritarianism in the name of individual rights, that altered this trend. Increasingly, conservatives found themselves allied with advocates of judicial restraint and legislative deference, while liberals and progressives appealed over the heads of elected bodies to more fundamental principles. For many who had been schooled in the skeptical ways of legal realism, the question was, Principles based on what? The answer might have been the Constitution, as in the case of Justice Hugo Black's libertarian defense of First Amendment rights. But the naked Constitution, following its bath in the "acid" of Oliver Wendell Holmesian skepticism and historicist criticism, seemed to many to be insufficient, given the new and expansive understanding of rights to which such students of the Court inclined.

It was at this opportune moment that John Rawls's *Theory of Justice* appeared, in a similar, if more purely academic climate of dissatisfaction with the morally skeptical impasse to which analytic philosophy had seemingly come.[5] Here at last was an intellectual approach that combined analytic rigor with interdisciplinary deference and the preferred political results—or so it seemed to a growing group of academic theorists from a variety of disciplines that, owing especially to the work of Ronald Dworkin, increasingly included law.[6]

The philosophic Godfather of this new approach was said to be Immanuel Kant. It is Kant's voice we hear in Justice William J. Brennan, Jr.'s, appeal to the "constitutional ideal of human dignity"; and it is Kant's voice we hear in Dworkin's more prosaic call for "equal concern and respect" (or, more recently, "integrity") as that which, according to Dworkin, it is the fundamental business of our Constitution to ensure.

Several questions naturally arise: What features of Kant's thought render it, or a part of it, so attractive? And how legitimately do his erstwhile philosophic and jurisprudential heirs come by their self-proclaimed legacy? Historically speaking the latter question is all the more pertinent, since Kant himself would in all likelihood have found the majority position of the *Lochner* court quite congenial. Finally, how useful is Kant's thought as a supplement to or replacement of the more traditional constitutional understanding of rights?

What one thinks rights are is inseparable from what one thinks a constitution is. Kant's thought provides not so much "new rights" as a new understanding of the grounding of rights in and by an ideal constitution. It is the business of actual, empirical constitutions to approximate or strive to actualize this ideal. The upshot is at once a sanctification of rights and a desanctification of actual constitutions. This is true both despite and because of Kant's vehement insistence on the binding authority—where questions of individual obedience are concerned—of positive law. Nevertheless, Kant's thought can make a worthwhile contribution to our understanding of rights as embodied in the American Constitution, a contribution to some extent invited by the Constitution itself.

New Kantianism

What then is Kant's position, and to what extent are his recent jurisprudential champions true to it? The jurisprudential Kantianism to which we have alluded above might be summarized in terms of two general tendencies. The first is a grounding of constitutionally guaranteed rights in—or an assimilation of them with—human dignity. All rights thus reduce fundamentally to a right to equal respect. The second is an understanding of rights that detaches them from, and renders them neutral toward, competing conceptions of the good. This understanding is sometimes coupled with an emphasis on procedure—an emphasis that may be said to represent another strand of Kantianism in its own right. To these, I would add a third implicitly Kantian trend in recent constitutional interpretation: a tendency to view the Constitution less as settled law than as an injunction or invitation to "aspire" to certain open-ended forms of civil and moral improvement.

As we shall see, the second of these tendencies, with its insistence on "neutrality" vis-à-vis the question of the good, is seriously misleading if taken as an accurate reflection of Kant's thought, and casts a shadow on the otherwise helpful representation of Kant's thought by the first. The third approach, newer than (and partially at odds with) the second, is rapidly gaining ground. It too, however, seriously distorts the meaning of Kant's moral "idealism," which, we will suggest, may give truer guidance to the meaning of the Constitution than do some contemporary theories it has inspired.

In understanding how and why contemporary self-styled Kantians use and abuse Kant, it is helpful to keep in mind that to which his thought was welcomed by many as antidote—utilitarianism and positivism whose implicit appeal to the will or interest of the majority could no longer be simply identified with enlightened sentiment in what Rawls called "reflective equilibrium," in the manner of earlier progressive thought. Somehow the claims of equality addressed by that earlier progressivism and the claims of the individual above the majority had both to be served. Rawls found an answer in "justice as fairness," as exemplified and clarified by the "original position." According to that ingenious device, the just underlying structures of a society are best understood as the outcome of a contract among mutually disinterested persons, screened by the "veil of ignorance" from knowledge of their future circumstances and abilities.

From such a starting point—implicit, according to Rawls, in our notion of legitimacy as deriving from "fair" consent—two sorts of principles were said to flow. First, individuals would choose to guarantee certain fundamental goods—preeminently liberty, consistent with the equal liberty of others, along with the minimal material conditions for its exercise. These goods constitute what Rawls called a "thin theory of the good."

Second, Rawls argued that such individuals would choose to maximize the lot of the least fortunate (with such attributes as talent or the willingness to work hard construed as "common assets" whose actual distribution is "morally arbitrary" and conveys no implication as to the right of individuals to their fruit).[7] Mindful of the possibility of drawing the short straw in life's lottery, individuals placed in the original position, Rawls held, would take out a kind of cosmic insurance policy, giving up some of the possible benefits of good luck as a hedge against the worst. As a consequence, they would, generally speaking, lay down structures that allowed the more happily endowed to reap the unearned reward of their good fortune only if such inequality would benefit the least well off.

Rawls's original position harbored many ambiguities and unresolved difficulties, which an army of critics were quick to point out. To begin with, his privileging of the least (rather than the less) well off seemed all too consistent with contemporary liberal prejudices favoring a racially coded "lower class" above the lower middle class and working poor—the very groups whose social and racial conservatism made the trumping of majoritarianism so attractive to liberals in the first place.[8] In addition, many pointed out that Rawls's theory of justice was less "neutral" vis-à-vis ways of life or overarching visions of the good than it pretended to be, since certain ways of life, such as some forms of religious piety and forms of Nietzschean self-assertion at the expense of others, were precluded at the outset. Perhaps the best known of Rawls's critics pointed to the ultimate absurdity of imagining selves as unencumbered by particularity, as those Rawls sought to envision. His hypothetical selves lacked in qualities of social and historical "embeddedness," without which questions of right and justice do not meaningfully apply.[9]

But probably the greatest difficulty lay with the essential baselessness of rights so understood. What, one could well ask, justified the individuals of Rawls's original position—and, by extension, real individuals—in their claim to have rights at all? Rawls's insistence on defending rights independent of and without reliance on any prior theory of the good was bound to appeal to skeptics and libertarians alike—to skeptics because of its minimalist profile, to libertarians for its rejection of the authority of any best way of life.

The downside of that appeal, however, was the detachment of rights from the account of human nature, and in particular from the natural sense of desert (or spiritedness) in which it had both morally and psychologically been rooted. In rejecting in the name of fairness (or a higher principle of desert) the common view that individuals "deserve" the fruits of their (unearned) talents and willingness to labor, Rawls struck a blow not only against the common understanding but also against his own principle of fairness as such. Stripped of common (however flawed) ideas about the relation between talent and effort on the one hand and about reward on the other hand, he was left without any meaningful standard for desert at all—any positive concept of fairness.[10]

Rawls knew that nature, with its haphazard distribution of life's chances, is not fair. Justice means the mitigation, insofar as socially possible, of the morally arbitrary distribution of nature's gifts. Yet such undeserved distribution can be construed as morally abhorrent only if one has some positive notion of the alternative. In Rawls's case, an underlying premise in favor of equality fills the bill. Since nothing that one is or does, in comparison with what others say or do, is intrinsically deserving, it is unfair for some to have more (or less) than others—unless the inequality can be justified by some overriding common interest. But Rawls's powerful claims on behalf of equality and his indignation at the cruelty of nature leave a tremendous void. For by his conception of justice as fairness we are left unsure of the basis for anyone's deserving anything in the first place.[11]

This fundamental lacuna in Rawls's thought results in what is from a more truly Kantian perspective a curious inversion. Rather than grounding rights as Kant did in the individual's absolute dignity and self-worth, Rawls suggested that a sense of self-worth is something we receive (and are indeed entitled to receive, along with other primary goods) from others. Our sense of our own dignity and with it our rights above society are themselves society's product.[12]

It is Rawls's curious insistence on the right not merely to respect but to self-respect (or to the "bases" thereof) that Dworkin and other juridical interpreters have found particularly compelling.[13] As legal rather than moral philosophers, they are less concerned with the basis of rights—after all, rights figure prominently in the Constitution and thus possess the authority of fundamental law—than with their meaning. And here Dworkin's formula of "equal concern and respect" as that to which individuals are, at bottom, constitutionally entitled is especially telling.[14] For his formula captures both an underlying agnosticism vis-à-vis the good and a frank admission of the dependence of an individual's sense of worth on the willingness of others to endorse or at least not condemn the way of life he chooses on what are, in the last analysis, arbitrary grounds.

A passage from Dworkin's later work, *A Matter of Principle,* is in this respect especially revealing. He calls for liberal government to "impose no sacrifice or constraint on any citizen in virtue of an argument that the citizen could not accept without abandoning his sense of equal worth." It follows, according to Dworkin, that a liberal must oppose the moralism of the new right, since "no self-respecting person who believes that a particular way to life is most valuable for him can accept that this way of life is base or degrading."[15]

More recently, Dworkin has championed what he calls "integrity" as the fundamental principle of legal interpretation, a principle that brings the formal principle of self-consistency to bear upon the shifting sands of historical meaning.[16] As Graham Walker has noted, Dworkin's complex conventionalism coexists uneasily with what appears to be a more absolutist commitment to the principle of equality of concern.[17] Thus, for example, in associating legal integrity with the Kantian ideal of "self-legislation," he leans on the affective resonance of the latter without precisely endorsing its truth.[18]

A similar evasiveness surrounds Dworkin's claim that a government which "accepts" the "abstract egalitarian principle" that "it must treat all citizens as equals" needs a "conception of equal concern"—a conception it must apply evenhandedly, since "integrity demands that government settle on a single conception that it will not disavow in any decision, including those of policy."[19] This formulation suggests that "law as integrity" is detachable from the particular principles of the legal tradition to which integrity applies. Thus integrity will require that a particular conception of equality be consistently enforced only where government accepts the abstract principle of equality.

Earlier in the volume, however, Dworkin suggests the relation between integrity and equality to be far more intimate. In defending his approach against the "conventionalism" and the "legal pragmatism" that he takes to be its relevant rivals, he argues that "law's constraints benefit society not just by providing predictability or procedural fairness . . . but by securing a kind of equality among citizens that makes their community more genuine and improves its moral justification for exercising the political power it does."[20]

Dworkin's justification of "law as integrity" thus rests on an extralegal, or substantively moral, claim concerning the basis of law's legitimacy. Significantly, however, Dworkin does not directly ask what makes a law just. Instead he attempts to argue from within. "Law as integrity" is to be preferred because it reveals law's contribution to equality and so to community. Law as integrity makes it easier for the law to justify itself morally, inasmuch as citizens subject to the law so interpreted and applied feel "secured" as equal members of the community.

In effect, Dworkin's notion of integrity represents another attempt, already familiar from Rawls, to appropriate Kant's universalizing formalism while leaving behind most of the substantive moral baggage with which it was originally endowed. What remains is a somewhat hazy commitment to equality—fleshed out, through the language of compassion that Kant himself would have abjured, as equality of "concern." Dworkin's ultimate human subject is not the "individual" of classical liberalism, but a fellow member of the communal hermeneutic circle, situated in a web of contextual, socially rooted meanings.[21] "Security" remains a basic justificatory aim of law; but security is no longer concerned with natural or otherwise fundamental substantive rights, but with equal consideration in relation to and on the part of other members of the group. What each essentially demands, in other words, is not to be left in peace, but to know that he or she counts and that others care.[22]

Where Dworkin pushes Kant's formalism in the direction of a historicizing communitarianism, David A. J. Richards would reconstruct a liberalism freed of its historical blemishes. This is not to say that Richards renounces history entirely. Rather, his intention is "to give appropriate weight to text, history, interpretive conventions, and political theory," the better to develop "in some detail a unified interpretive account of the American constitutional law of religious liberty, free speech, and constitutional privacy."[23]

By "political theory" Richards seems ultimately to mean the identification of broad principles that he traces to the founders or thinkers upon whom the founders generally relied. Richards's complex and nuanced reading of a variety of historical texts from before and after the time of the founding is intended to show how an expanded understanding of rights—such as the unenumerated right to privacy championed in *Griswold v. Connecticut*, or robust versions of affirmative action—arises legitimately from the Constitution, when it is interpreted according to a methodology that the framers themselves implicitly called for.

Richards's subtle "interpretive" blending of theory and history comes ultimately to rest, however, in an identification of the founders' "community of principle" with "a moral community of free and equal persons capable of respecting one another because they have been *guaranteed the resources to respect themselves*" (emphasis in the original). On the basis of this resting point, so close to the positions of Rawls and Dworkin in its treatment of self-respect as an external resource, Richards ultimately justifies the thrust of his enterprise. Here the search for historical sources gives way to an otherwise unsubstantiated moral animus, one requiring "struggle to include outcasts into a more critically humane community or principle." The central vision of the Constitution is thus said to be fundamentally "aspirational," bent on expanding the community of "free and equal persons" by guaranteeing the resources of self-respect that make it possible to respect others. Richards continues, however, with a further nod to the openended processes of history, inasmuch as we have "both the interpretive right and duty to make the most reasonable sense we can of that vision by our lights and in our circumstances."[24]

A final coda, moreover, reveals Richards's constitutional vision to be historically rooted in a way that he may not intend. In the last page of *Foundations of American Constitutionalism* he links his approach to the "hunger" experienced by "educated Americans" who gravitate toward two "attractive but apparently inconsistent claims," the first calling for "a deeper sense of community," the second for "higher standards of critical argument and learning." In naming and partly satisfying this contradictory (yet familiar) hunger, the author shows himself less a student of American history than an example of a peculiar, currently fashionable intellectual type—one who longs for community even as he or she "critically" rejects the one of which he or she is actually a part. In any case, it remains both philosophically and historically problematic to assume that the central aspiration of the founders (let alone of Locke, upon whose reconstruction Richards claims to rely) was to guarantee persons the "resources to respect themselves."[25]

Richards's "aspirational" approach to constitutional interpretation identifies fidelity to the Constitution with the pursuit of an egalitarian communitarianism that is for a variety of reasons attractive today to many "educated Americans." Richards, like others who share in his aspirational approach, understands the essential meaning of the Constitution to lie in a certain ideal for which it stands.[26] At the same time, constitutional principle for Richards is intrinsically dynamic—bent in its very essence on promoting ever stronger and more inclusive ties of mutual respect, but also open to new vistas of social and historical meaning.

Justice Brennan has similarly located the essential meaning of the Constitution in an "aspirational" ideal centered on a progressive realization of equal respect or, as Brennan puts it, "human dignity." The Constitution, he has argued, "embodies the aspiration to social justice, brotherhood, and human dignity that brought this nation into being," an equality of right and dignity, however, that has in part "been more pretension than realized fact."[27] But we are, he continues, "an aspiring people, a people with faith in progress. Our amended Constitution is the lodestar of our aspirations. Like every text worth reading, it is not crystalline. The phrasing is broad and the limitations of its provisions are not clearly marked. Its majestic generalities and ennobling pronouncements are both luminous and obscure." To be faithful to the Constitution is to "account for the existence of . . . fundamental value choices" and at the same time to "accept the ambiguity inherent in the effort to apply them to modern circumstances."[28] The "fundamental principles" discerned by the founders through their historically particularized struggles assumed precise and at times anachronistic contours, which in themselves ought not to bind us.[29] The fundamental principles of the Constitution are thus less a settled injunction than part of the "pattern of liberal government in the eighteenth century" that we adopt as our guide "in evaluating quite different historical practices."[30] The "genius of the Constitution," then, lies not "in any static meaning it might have had," but "in the adaptability of its great principles to cope with current problems."

Among these principles and value choices the "constitutional ideal of human dignity" assumes for Brennan singular importance. Human dignity is a goal both infinite and openended. If there is one thing that Brennan's own judicial experience confirms it is that "the demands of human dignity will never cease to evolve."[31] This evolutionary process he calls both "inevitable" and the "true interpretive genius of the text":

> If we are to be as a shining city upon a hill, it will be because of our ceaseless pursuit of the constitutional ideal of human dignity. For the political and legal ideals that form the foundation of much that is best in American institutions— ideals jealously preserved and guarded throughout our history—still form the vital force in creative political thought and activity within the nation today. As we adapt our institutions to the ever-changing conditions of national and international life, those ideals of human dignity—liberty and justice for all individuals—will continue to inspire and guide us because they are entrenched in the Constitution."[32]

These personal remarks by a liberal member of the Court are remarkable for their identification of the Constitution, in its essence, with the ideal of "human dignity"; equally remarkable, however, is the vagueness of that ideal, along with its seemingly limitless adaptability to new historical circumstances.

In light of the above tendencies in constitutional interpretation, it is useful to turn briefly to the grand philosophic scheme from which disparate elements of those tendencies are drawn—the scheme in which a certain kind of constitutional idealism—legal "neutrality" vis-à-vis the good—and the contemporary notion of "human dignity" largely originate. What follows can in no way be taken as even a partial summary of Kant's thought. Instead I mean to sketch out for two reasons the complex context from which each of these strands is drawn. I do so first because Kant has thought through certain issues more deeply and persuasively than many contemporary thinkers who claim to go beyond him. Second, a fuller consideration of such issues may better reveal both the strengths and the limitations of a Kantian approach to constitutional rights.

Kant and the Community of Respect

The current communitarian attack on "Kantian" (that is, Rawlsian) individualism is ironic, for Kant was the first thinker to show compellingly that individuality and community, far from being opposed, necessarily imply each other. This mutual implication is true for Kant on both a metaphysical and a moral scale. Metaphysically, individuals have worldly existence only insofar as they engage interactively with other individuals. Morally, this engagement takes the form in the first instance of a common will in whose necessitating dictates each individual participates. Thus subjected to the law of its own making, each is at once self-subsistent and connected to a larger whole. The independence or freedom upon which individuality ultimately rests is thus inseparable from the individual's community with others.[33]

This conception of moral community contrasts with the community of nature, constituted by analogously interactive laws—laws, however, whose exchanges ultimately threaten and dissolve (in the most literal sense) rather than uphold human individuals. In nature's "economy," to use Kant's terms, human interests and concerns do not "reckon." It is against the backdrop of this natural economy and of Hobbes's analogous human marketplace—in which "man's worth is his price"—that the "absolute worth" or "dignity" of man must be understood. Moral freedom lifts man beyond the economies of nature and a merely natural society into a moral economy in which no one can be a mere means to another.

In such a moral community, each is infinitely, hence equally, worthy. Here the laws are consistent with (rather than at odds with, like the laws of the physical "community") the self-subsistence by which individuality is ultimately defined. More simply stated, only by virtue of our moral community with others are we genuinely self-subsistent as individuals, or free.[34]

The grounds of human self-respect, along with the rights that flow from it, are thus ineluctably communal. But the community at issue is one radically divorced from nature—indeed, beyond the bounds of space and time—an ideal of reason, in short, that cannot be identified with any actual human society. The notion that self-respect is derived from others would have been anathema to Kant. It undercuts the self-sufficiency—the radical independence of the individual, at least for moral purposes, with respect to all natural attachments—upon which human dignity ultimately rests. In short, where "new Kantians" find the sources of self-respect in the solicitude, or "equal concern and respect," of others, true Kantians locate the source of self-respect in the radical, moral freedom of the individual.[35]

Many will find Kant's derivation of human dignity exaggerated or bizarre, and it is not my intention to explore or defend it more fully here.[36] Kant's presentation does, however, usefully highlight the dangers involved in identifying what is respectable with what happens to be respected. The community upon which Kantian individuality depends is not just a mutual admiration society. The right to respect flows from one's inherent worthiness. To the extent that the good opinion of others is thought of as a source of human worth, man's dignity and the basis of his rights are irrevocably breached.

Juridical community is the external counterpart of moral community, whose common will enjoins us to establish laws protecting persons in the external exercise of their freedom. The "idea" of this community of right, which Kant associates with Plato's ideal republic, calls for a reciprocal union. This union provides for the greatest liberty of each consistent with the greatest liberty of all the rest. The ensuing constitution, which Kant compares with Plato's ideal republic, is a pure idea of reason.[37]

This ideal constitution calls, among other things, for republican self-government and the separation of legislative, executive, and judicial powers. It also entails intellectual and religious freedom, combined with strict protection of property rights along free market lines.[38] Welfare is permitted in the name of preserving civil society rather than as a matter of individual entitlement, the "uniform equality of human beings as subjects of the state" being perfectly compatible, as Kant puts it, with "the utmost inequality of the mass" in their possessions "physical or mental."[39]

Human dignity, then, does not require material equality or even its approximation, although Kant would reserve active citizenship to male adults capable of supporting themselves as free rather than wage laborers.[40] Like his moral elevation of the ideal constitution of reason above any actual constitution to which people may happen historically to have consented, Kant's restriction of the franchise suggests the relative insignificance of political activity to his conception of individual freedom. The truly public figures for Kant are thinkers and writers—not politicians and civil servants—who contribute to the process of cultural enlightenment by means of which the people, civilly united by external laws, can progressively realize moral community as well.[41] In this way, Kant hopes, a juridical community of means will gradually transform itself, without breach of law, into an ethical "kingdom of ends."

Kant and State Neutrality Vis-à-Vis the Good

Kant's name is sometimes invoked in connection with the relativist argument that the state should be neutral toward competing ways of life because no way of life is ascertainably the best. This association is in some ways curious. Probably no secular philosopher has been surer than Kant that there is a best way of life, a single model by which to set one's store, open in principle to all human beings.[42] It is, moreover, for Kant, only on the basis of this best way of life that rights as such have any genuine meaning or rational foundation. Where Kant comes closest to the claim falsely attributed to him is in his insistence that the state has no direct charge to realize the particular ends of its citizens (including moral ones), but only to ensure that each is free to pursue his ends to the maximum extent possible, consistent with the equal freedom of others.

The reasons Kant advances for this position, however, reveal his distance from the "value neutrality" of many who today claim Kant's mantle. The first and less important of these reasons flows from what Kant regards as the fundamental indeterminacy of happiness for human beings, and hence the unsuitability of happiness as a fundamental juridical principle.[43] In a word, the notion of happiness lacks determinate content and hence cannot furnish the obligatory or necessitating guidance implicit in a legal order.

The second and ultimately more important reason flows from what is necessarily implied by the moral way of life, whose absolute choice-worthiness Kant contrasts with the merely relative value of happiness and its pursuit. For the choice-worthiness of the moral way of life is inseparable from the idea of inner freedom that it implies—a freedom that cannot be externally coerced or otherwise imparted from without. It would be contradictory for the law to try to force that inner state of moral grace, our potentiality for which gives law its ultimate ground. Instead, laws of right leave persons free to pursue ends of their own choosing, in the not unsupported hope that the ensuing culture of enlightenment will facilitate—without actually effecting—this inner transformation.

When Kant says that the laws of right have nothing to do with

159

"the ends men have by nature," he does not mean that happiness has nothing to do with justice. On the quasi-cosmic scales of the all-wise judge to whom he sometimes rhetorically refers, virtue alone is insufficient—at least as an ultimate goal of moral aspiration. The supreme good toward which humanity is enjoined to strive is not virtue alone, but happiness conjoined with virtue or worthiness to be happy.[44] If justice means that each gets his due, nothing less than happiness is a sufficient reward for virtue. But for justice on so cosmic a scale we can hope only with God's help.

It is to justice on a human scale—the due that we owe to and are owed by other human beings—that Kant's juridical constitution specifically addresses itself; and here Kant's demands upon the human spirit become more modest. It is this modesty that lies at the heart of the curious convergence of Kant's juridical system with that of Hobbes, a convergence in which Kant took some comfort. For if at least some moral ends, such as public security or peace, can be achieved by amoral or even immoral means—that is, by "nature herself"—then there is new ground for moral hope. This ground is supported not only by belief in God but also by a judicious, albeit provisional interpretation of human history.

If the problem of politics can be solved for a nation of devils if only they are intelligent, then there is good reason to suppose that man's baser impulses, however evil in themselves, may ultimately serve moral ends.[45] Equally significant, there is every reason to suppose that our moral efforts will not be futile, supported as they are by the workings of man's animal nature. It is this external convergence between Kant and Hobbes that has encouraged some contemporary neo-Kantians to try to have it both ways—to surround a fundamentally Hobbesian moral skepticism and conventionalism with appeals to human dignity and worth that are inseparable, in their original Kantian context, from the moral absolutism of the categorical imperative.

They are, to be sure, aided in this obfuscation by the efforts of Hegel and his followers to blur the line between right and virtue, nature and morality, and—to some extent—by the rigidity of Kant himself, whose identification of human dignity with the untrammeled right of individuals to contract freely (except in sexual matters [!]) might well give the most devoted of Kantians pause. Somehow, human rights seem to require a more substantive admission of human neediness, and with it a larger claim upon the material resources of our fellows, than Kant is willing to allow. For Kant a starving man, so long as he has not been robbed or defrauded of his property, has only nature or himself to blame. While for Locke the right to property includes the right to life, for Kant the right to property, at least in principle, trumps it. In practice, however, no man can be legally compelled to give up his life; hence the starving man's juridical duty to refrain from taking the property of others is, strictly speaking, unenforceable.

Still, Kant's defense of freedom of contract in the name of human dignity points to the dangers involved in treating laudable and prudent aid to the indigent, along with other forms of public investment, as matters of strict entitlement. Contemporary efforts to treat welfare benefits as entrenched rights ultimately threaten the very private sphere upon which meaningful individualism hinges.[46] It is thus ironic that the same interpretive premises used today to carve out a substantive constitutional right to privacy are also used to breach the fragile wall that has historically guarded the private sphere by separating state and society.

Kant's rigorous defense of property rights is offset—and in some measure softened—by his understanding of the relation between law and culture. Where law separates, guarding the absolute juridical integrity of individual persons, culture unites, by stimulating the mutual attachments of civility and taste. Like George Bush's "thousand points of light," civility, according to Kant, encourages a general atmosphere of benevolence, which Kant especially associates with feminine good works.[47]

Kant's distinction between law and culture, moreover, overrides in otherwise useful ways the more traditional distinction between public and private. "Public" no longer means that which pertains to government, but rather all that is "publicized," thereby contributing to both legal and cultural progress in the widest sense. Scholars and other citizens of the republic of letters, rather than government officials, are the proper guardians of this most truly public sphere. Kant's concept of a civil culture in this way usefully anticipates our own notion of "society" (as in "society pages"), along with the so-called fifth estate—both quasi-private institutions performing public roles.

To be sure, Kant in so recasting the public sphere is also pleading for intellectual freedom from a monarch in a position to deny it. There is thus every reason for him to play down the importance of genuine political power for true citizenship, just as he plays down the importance of government by the actual consent of the governed. As a partial surrogate for political independence, intellectual freedom is to be granted in exchange for political quiescence. The empirical constitution—the laws of the land—have absolute claim to the obedience of all citizens. But the citizens in turn are to be granted the

161

freedom to argue and, if possible, persuade the prevailing powers peacefully, and without breaching the continuity of lawful governance, to amend themselves. Such at least was the implicit deal that Kant attempted to strike with Frederick the Great and, less successfully, with his successor: "Argue as much as you want, and about whatever you want, only obey!"[48]

Kant and Constitutional Aspiration

Hence Kant's peculiarly two-sided approach to constitutionalism—an approach that differentiates the rational constitution from its imperfect empirical embodiments, while at the same time insisting on their underlying unity.[49] The rational constitution is for Kant the *telos* of the law, the principle that substantially informs (in a quasi-scholastic sense) all actual states. The constitution so conceived is a fence, in its particulars, against despotism of both the few and the many—for the formlessness of untrammeled popular will renders it indistinguishable, for Kant, from tyranny. It is at the same time an ideal that actual governments are enjoined progressively to approach, through gradual and law-abiding self-transformation.[50] Republicanism—Kant's name for the ideal form that all empirical constitutions, whatever their actual laws, implicitly share—can thus be honored both in letter and, until such time as that is possible, in spirit, as is done by enlightened monarchies that govern (Kant is no doubt again looking over his political shoulder) "in a republican manner."[51]

To what extent is Kant's metaphysically and morally enriched constitutionalism a useful guide to American constitutional rights? Leaving aside Kant's personal admiration for our system of government, it does seem that the American Constitution, taken together with the Declaration of Independence, performs a dual role reminiscent of the Kantian distinction between the empirical and the ideal.

The Kantian flavor of the American Constitution is perhaps nowhere clearer than in Lincoln's designation of it as the "silver frame" around the Declaration's "golden apple." Without forbidding slavery (or explicitly endorsing it), the Constitution somehow pointed in the direction of slavery's eventual elimination, and thus set forth a goal to be realized, it was hoped, not by breaching the letter of the law but by a gradual change of attitude or "culture."[52]

Today as well, the American Constitution plays a dual role—a more narrowly legal function, which sets forth the limits of governmental power, and a broader political function, which sets forth goals toward which citizens are implicitly enjoined to strive. Indeed, these two functions cannot be strictly separated. "Equal protection of the laws," for example, is both a restraint on existing legislative power and the embodiment of a certain ideal, an underlying conception of justice, which judicial interpretation, however strictly it may want to adhere to the meaning of language or the "simple" intention of the founders, cannot ignore.

For that intention is bound up with an overall scheme and a set of purposes—along with a set of principles, partly, but not exhaustively, enumerated in the Declaration. To discover the meaning of the Constitution is, in a limited number of cases, necessarily to raise more general philosophic questions of a sort that Kant, among others, sought to answer. The risks involved, of which current literature gives not a few examples, cannot entirely be avoided. Such risks can, however, be mitigated by a due attention to the language of the document as primary evidence of the intentions, in both the narrower and the broader senses, of its authors. Such attention would secure, among other things, a suitable regard for the relation between human dignity and self-reliance.

In any case, it is clear that the content of the Declaration and thus by implication the core principles of the Constitution are not simply identical with Kant's "idea of reason." Nor do the rights of the Declaration appeal directly to the categorical imperative. Perhaps this, then, is the essential difference between the Kantian approach to constitutional rights and that of the founders: for the former, rights stem from the moral law grasped as a fundamental "fact of reason"; for the latter, rights stem from nature or nature's God, as mediated by the actual consent of the governed.

Still, given the crucial and at times uneasy relation between the liberal, mainly Lockean thought of the founders and a more traditional religiosity that has also defined our national experience, some form of Kantianism may well perform—as it has in the past—a useful and evocative role. As Lincoln drew upon the cadences of the Bible, so Kant's transcendental grounding of human rights can remind us of the burden as well as the glory of freedom. Whether the morally neutered and historicized Kant currently in vogue is what is called for remains more doubtful.

8

Implied Protections and Protections Presupposed—Or, Not Every Right That Looks New Is New

Henry Shue

"New right" is frequently a sneer. The immediate reason for calling a right new is to insinuate that it is made up—invented for convenience, at best—and therefore bogus, while an old right is implied to have been discovered somehow in the nature of things and therefore to be genuine. The notion of simply discovering a right in the nature of things usually depends on either a protopositivist epistemology that finds rights lying on the surface of reality, unencumbered by theoretical grounding—the right is "just there"—or an intuitionist epistemology that is mysterious and undiscussable—one must "just see" the right. Yet we have other and far better reasons than supposed newness to resist the proliferation of rights claims and the rights inflation produced by illegitimate coinage of rights.

Chronology versus Substance

Everyone has his favorite manufactured right. Mine is the right to first use of nuclear weapons, conveniently discovered in the nature of international relations by the staff of the U.S. National Security Council during the late 1940s:

> The United States not only maintains a right to use atomic bombs, but does in fact now plan to use them in the event

164

of major war, and this plan is not at present dependent upon the prior use of such weapons by any possible aggressor.[1]

Had it any basis beyond mere assertion, this would have been a right not to self-defense but to a massive retaliation against civilians—the only kind of attack of which the United States was capable at the time. Preposterous, ungrounded claims—such as this one to a general entitlement to kill civilians massively and indiscriminately—have led to a search for reasonable and systematic ways to distinguish between the authentic and the phony.

Philip Alston, for example, has suggested that the General Assembly of the United Nations should institute a "system of *appellations controlees*" by "mandating a precise modus operandi to be followed when the proclamation of a new human right has been proposed."[2] If such a screening of proposals were rigorous, it could not hurt. Nor could it help much. The fundamental problem is not susceptible to procedural solution. We need instead a consensus upon the concept of a right and a consensus upon the standards for the adequate protection of a right.

The baseless ways in which "old rights" and "new rights" are discussed fail even to be coherent. A second way of proceeding boils down to the arbitrary stipulation that to be counted as old a right must have been articulated before around 1800. This viewpoint supposes that all new rights, articulated since 1800, are fake.

The first step is as unobjectionable as it is unhelpful: we could certainly adopt the convention of calling seventeenth- and eighteenth-century rights the old ones, and nineteenth- and twentieth-century rights the new ones. All the weight then shifts to the second step: establishing the contention that everything new in precisely this sense is ersatz. It would be purely circular and entirely question begging to specify even a completely accurate list of features distinctive of the old rights and then to declare the new rights illegitimate *because* they lacked the features common to the old ones. This is no argument.

What is needed is an argument to show that each of the features shared by the old rights is a necessary condition of being a right, not just of being an "old" right; they are of course necessary for being an old right, by the stipulation in the first step. They must be demonstrated as requisite to being a right at all. The features common to old rights might specify a conception of an old right, but one cannot convincingly announce without argument that all those features belong to the very concept of a right. It would have to be shown that any authentic right must fit perfectly into the eighteenth-century conception of a right.

People sometimes believe that everything worth knowing about rights was already known by 1800 and that the only useful undertaking for us now is to decipher the intent of those who wrote before that date. This is particularly implausible if rights are natural in the sense that they are based upon the nature of human society, for it presupposes that nothing worth knowing about human social nature has been understood during the last two centuries. Would John Locke, Alexander Hamilton, and James Madison have learned nothing from Charles Darwin, John Stuart Mill, Fyodor Dostoyevsky, Sigmund Freud, or Max Weber about which rights need protection and how best to protect them?

In chapter 5, Harvey C. Mansfield, Jr., suggests making Friedrich Nietzsche the historical pivot of conceptions of rights. I would suggest on the contrary that current debates about rights have virtually nothing to do with Nietzsche. Mansfield's central historical thesis, reflected in his chapter's title, is that "as theory the new rights were born in Friedrich Nietzsche's doctrine of the creative self."[3] Mansfield apparently offers John Rawls as his example of an advocate of "new rights" whose theory somehow rests upon a Nietzschean creative self.[4]

Mansfield's speculation about Nietzschean influence depends on two highly doubtful connections. First, he presents Nietzsche's doctrine of the creative self as "decisive in American pragmatism."[5] But since pragmatism defines truth in terms of the socially useful and Nietzsche had only contempt for the socially useful, their respective accounts of truth and reality are too deeply opposed for Mansfield's hypothesis to be plausible. Second, pragmatism has had little influence on the rights debates of recent decades. British jurisprudence, as exemplified by H. L. A. Hart, for example, has been more influential than American pragmatism.

Rawls in particular is most deeply influenced by Immanuel Kant and David Hume.[6] Of course, since neither Hume nor Kant took the self to be the straightforward, natural "given" that Mansfield apparently would like, they too may be closet Nietzscheans, by Mansfield's standard! The specific parallel between Nietzsche and Rawls is claimed to lie in the following: "Instead of the strong and the weak we have the equalizers and the equalized—called by John Rawls the 'least advantaged.'"[7] But what is supposed to be the parallel?

First, Nietzsche's "strong" scorn his "weak" and disregard their interests, while Rawls's so-called "equalizers" and "equalized" cooperate with each other on terms that all sides (there are of course more than two relevant groups) consider fair. Second, the Rawlsian principle that deals with the least advantaged is lexically subordinate to a prior principle that guarantees equal basic liberties to all individuals and protects them against inordinate influence by others. Rawls's basic liberties are thoroughly traditional, although they do include Benjamin Constant's "liberty of the moderns" as well as his "liberty of the ancients."[8] I see no parallel with Nietzsche and little reason to call those people "equalizers" who do well economically while pursuing their own interests within a fair set of rules.

Perhaps one should not rest so much weight on the fact that Rawls is the first contemporary theorist discussed by Mansfield after he states his Nietzschean thesis. The most natural interpretation of his general thesis would be that rights which are fundamentally Nietzschean are new and rights uncorrupted by Nietzsche are old. Let us then consider an alleged right that I consider a paradigm of a "new" right, if not the *bête noire* of those who are exercised about new rights: the right to privacy. In their famous essay "The Right to Privacy," Samuel D. Warren and Louis D. Brandeis gave this characterization of the right:

> These considerations lead to the conclusion that the protection afforded to thoughts, sentiments, and emotions, expressed through the medium of writing or of the arts, so far as it consists in preventing publication, is merely an instance of the enforcement of the more general right of the individual to be let alone. . . . The principle which protects personal writings and all other personal productions, not against theft and physical appropriation, but against publication in any form, is in reality not the principle of private property, but that of an inviolate personality.[9]

Although many critics of the right to privacy do their best to leave the impression that it was cut out of whole cloth by the dreaded Earl Warren court, this seminal law review article articulating a conception of it appeared in 1890.[10] Is the "inviolate personality" appealed to by Samuel Warren and Brandeis the Nietzschean "creative self" that Mansfield says lies behind new rights? I do not believe that anyone who reads their article will think so. But if the right to privacy is not "born in Friedrich Nietzsche's doctrine of the creative self," it does not qualify as a new right by what would appear to be the most natural reading of Mansfield's suggestion. Yet if the right to privacy is not a new right, then what is?

We have been given no single, coherent account of where to draw the line between new and old. "New rights" remains a loose term of abuse with no determinate reference.

It was a mistake, I have already suggested, to try to distinguish between new and old rights before reflecting about the concept of a right. What is a right, then? Mansfield suggests the following: "A right is permission to do a range of things that an individual is able to do."[11]

This will not do at all. The content of a right may include not only doing things but having things (like private property in an adequate diet or ready access to procedures of habeas corpus) and believing things (like religious or metaphysical views that have no implications about doing anything). A right is far more than a permission. If a right were only a permission, it would be hard to imagine any good reason for governments to have been instituted. Mill, who must belong with the uncorrupted old rather than the corrupted new, seems much closer to the mark: "To have a right, then, is, I conceive, to have something which society ought to defend me in the possession of."[12]

Rights ground demands for protection, often institutional and sometimes governmental. An implemented right is something defended or protected, or an enjoyment—of doing, having, believing, or whatever—that is socially guaranteed.[13] The social guarantees may, but need not, be governmental. A morally grounded right may or may not require legally enforceable protection, but it does require effective protection.

Why it is mistaken to conceive of a right as a mere permission was carefully argued in Wesley Hohfeld's 1923 classic *Fundamental Legal Conceptions*.[14] Consider two cases. In the first case you and I are walking along and see on the sidewalk a twenty-dollar bill, which never belonged to either of us. If there is no way to establish to whom it did belong, we are each at liberty, or permitted, to pick up the bill. This means that if you pick it up before I do and insist upon keeping it, I have no grounds for complaint, any more than you have if I get there first. I have no right to this bill, although I am permitted to grab it if I am able. In the second case, the bill does belong to me and was inadvertently dropped earlier when I was walking in the opposite direction. Now I am not simply permitted to pick it up if I am able: I have a right to it. If you pick it up before I do and insist upon keeping it, I do have grounds for complaint. And there can be legal procedures for protecting my right and enforcing it against you.

A permission and a right are quite distinct. First, it can make perfect sense to protect a right, but there is nothing to protect in the case of the permission. A protected permission would be much more than a permission—it would have been transformed, wisely or unwisely, into a right when the protection was granted. People have not fought and died to gain their unprotected permissions.

Second, rights entail correlative duties upon other parties, and permissions do not. Protection must be provided by someone other than the person whose right is threatened and the person threatening it. Mansfield appears to be confusing (a) simply being at liberty, which is constituted merely by the contingent fact that no second party happens to be preventing one from doing something, with (b) enjoying a right to liberty, which is partly constituted by third parties protecting one against second-party interference.

When one has an implemented right to liberty, social institutions provide effective protection for one's liberty, or for whatever else the right is a right to—not all rights are rights to liberties. Implemented rights are profoundly social, because the protections are social. Where rights are respected, people protect each other's rights. Our brief, partial look at the concept of a right tells us, then, that we must pay attention to the social guarantees, or institutionalized protections, that distinguish genuine rights from the mere permissions considered by Mansfield.[15]

I want throughout this brief essay to look at *forms* that good arguments can take rather than to devote all my space to working out a single argument fully. One cannot whisk a right into, or out of, existence with the turning of a page. Thus I will not try to establish whether there are rights of the putative kinds I mention. Instead I will try to indicate how one can responsibly go about considering whether to institute new forms of protection for rights, protection that will sometimes but not always involve recognizing additional rights.

One abiding and fundamental human interest is physical security, and no right is more basic than the right to physical security. It is a moral right. A constitution that did not provide a basis for adequate legal protections for physical security would be inadequate, in need of reform in the area of providing for individual safety from certain, not all, kinds of physical threats.

Many, many laws provide protection for the physical security to which every person has a moral right: laws against battery, laws against assault, laws against aggravated assault, laws against rape, laws against various types and degrees of killing, and so on. One simple but fundamental problem with the current fashion of trying to divide rights into old and new is that, to my knowledge, no one has yet even tried to say how rights are to be individuated for purposes of counting. Are there as many rights as there are separately defined crimes with distinguishable penalties, such that, for example, a person has one right not to be subject to battery, a second right not to be subject to assault, a third not to be subject to murder in the first degree, and so on? Or shall we say that a person has a single basic right to physical security, for which there are many protections against many specific threats?

Now this counting problem may seem, and in most respects is, a bit silly; but it is an unavoidable problem for those who label rights as old or new. Before one can coherently label one right as old and another as new, one logically must have established that there are two rights, not one. The labelers bear the burden of specifying a counting rule.

Here is an example of the practical import of this abstract point. In several states and in many countries, a husband may coerce his wife to have sex with him against her will without violating any law. Where laws against assault and battery exist, he commits a crime if he assaults or batters her in the process. But where the various types of rape are all defined so as to exclude by definition the rape of a spouse, he commits no crime in subjecting his wife to coerced sex of a kind that would constitute a rape if he subjected any other woman to it. In these jurisdictions there is no legal protection for this aspect of physical security—namely, to be secure against the coercive infliction of sexual acts that one has attempted to reject.

As I have already indicated, I make no attempt fully to canvass the arguments in any of my examples. The only question I ask is, Would a right against marital rape be a new right in any meaningful sense? If a legislature in a state where marital rape is impossible by definition chooses to grant legal protection to the physical security of wives against this threat of coercion by their husbands, is the legislature creating a new right? This is my question—this and the unavoidably presupposed questions: How does one decide when there is one right with an additional form of protection and when there are two rights? And for cases in which the first question has a clear answer, how does one decide whether the second right is new? Would the introduction of legal protection against marital rape constitute the recognition of a new right, and how do we know?

Those who wish to scorn all new rights face a very uncomfortable dilemma: the more reason we have to think the right to physical security against spousal rape would be new, the more reason we would have to think it would be an excellent idea. It turns out to be very difficult indeed to argue that the conception of a marital rape is both a new idea and a bad idea—the newer it is, the better it is.

Consider a jurisdiction in which marital rape is definitionally impossible because a wife is treated as a husband's sexual property.

She is not his property *tout court*—not a slave whom he can, for example, buy or sell. She is, however, his sexual slave. In sexual matters her actual, continuing consent counts for nothing, and his will counts for everything—this is the paradigm of slavery.

The example chosen could have been more or less extreme than this one. Clearly, the more extreme the case, the more alien the idea that a married woman retains a basic right to the security and integrity of her own body. Therefore, the more urgent is the need for legal protection against her body's being used contrary to her expressed wishes for the purposes of another person, her husband. Accordingly, to the extent that a right against marital rape would be a new right, it ought to be recognized and instituted.

On the far less consequential question of whether this right would be new, I see no clear answer because I see no clear question about age. I am inclined to respond that every person has a basic moral right to physical security—to the integrity of one's own body. I see no meaningful question whether the right to physical security is itself new or old.

Many interesting questions arise, however, about its articulation, formulation, recognition, and implementation. Hobbes, for example, sharply recognized a right to physical security and formulated some of but not all its aspects. Some theorists—Hart and Rawls, for example—obscure it by sometimes writing as if all rights were rights to liberties and a liberty were the only possible content of a right. In theory people could someday forget about the right to physical security, so that another theorist would have to rediscover and freshly articulate it.

None of this tells us anything, however, about the age of the underlying right, if indeed rights have ages. I think of the basis for moral rights as being already determined at a given time by the facts of human social interaction at that time—the fundamental interests at stake and the standard threats to them at that time. The precise articulation of the rights awaits philosophical, political, and legal insight, arising from attempts to build principled consensus. This, however, may well be some superfluous Platonism with no practical importance.

But many intellectual, legal, and political developments concerning rights are datable in a manner that permits meaningful discussion of new and old. When did it first occur to Saint Thomas that the acceptability of private property might be contingent upon satisfaction of the material needs of all persons? When did a majority realize that women morally ought to be given a legal right to vote? When did Haitians realize that slavery ought to be abolished in their country?

When was this or that constitution, constitutional amendment, law, or highest court decision adopted here or there? Judicial interpretations, laws, and constitutions are all datable and therefore relatively new or old. Legal rights come and go, are born and die, flourish and wither—indeed, are abolished and introduced.

So we can usefully ask, When did marital rape become a crime in the state of New York? Just as we can ask, When was slavery prohibited in the state of Missouri? But if someone asks, When did the right to physical security come to include all rape? I am torn between answering, "Always did, although it took some people a long while to realize it," or answering, "Why do you ask—what do you suppose turns upon the answer?"

Either way, the sheer newness of the legal right would be no ground for opposition to its introduction into the statute books. Indeed, as I have shown, its unfamiliarity may make its introduction all the more urgent. Since some moral rights should, and some should not, be implemented as legal rights, there could of course be other, entirely different reasons not to create the legal right. I doubt they are significant in this case, but I cannot pursue the substantive merits here. The point, however, is precisely that one must consider the substantive merits rather than worrying about new versus old.

Let us examine a small selection of the issues a little more systematically. Recognized rights can imply genuine rights that have not yet been recognized, and recognized rights can presuppose genuine rights that have not yet been recognized. Implication and presupposition deserve at least brief separate consideration.

Implied Protections

Insofar as rights are based upon the nature of human society, some genuinely new rights might well become necessary as society changes. From the evident fact that we need to control the proliferation of groundless assertions of rights—such as the right to use atomic bombs—it by no means follows that the only good right is an old right.

Government institutions, commercial enterprises, communications and surveillance technology, military and medical technology, and most other forms of human enterprise and organization evolve through the decades. We face new diseases and new cures, new energy sources and new environmental pollutants. I cannot imagine how one could know a priori that none of these changes in human society have created, or will create, new vulnerabilities against which it would be rational for us to protect each other through the social guarantees that partly constitute rights.

For example, suppose it is indeed reasonable that we recognize a moral and a legal right to die—at least the name of which might well have sounded absurd to John Locke. It is then perhaps a matter less of a new insight into individual liberty than of new medical technologies creating undreamed-of possibilities for the cruel, unusual, and gratuitous infliction of pain and suffering by doctors eager to install them but unwilling to exercise any judgment about removing them.[16] Having noted above the protopositivism of some attempts to make sense of natural rights, I hasten to add that one cannot push too hard on the distinction between changed circumstances and changed comprehension, without relying upon an untenably sharp distinction between empirical and conceptual.

Any new technology must also be comprehended, thereby bringing conceptual as well as empirical change. Nevertheless, the argument for the recognition of a right to die depends little on any allegedly new insight—that control over one's life involves not having strangers seize control over the circumstances of one's death, even if the strangers claim to have come to help you. We knew that already. Rather, it turns on the increasing power of medical technology to inflict upon helpless subjects months and years of living death that serve only the interests of people other than the totally vulnerable victim of the uncontrolled technology.

Thus the standard threats, against which we can sometimes protect each other through the implementation of rights, themselves change.[17] While new medical technology brings some great benefits, it also creates unprecedented and horrifying possibilities for manipulation and control. It certainly seems reasonable that protection should be provided, irrespective of whether the rights that would have to be recognized in order to provide it were old or new. The fact that changing threats to unchanged interests can ground new rights is one correct explanation of the changing conceptions of rights for which Mansfield comes up with his undocumented hypothesis about Nietzschean influence on rights theorists. It is groundless to invoke "the abandonment of human nature" when people are simply responding to new threats with new protections.[18]

I will not pursue any further the point that no good reasons have been produced to establish anything inherently suspect about a new right recognized in order to protect fundamental human interests against new standard threats. I will instead address the point that, although rights need not be old in order to be legitimate, some rights that appear to be new are actually old, in that they entail or are entailed by rights that are indisputably old. For example, a so-called new right may turn out to be essential for the adequate protection of an old right; in that case the recognition and articulation are new, but the right itself is old. The existence or importance of the new right had been overlooked, because the nature of the old right had not been fully comprehended. Surely no defender of natural rights is prepared to state and prove the theorem that the list of rights was complete either in 1800 or in 1960.

Even Robert Bork acknowledges, for the case of constitutional rights, that "courts often give protection to a constitutional freedom by creating a buffer zone, by prohibiting a government from doing something not in itself forbidden but likely to lead to an invasion of a right specified in the Constitution."[19] David Luban, in the 1991 Bertram Morris colloquium, calls the general category of approach that acknowledges something like Bork's buffer zone "the prospectivist theory of rights," as contrasted with "the reactivist theory," because of its devotion to the actual prevention of rights violations rather than the distantly second-best goal of compensation after the fact of violation.[20]

Luban and Bork are of course discussing constitutional rights, some of which have moral grounds; I am mainly discussing moral rights. Yet I have made the analogous point about moral rights: sometimes in order to protect a well-recognized moral right like the right to physical security it is essential to recognize explicitly an implied moral right that has previously gone unremarked. And not always but often, the newly recognized moral right constitutes good reason to institute new legal protections, especially where highly vulnerable persons need assistance against coercion that they cannot safely resist on their own.

And if the Constitution does not contain grounds for prospective protections, one may have reason to introduce a statute, although each proposed protection must be argued out specifically and substantively. Some statutes create new legal rights. The secure protection of our rights *before* they are violated is one of the main purposes of legislatures—indeed, of government in general.

Even if by some miraculous process the list of rights could be certified already to be complete at a particular date, what are the arguments to show that comprehension of the features and implications of those rights could never deepen? Even if someone (who?) had definitively (how?) closed the list, our understanding of it could change, for better or for worse. I rely upon no assumption of progressive enlightenment. Of course we also may forget some of what was once understood, and of course new enthusiasms may lead us off the track into misguided meanderings. This is why we must insist on being told the reasons for assertions made about rights, including the concept of a right and the standard of protection being assumed.

Thus, although being fundamentally new need not embarrass a genuine right, I will concentrate in the remainder of this chapter on the rights that seem new but are not, because we have only recently come to understand their necessity for civilized society. These rights are old in that the crucial consideration is not that the circumstances of human society have changed in a fundamental way, creating a new threat to human interests, but that we have newly realized that certain measures were needed all along.

This point has major practical significance. If the suggestion that some newly articulated rights may be essential elements of old rights has been given any plausibility, then the mere fact that a right has only recently been articulated is insufficient reason to conclude that it is a new right, much less that it is suspect. Judgments about which rights are new and which are old are substantive judgments that turn upon the concept of a right, the content of the specific putative rights in question, and what it would mean concretely to give them adequate protection. Where and by whom the rights were first mentioned is of minor consequence. What is needed is not a chronological account, but a practical and conceptual analysis.

Protections Presupposed

Again I want to draw an analogy between forms of reasoning about moral rights and forms of reasoning about constitutional rights. For the analogy to hold, it need not fail to distinguish moral rights from constitutional rights. Some constitutions embody more moral rights than others do; whether this is advisable depends on whether, in the face of the threats to those rights in that society's circumstances, the secure enjoyment of the contents of the rights requires legal protections. In any case that is another question, and I am drawing the analogy for only one formal feature. It may be necessary to emphasize that this is a *non*relativistic theory acknowledging that what is objectively appropriate depends upon reality, which is not everywhere the same.

In a fascinating section of "The Warren Court and the Concept of a Right," David Luban presents a daring interpretation of Justice William O. Douglas's notorious penumbra metaphor in *Griswold*. In the process he plausibly argues that Bork's criticism of Douglas misinterprets Douglas's much-ridiculed sentence through a failure to appreciate the point of the central metaphor of penumbra. While I am in no special position to judge the merits of the constitutional question, what Luban says about it strikes me as exactly correct for the case of moral rights. Douglas's infamous sentence, which has given the world much law-student hilarity on the subject of emanations, is as follows:

> Specific guarantees in the Bill of Rights have penumbras, formed by emanations from those guarantees that help give them life and substance.[21]

Bork maintains, as we saw above, that courts do indeed secure constitutional rights by "creating" surrounding protections, for which he aptly introduces the military metaphor of a buffer zone designed to prevent "an invasion of a right specified in the Constitution."[22] Bork's mistake, according to Luban, is to think that his buffer zones are Douglas's penumbras.

What I take to be Bork's fundamental criticism of Douglas's specific reasoning is this:

> Justice Douglas bypassed that seemingly insuperable difficulty by simply asserting that the various separate "zones of privacy" created by each separate provision of the Bill of Rights somehow created a general but wholly undefined "right of privacy" that is independent of and lies outside any right or "zone of privacy" to be found in the Constitution.[23]

That there are protective zones—whether or not of privacy—around specified rights is not, according to Bork, in dispute. The fallacious inference made by Douglas is from specific protective zones, given some definition by the particular right that they each respectively protect, to one big sloppy "general but wholly undefined" zone. It is the messy merge of the separate zones, not their independent existences, that is challenged. And of course if there is no large general zone, there is nothing that needs to be denominated as the right to privacy.

According to Luban, in the Douglas sentence that introduced the penumbra metaphor Bork interprets "those guarantees" in the second clause merely to refer back to the "specific guarantees in the Bill of Rights" in the first clause. Bork's reading of Douglas's sentence, according to Luban, is:

> Specific guarantees in the Bill of Rights create penumbras that help give the specific guarantees life and substance.[24]

Richard Mohr had, however, earlier suggested that the correct—and certainly richest—reading of Douglas's sentence is:

> Specific guarantees [in the Bill of Rights] have penumbras
> that are formed by emanations from those *general* guarantees
> that help give the specific guarantees life and substance.[25]

This has the startling implication, drawn out by Luban, that, *pace* Bork, rather than the First, Third, Fourth, and Fifth Amendments having their own respective penumbras, which must execute a messy merge to create what could then be called the right of privacy, the First, Third, Fourth, and Fifth Amendments are the specific guarantees that are themselves the penumbras of an underlying general right of privacy! The right against having soldiers quartered in private homes during peacetime, like the right against forced self-incrimination, is a specific prospective protection of privacy against an all-too-standard governmental threat.

The light in the penumbra of the moon is cast not by the moon but by the sun. The physics of penumbras is, therefore, as Luban notes, on the side of Mohr and of Douglas as Mohr reads him. What Mohr calls Douglas's "careful metaphor" certainly makes incomparably more sense on Mohr's reading than on Bork's. Physical law and constitutional law are, however, separate matters, and I now leave them each to those who know them better than I.

My purpose in introducing this brief account of an enormously complex issue in constitutional law is to indicate dramatically a form of reasoning that is perfectly standard in all theoretical areas with which I am acquainted—namely, reasoning backwards from *explicandum* to *explicans*. Temporally speaking, one is moving from conclusion to premises—in only this precise sense is one reasoning backwards, in that one's thoughts are moving logically upstream.[26]

One sees a phenomenon like a lunar penumbra, which is neither total darkness nor total light, and one asks, How can this be fully explained? Why is there no more light? Because of the moon. Why is there no less light? Because of the sun. The positions of the sun and the moon explain the lunar penumbra because from an adequate description of the sun and the moon plus the relevant principles, one could infer the description of the lunar penumbra—from which, however, one in fact began the search for the explanation.

This is reasoning to presuppositions, a form of reasoning used since time immemorial by philosophy, science, and other theoretical inquiries.[27] Its obvious problem is that there is almost always more than one possible explanation for any given phenomenon and more than one set of premises that yield any given conclusion. Hence, one's theoretical work is by no means done as soon as one thinks of a plausible explanation; that explanation must perpetually be com-

177

pared with others, and there is no way in science, philosophy, jurisprudence, or anywhere else to impose closure by proving somehow that no other alternative accounts will emerge to rival the one currently favored. This is, therefore, an indispensable but limited form of reasoning.

In spite of its undeniable limitations, however, this form of reasoning is a perfectly legitimate means of articulating rights that, since their articulation is new, will reflexively be denounced by some as new rights. The articulation of such a right is, *ex hypothesi*, new. But the right itself need not be new, any more than the sun need have been born on the day that someone figured out it was the source of the light in the lunar penumbra. If those who ratified the Third Amendment intended to protect the privacy of the home and saw the quartering of soldiers during peacetime as an "ordinary and serious but remediable" threat to that fundamental interest in privacy, this would help to explain the ratification. I hardly need add that this is not the only available explanation, nor that it is a new explanation. What matters is that its newness does not in itself count against its theoretical appropriateness or explanatory power.

I am not trying to prove either a moral or a constitutional right to privacy, any more than I was earlier trying to prove a moral or constitutional right against marital rape. I am sketching two general ways one can reasonably move to new formulations of what may or may not be new rights. Contrary to the speculations by Mansfield, we have encountered neither need nor temptation to deny the existence of abiding human interests or to invoke the existence of Nietzschean selves engaged in irresponsible self-expression.

One final contrast may be helpful. Reasoning to an implied protection moves logically downstream, while reasoning to a presupposed right moves logically upstream. Reasoning from an established right to the need for a new protection moves from the more general to the more specific, while reasoning from an established right to a previously unrecognized, underlying right moves from the more specific to the more general. It would be the general right to physical security that implied the specific right against marital rape and a general right to liberty that implied the specific right to die—that is, the right not to have other persons arrogate control over the circumstances of one's death. By contrast, it would be the specific right against unreasonable searches and seizures and the specific right against the insertion of troops into homes that presupposed, as a theoretically unifying concept, a general right to privacy.

Anyone who has followed the argument so far will already have seen the next step. In no theoretical endeavor does one reason only from particular to general or only from general to particular. One reasons, in the Socratic sense, dialectically: one tests in both directions. This will be true of any comprehensive and rigorous theory of rights. Sometimes one will argue, If this is the general right presupposed by that putative specific right, then the specific right is unacceptable. At other times one will argue, If this is the specific right implied by that putative general right, then the general right is unacceptable. Theory construction has no algorithms, and one of the algorithms it does not have is, Always reject new conceptions.

Notes

Chapter 1: Introduction

1. In *The Mind of the Founder*, Marvin Meyers, ed. (New York: Brandeis University Press, 1981) p. 7.

2. See Allan Bloom, *Rousseau's Emile*, pp. 4, 5, in Allan Bloom, trans., *Emile* (New York: Basic Books, 1979).

Chapter 2: Present Conceptions of Human Rights

1. See, *inter alia*, Donald Lutz, "The U.S. Bill of Rights in Historical Perspective," in *Publius*, vol. 22 (Spring 1992). (See also Donald Lutz and Jack D. Warden, *A Covenanted People: The Religious Traditions and the Origins of American Constitutionalism* (Providence: John Carter Brown Library, 1987); and Donald Lutz, ed., *Documents of Political Foundation Written by Colonial Americans* (Philadelphia: Institute for the Study of Human Issues, 1986).

2. Daniel J. Elazar, *The American Constitutional Tradition* (Lincoln: University of Nebraska Press, 1988).

3. Ibid., pp. 124–39.

4. Donald Lutz, *Popular Consent and Popular Control: Whig Political Theory in the Early State Constitutions* (Baton Rouge: Louisiana State University Press, 1980).

5. Elazar, *The American Constitutional Tradition*.

6. On institutions as protectors of rights, see James Madison's letter to Thomas Jefferson of October 17, 1788, in Marvin Meyers, ed., *The Mind of the Founder: Sources of the Political Thought of James Madison* (New York: Bobbs-Merrill, 1973), pp. 205–09; Martin Diamond, Winston Mills Fisk, and Herbert Garfinkel, *The Democratic Republic: An Introduction to American National Government*, 2nd edition (Chicago: Rand McNally, 1972); and Martin Diamond, "The Separation of Powers and the Mixed Regime," in *Publius*, vol. 8 (Summer 1978), pp. 33–43.

7. I am indebted to Robert Licht for this felicitous way of encapsulating the difference.

8. See Alan Tarr, "American State Constitutionalism and 'First Amendment Rights,' " in *Publius*, vol. 22 (Spring 1992).

9. I elaborate on this in Daniel J. Elazar, "Obligations and Rights in the Jewish Political Tradition: Some Preliminary Observations," and, "Is There a Practical Way to Bridge the Gap Between Jewish and Modern Expectations of Rights and Obligations?" *Jewish Political Studies Review*, vol. 3 (Fall 1991).

10. Dworkin as a moral and legal theorist appears to believe that his theory is rationally grounded and thus not "relativistic." Its consequence, however, is a universal tolerance that cannot be distinguished from moral relativism. See Ronald Dworkin, *Taking Rights Seriously* (Cambridge, Mass.: Harvard University Press, 1978).

CHAPTER 3: BETWEEN PHILOSOPHY AND HISTORY

1. Judith Shklar, *Ordinary Vices* (Cambridge, Mass.: Harvard University Press, 1984), p. 237.

2. H. L. A. Hart, *The Concept of Law* (Oxford: Clarendon Press, 1961), chapter 9. Important discussions of Hobbesian arguments are found in Leo Strauss, *Natural Right and History* (Chicago: University of Chicago Press, 1953), chapter 5 (A); Ian Shapiro, *The Evolution of Rights in Liberal Theory* (Cambridge: Cambridge University Press, 1986), chapter 2; Richard Tuck, *Natural Rights Theories: Their Origin and Development* (Cambridge: Cambridge University Press, 1979).

3. For a clear characterization of the American significance of Locke's religious thought, see Walter Berns, "Religion and the Founding Principle," in Robert H. Horwitz, ed., *The Moral Foundations of the American Republic* (Charlottesville: University Press of Virginia, 1977), pp. 157–82. David A. J. Richards offers a survey with constitutional applications in *Toleration and the Constitution* (New York: Oxford University Press, 1986), chapters 4 and 5. A valuable collection of diverse essays is found in Robert A. Goldwin and Art Kaufman, eds., *How Does the Constitution Protect Religious Freedom?* (Washington, D.C.: AEI Press, 1987). I have explored the roots and consequences of Locke's argument in "Liberalism and Public Morality," Alfonso J. Damico, ed., *Liberals on Liberalism* (Totowa, N.J.: Rowman & Littlefield, 1986), pp. 129–47. Stephen Holmes has traced parallel developments in the thought of the sixteenth-century French thinker Jean Bodin, in "Jean Bodin: The Paradox of Sovereignty and the Privatization of Religion," J. Roland Pennock and John W. Chapman, eds., *Religion, Morality, and the Law: Nomos XXX* (New York: New York University Press, 1988), pp. 5–45. The late George Kelly has done the same for Pierre Bayle in "Bayle's Commonwealth of Atheists Revisited," Pennock and Chapman, pp. 78–109.

4. "Debates on the Putney Project," in Alphaeus Thomas Mason, *Free Government in the Making* (3rd ed.; New York: Oxford University Press, 1965), p. 13.

5. Gregory Vlastos, "Justice and Equality," in Jeremy Waldron, ed., *Theories of Rights* (Oxford: Oxford University Press, 1984), pp. 41–76. See also Joel Feinberg, *Social Philosophy* (Englewood Cliffs, N.J.: Prentice-Hall, 1973), pp. 88–94.

6. The literature on this topic is unfathomably vast. For the seventeenth-century context, readers may begin with: Strauss, *Natural Right and History*, chapter 5 (B); Shapiro, *The Evolution of Rights in Liberal Theory*, chapters 2–3; C. B. Macpherson, *The Political Theory of Possessive Individualism: Hobbes to Locke* (Oxford: Oxford University Press, 1962); James Tully, *A Discourse on Property: John Locke and His Adversaries* (Cambridge: Cambridge University Press, 1980); Richard Ashcraft, *Revolutionary Politics and Locke's Two Treatises of Government* (Princeton: Princeton University Press, 1986); Richard B. Schlatter, *Private Property: The History of an Idea* (London: Allen & Unwin, 1951). Important contemporary treatments include: Alan Ryan, *Property* (Minneapolis: University of Minnesota Press, 1987) and *Property and Political Theory* (Oxford: Basil Blackwell, 1984); Lawrence Becker, *Property Rights: Philosophic Foundations* (London: Routledge and Kegan Paul, 1971); John W. Chapman, *Property* (New York: New York University Press, 1980); Jeremy Waldron, *The Right to Private Property* (Oxford: Clarendon Press, 1988). Two provocative and philosophically informed discussions within the constitutional context are Bruce A. Ackerman, *Private Property and the Constitution* (New Haven: Yale University Press, 1977) and Richard Epstein, *Takings* (Cambridge, Mass.: Harvard University Press, 1986).

7. See below, notes 18 and 19.

8. See especially Herbert Croly, *The Promise of American Life* (New York: Capricorn Books, 1964).

9. Arguably, this tension can be resolved if both teachings are seen as rooted in a deeper Lockean conception of rational liberty or self-direction, and of government as having the right to provide all individuals with the internal and external requisites for the development and exercise of self-direction. See Rogers Smith, *Liberalism and American Constitutional Law* (Cambridge, Mass.: Harvard University Press, 1985).

10. For more developed speculations along these lines, see my "Moral Personality and Liberal Theory: John Rawls's 'Dewey Lectures,' " *Political Theory*, vol. 10 (1982), pp. 492–519.

11. For this, see especially George Kateb, "Democratic Individuality and the Claims of Politics," *Political Theory*, vol. 12 (1984), pp. 331–60.

12. See Bernard Williams, "Persons, Character and Morality," in *Moral Luck* (Cambridge: Cambridge University Press, 1981), pp. 1–19, and "A Critique of Utilitarianism," in J. J. C. Smart and Bernard Williams, *Utilitarianism: For and Against* (Cambridge: Cambridge University Press, 1973).

13. See, for example, Benjamin R. Barber, *Strong Democracy: Participatory Politics for a New Age* (Berkeley: University of California Press, 1984), *The Conquest of Politics* (Princeton: Princeton University Press, 1988), and "Liberal Democracy and the Costs of Consent," in Rosenblum, *Liberalism and the Moral Life*, pp. 54–68; Michael Walzer, "Philosophy and Democracy," *Political*

Theory, vol. 9 (August 1981), pp. 379–99, and "Liberalism and the Art of Separation," *Political Theory*, vol. 12 (August 1984); pp. 315–30. While this line of argument is most frequently associated with the participatory left, portions also make their appearance in the populist majoritarianism of the New Right, typically in response to what it views as "judicial activism." For an illuminating exposition and critique, see Stephen Macedo, *The New Right v. the Constitution* (Washington, D.C.: The Cato Institute, 1987).

14. Barber, *The Conquest of Politics*, p. 7.

15. For a more detailed discussion of the relation between egoism and rights, see Jeremy Waldron, *Nonsense upon Stilts: Bentham, Burke and Marx on the Rights of Man* (London and New York: Methuen, 1987), pp. 190–209. The philosophical version of this issue goes back at least to Hobbes. In *Morals by Agreement* (Oxford: Oxford University Press, 1986), David Gauthier tries to reinvigorate the Hobbesian argument that individuals moved by no more than rational self-interest would assent to moral constraints on their behavior, including the rights of others to certain kinds of noninterference. This thesis has been subjected to numerous searching criticisms, many of which are usefully collected in Ellen Frankel Paul et al., eds., *The New Social Contract: Essays on Gauthier* (Oxford: Basil Blackwell, 1988). In his post-*Theory of Justice* phase, John Rawls has denied with increasing fervor that rational self-interest, even when constrained by forms of ignorance and uncertainty, is enough to generate liberal principles. The distinction between the "rational" (forming and pursuing a conception of the good) and the "reasonable" (acting to honor fair terms of social cooperation) is intended to rule out the possibility that principles of justice can be selected "purely on the basis of a conception of rational choice as understood in economics or decision theory" ["The Basic Liberties and Their Priority," in Sterling M. McMurrin, ed., *The Tanner Lectures on Human Values*, vol. 3 (Salt Lake City: University of Utah Press, 1982), p. 21n.]. Judith Shklar has also forcefully argued against the egoism thesis: "Since the eighteenth century, . . . critics of liberalism have pictured it as a doctrine that achieves its public goods, peace, prosperity, and security, by encouraging private vice. Selfishness in all its possible forms is said to be its essence, purpose, and outcome. . . . Nothing could be more remote from the truth. The very refusal to use public coercion to impose creedal unanimity and uniform standards of behavior demands an enormous degree of self-control. Tolerance consistently applied is more difficult and morally more demanding than repression. . . . Far from being an amoral free-for-all, liberalism is, in fact, extremely difficult and constraining, far too much so for those who cannot endure contradiction, complexity, diversity, and the risks of freedom" [*Ordinary Vices*, pp. 4–5. Shklar's comments on Kantian liberal character, pp. 232–36, are also pertinent in this connection].

16. Fred Siegel, "Nothing in Moderation," *The Atlantic*, vol. 265 (May 1990), pp. 108–09.

17. In the U.S. context, this issue is further complicated by the question of federalism. One indisputable outcome of the Civil War was the victory of a conception of national citizenship and of a mechanism for its protection. The

question then becomes, What rights does national citizenship entail? The answer will draw the line between legitimate and illegitimate uses of state and local public power. National rights of voting, participation, and conscience are now regarded as settled and enforceable against local majorities. But issues such as abortion, pornography, and homosexuality remain embroiled in the struggle between proponents of uniform, judicially enforced national rights and proponents of local (hence variable) legislative authority.

18. For useful historical surveys, see: Stefan Collini, *Liberalism and Sociology: L. T. Hobhouse and Political Argument in England, 1880–1914* (Cambridge: Cambridge University Press, 1979); Michael Freeden, *The New Liberalism: An Ideology of Social Reform* (Oxford: Clarendon Press, 1978); and Gerald F. Gaus, *The Modern Liberal Theory of Man* (London & Canberra: Croom Helm, 1983), esp. chapter 7.

19. For philosophical arguments in favor of welfare rights, variously construed, see: C. J. G. Sampford and D. J. Galligan, eds., *Law, Rights and the Welfare State* (London: Croom Helm, 1986), especially chapters by Raymond Plant and Wojciech Sadurski); Carl Wellman, *Welfare Rights* (Totowa, N.J.: Rowman and Littlefield, 1982); D. D. Raphael, "Human Rights, Old and New," in Raphael, ed., *Political Theory and the Rights of Man* (London: Macmillan, 1967). Martin P. Golding argues for an even stronger proposition, that "if there are any rights at all, there are welfare rights . . . [and] that the notion of welfare rights has a theoretical primacy, conceptually and normatively, over option rights" ["The Primacy of Welfare Rights," *Social Philosophy and Policy*, vol. 1 (Spring 1984), p. 135]. For an effort to incorporate this concept into the U.S. Constitution, see Frank I. Michelman, "In Pursuit of Constitutional Welfare Rights: One View of Rawls's Theory of Justice," *University of Pennsylvania Law Review*, vol. 12 (1973) and "Constitutional Welfare Rights and *A Theory of Justice*," in Daniels, ed., *Reading Rawls*, pp. 319–47. For an extension into the international arena, see Henry Shue, *Basic Rights: Subsistence, Affluence, and U.S. Foreign Policy* (Princeton: Princeton University Press, 1980). Maurice Cranston offers a counterargument in "Human Rights, Real and Supposed," Raphael, pp. 43–53. Of course, Robert Nozick's *Anarchy, State, and Utopia* (New York: Basic Books, 1974) may be read as a sustained critique of the proposition that rights and welfare can be conjoined. Waldron offers a useful summary discussion in *Nonsense upon Stilts*, pp. 156–59.

20. Amartya Sen, "Individual Freedom as a Social Commitment," *The New York Review of Books*, vol. 37 (June 14, 1990), p. 50.

21. Norman Daniels has offered an even more far-reaching argument to the effect that the equal political and social liberties affirmed in Rawls's first principle of justice will not be truly choiceworthy unless their worth to all individuals is more or less equal, a requirement that would require a substantial reduction in the range of economic and welfare inequalities permitted by Rawls's Difference Principle. ["Equal Liberty and the Unequal Worth of Liberty," in Daniels, ed., *Reading Rawls* (New York: Basic Books, n.d.), pp. 253–281.] Another strategy would be to more effectively insulate the

political process from such inequalities, which might well require reversing Buckley v. Valeo and related decisions. See Rawls's discussion of this option in "The Basic Liberties and Their Priority," pp. 74–9.

22. For a moderate and balanced statement of this position, see Charles Taylor, "Cross-Purposes," in Nancy Rosenblum, ed., *Liberalism and the Moral Life* (Cambridge, Mass.: Harvard University Press, 1989), pp. 159–82. A more radical critique of rights-based community is offered by feminists who argue that the essentially abstract and adversarial language of rights distorts, or makes impossible, discussion of crucial issues of caring and degradation. Other feminists argue that the problem is not so much the language of rights as it is a political failure to define them appropriately and extend their protections to all members of the community. See Susan Moller Okin's "Humanist Liberalism," in Rosenblum, pp. 21–53, and her "Feminism, the Individual, and Contract Theory," *Ethics*, vol. 100 (April 1990), pp. 658–69. Two important recent collections bearing on this question are Deborah Rhode, ed., *Theoretical Perspectives on Difference* (New Haven: Yale University Press, 1989), and the "Symposium on Feminism and Political Theory," *Ethics*, vol. 99 (January 1989), pp. 219–406. See also the discussion in Waldron, *Nonsense upon Stilts*, pp. 159–60.

23. Jeremy Waldron, "When Justice Replaces Affection: The Need for Rights," *Harvard Journal of Law and Public Policy*, vol. 11 (1988), pp. 625–47.

24. See Roberto Unger, *False Necessity: Anti-necessitarian Social Theory in the Service of Radical Democracy* (Cambridge: Cambridge University Press, 1987). For discussions of this thesis from various points of view, see Robin W. Lovin and Michael J. Perry, eds., *Critique and Construction: A Symposium on Roberto Unger's Politics* (Cambridge: Cambridge University Press, 1990). Lovin's "Introduction," pp. 3–6, is a useful guide.

25. Mark Tushnet, "An Essay on Rights," *Texas Law Review*, vol. 62 (May 1984), pp. 1363–1403. Tushnet also offers an external substantive critique to the effect that rights-talk impedes advances by (what he terms) progressive social forces. His argument is in turn criticized by Michael J. Perry, "Taking Neither Rights-Talk Nor the 'Critique of Rights' Too Seriously," *Texas Law Review*, vol. 62 (May 1984), pp. 1405–16.

26. See especially Jeremy Bentham's *Anarchical Fallacies*, portions of which are reprinted in Waldron, *Nonsense upon Stilts*, pp. 46–76.

27. For a recent defense of Mill that manages to cite a substantial fraction of the writings on this subject, see John Gray, "John Stuart Mill on Liberty, Utility, and Rights," in J. Roland Pennock and John W. Chapman, eds., *Human Rights: Nomos XXIII* (New York and London: New York University Press, 1981), pp. 80–116. Gray's note 11 is an especially valuable compilation of sources.

28. An excellent collection of recent essays on this topic may be found in R. G. Frey, ed., *Utility and Rights* (Minneapolis: University of Minnesota Press, 1984). Other important contributions include Lawrence Haworth, "Utility and Rights," in Nicholas Rescher, ed., *Studies in Moral Philosophy* (Oxford: Basil Blackwell, 1968), pp. 64–85; David Lyons, "Human Rights

and the General Welfare," *Philosophy and Public Affairs*, vol. 6 (Winter 1977), pp. 113–28, and "Utility and Rights," in Jeremy Waldron, ed., *Theories of Rights* (Oxford: Oxford University Press, 1984), pp. 110–36; T. M. Scanlon, "Rights, Goals, and Fairness," also in Waldron, *Theories of Rights*, pp. 137–52; H. L. A. Hart, "Between Utility and Rights," in Alan Ryan, ed., *The Idea of Freedom: Essays in Honour of Isaiah Berlin* (Oxford: Oxford University Press, 1979), pp. 77–98. Waldron's *Nonsense upon Stilts*, p. 228, offers a list of additional readings on this topic.

29. Nozick, *Anarchy, State, and Utopia*, pp. 28–35; Ronald Dworkin, *Taking Rights Seriously* (Cambridge, Mass.: Harvard University Press, 1978), chapter 7, and *A Matter of Principle* (Cambridge, Mass.: Harvard University Press, 1985), chapter 17.

30. John Rawls, *A Theory of Justice* (Cambridge, Mass.: Harvard University Press, 1971); Ronald Dworkin, "The Original Position," in Norman Daniels, ed., *Reading Rawls*, pp. 16–53. Rawls takes issue with Dworkin's interpretation in "Justice as Fairness: Political not Metaphysical," pp. 236n–237n, but does not firmly reject it. Indeed, Rawls remarks, "Others may prefer his account."

31. For discussions of such tradeoffs, see Brian Barry, *Political Argument* (London: Routledge & Kegan Paul, 1965), pp. 3–8; James S. Fishkin, *Justice, Equal Opportunity, and the Family* (New Haven: Yale University Press, 1983), pp. 169–93; Charles E. Larmore, *Patterns of Moral Complexity* (Cambridge: Cambridge University Press, 1987), chapter 6.

32. G. A. Cohen, "Self-Ownership, World Ownership, and Equality," in Frank S. Lucash, ed., *Justice and Equality Here and Now* (Ithaca: Cornell University Press, 1986), pp. 109, 111.

33. Clinton Rossiter, ed., *The Federalist* (New York: New American Library, 1961), no. 84, p. 515.

34. See Arthur E. Wilmarth, Jr., "The Original Purpose of the Bill of Rights: James Madison and the Founders' Search for a Workable Balance between Federal and State Power," *American Criminal Law Review*, vol. 26 (1989), pp. 1290–91.

35. Madison's speech to the House of Representatives of June 8, 1789; quoted in Wilmarth, "The Original Purpose of the Bill of Rights," p. 1293.

36. Nozick, *Anarchy, State, and Utopia*, pp. 28–29.

37. Leo Strauss, *Natural Right and History* (Chicago: University of Chicago Press, 1953), p. 182.

38. Dworkin, "The Original Position," p. 40. I cannot here assess Kymlicka's intriguing assertion that Dworkin has in effect subsequently repudiated this system of classification. See *Liberalism, Community, and Culture*, p. 75.

39. For those inclined to take a deeper plunge into this topic, the place to begin is Rex Martin and James W. Nickel, "Recent Work on the Concept of Rights," *American Philosophical Quarterly*, vol. 17 (July 1980), pp. 165–67.

40. I do not mean to suggest that this coexistence is altogether untroubled. For some reasons why not, see my "Defending Liberalism," *American Political*

Science Review, vol. 76 (1982), pp. 621–29, and *Kant and the Problem of History* (Chicago: University of Chicago Press, 1975), pp. 195–202.

41. For the philosophical underpinnings of constitutional rights, see John Rawls, "The Basic Liberties and Their Priority," in Sterling M. McMurrin, ed., *The Tanner Lectures on Human Values: III* (Salt Lake City: University of Utah Press, 1982), pp. 1–87. Natural duty is discussed in *A Theory of Justice*, sections 19 and 51. The capacity for a sense of justice is stressed in "Kantian Constructivism in Moral Theory: The Dewey Lectures 1980," *Journal of Philosophy*, vol. 77, pp. 515–72.

42. Waldron, *Nonsense upon Stilts*, chapter 6. This is not to say, however, that there is a full-blown right to do wrong. Readers interested in this issue may consult Waldron, "A Right to Do Wrong," *Ethics*, vol. 92 (1981), pp. 21–39, and the ensuing exchange between Waldron and myself, "On the Alleged Right to Do Wrong: A Response to Waldron" and "Galston on Rights," both appearing in *Ethics*, vol. 93 (January 1983), pp. 320 ff.

43. Joseph Raz, "Right-based Moralities," in Waldron, ed., *Theories of Rights*, pp. 182–200.

44. Raz, "Right-based Moralities," p. 182. This immediately raises the question whether these basic moral categories form a harmonious system and, if not, how the conflicts among them are to be adjudicated. Raz provides some sense of direction in *The Morality of Freedom* (Oxford: Clarendon Press, 1986), especially chapters 11–15.

45. Shklar, *Ordinary Vices*, chapter 6; "The Liberalism of Fear," in Rosenblum, *Liberalism and the Moral Life*, chapter 1; "Injustice, Injury, and Inequality: An Introduction," in Lucash, *Justice and Equality Here and Now*, pp. 13–33; "Giving Injustice Its Due," *Yale Law Journal*, vol. 98 (1989), pp. 1135–51.

46. Waldron, *Nonsense upon Stilts*, p. 179; "When Justice Replaces Affection," pp. 625–47.

47. Dworkin, *Taking Rights Seriously*, pp. xi, 188.

48. For a clear discussion of will and interest theories, see James W. Nickel, *Making Sense of Human Rights* (Berkeley: University of California Press, 1987), pp. 19–23. Nickel links these categories to the Kantian and utilitarian traditions, respectively, not implausibly; but there are also non-Kantian will theories and non-utilitarian interest theories. See, for example, Joseph Raz's discussion of the links between rights and interests in *The Morality of Freedom*, chapter 7.

49. Joel Feinberg, "The Nature and Value of Rights," in David Lyons, ed., *Rights* (Belmont, Calif.: Wadsworth, 1979), pp. 84, 87.

50. Thomas E. Hill, Jr., "Servility and Self-Respect," in Lyons, *Rights*, pp. 111–24.

51. Dworkin, *Taking Rights Seriously*, chapter 12.

52. Joel Feinberg, *Social Philosophy* (Englewood Cliffs, N.J.: Prentice-Hall, 1973), pp. 96–97.

53. Stuart Hampshire, *Innocence and Experience* (Cambridge, Mass.: Harvard University Press, 1989), pp. 72–78, 107–09. While the form of adjudication enjoys universal validity, Hampshire suggests, its content will be

strongly influenced by the "practices, the moral principles, and the precedents that prevail in a particular culture or community" (p. 61).

54. These five headings summarize what I believe most Americans would intuitively take to be the incontrovertible heart of the matter. They are also congruent with and systematize Benjamin Constant's famous description of the "liberty of the moderns": "It is the right to be subjected only to the laws, and to be neither arrested, detained, put to death or maltreated in any way by the arbitrary will of one or more individuals. It is the right of everyone to express their opinion, choose a profession and practice it, to dispose of their property, and even to abuse it; to come and go without permission, and without having to account for their motives or undertakings. It is everyone's right to associate with other individuals, either to discuss their interests, or to profess the religion which they and their associates prefer, or even to occupy their days or hours in a way which is most compatible with their inclinations or whims. Finally it is everyone's right to exercise some influence on the administration of the government, either by electing all or particular officials, or through representations, petitions, demands to which the authorities are more or less compelled to pay heed." Biancamaria Fontana, *Political Writings* (Cambridge: Cambridge University Press, 1988), pp. 310–11. For the most nuanced discussion of Constant's contribution to liberal rights, see Stephen Holmes, *Benjamin Constant and the Making of Modern Liberalism* (New Haven: Yale University Press, 1984), especially chapters 1 and 2.

55. On all this, see Richard A. Wasserstrom, ed., *Morality and the Law* (Belmont, Calif.: Wadsworth, 1971); Ronald Dworkin, *A Matter of Principle* (Cambridge, Mass.: Harvard University Press, 1985), chapter 17 and *Taking Rights Seriously*, chapter 10; *California Law Review*, vol. 77 (May 1989), pp. 479–594; Stephen Macedo, *Liberal Virtues: Citizenship, Virtue, and Community in Liberal Constitutionalism* (Oxford: Clarendon Press, 1990), pp. 193–97.

56. Nozick, *Anarchy, State, and Utopia*, pp. 150–82; Loren Lomasky, *Persons, Rights, and the Moral Community* (Oxford: Oxford University Press, 1987), chapter 6; Nickel, *Making Sense of Human Rights*, pp. 100, 151–56; Rolf Sartorius, "Persons and Property," in R. G. Frey, ed., *Utility and Rights* (Minneapolis: University of Minnesota Press, 1984), pp. 196–214; Alan Ryan, "Utility and Ownership," in Frey, pp. 175–195.

57. Nickel, *Making Sense of Human Rights*, pp. 152–56.

58. See Richard Epstein, *Takings: Private Property and the Power of Eminent Domain* (Cambridge, Mass.: Harvard University Press, 1985).

59. See notes 18 and 19.

60. The literature on these topics is now vast, and I cannot even begin to cover it. Useful points of departure are Lomasky, *Persons, Rights, and the Moral Community*, chapters 7 and 8; Kent Greenawalt, *Religious Convictions and Political Choice* (New York: Oxford University Press, 1988), chapters 6 and 7; Joel Feinberg, *Rights, Justice, and the Bounds of Liberty* (Princeton: Princeton University Press, 1980), pp. 159–206; Flathman, *Toward a Liberalism*, chapter 6; Kurt Baier, "When Does the Right to Life Begin?" in Pennock and Chapman, *Human Rights*, pp. 201–29.

61. Wills, *Inventing America*, chapters 21–23. For a sophisticated discussion of this issue, see Nathan Tarcov, "American Constitutionalism and Individual Rights," in Robert Goldwin and William Schambra, eds., *How Does the Constitution Secure Rights?* (Washington, D.C.: AEI Press, 1985), pp. 105–08.

62. Once again, the literature in this area is vast and burgeoning. For a start, see Marshall Cohen, Thomas Nagel, and Thomas Scanlon, eds., *Equality and Preferential Treatment* (Princeton: Princeton University Press, 1977), especially Owen Fiss's "Groups and the Equal Protection Clause"; Paul et al., *Equal Opportunity*; Nathan Glazer, "Individual Rights against Group Rights," in Eugene Kamenka and Alice Erh-Soon Tay, eds., *Human Rights* (London: Edward Arnold, 1978), pp. 87–103; Will Kymlicka, *Liberalism, Community, and Culture* (Oxford: Clarendon Press, 1989), chapters 7–10; and Robert K. Fullinwider, *The Reverse Discrimination Controversy: A Moral and Legal Analysis* (Totowa, N.J.: Rowman & Allanheld, 1980), chapter 5.

CHAPTER 4: IS THERE A RIGHT TO DIE?

1. There is another still more powerful reason for resisting this temptation. Is it not unreasonably paternalistic of me to try to order the world so as to free my children from the usual intergenerational experiences, ties, obligations, and burdens? What principle of family life am I enacting and endorsing with my "altruistic suicide"?

2. Here is a recent example, from a professor of sociology, who objected to my condemnation of Derek Humphry's *Final Exit*:

> Is Mr. Kass absolutely opposed to suicide? Would he have dissuaded Hitler? Would he disapprove of suicide by Pol Pot? . . . If we would welcome suicide by certain figures on limited occasions, should we prolong the lives of people who lived useless, degrading or dehumanized lives; who inflicted these indignities upon others; or who led vital lives but were being reduced to uselessness and degradation by incurable disease? [*Commentary*, May 1992, p. 12]

3. Harvey C. Mansfield, Jr., "The Old Rights and the New: Responsibility vs. Self-Expression," chapter 5 of this volume.

4. Hans Jonas, "The Right to Die," *Hastings Center Report*, August 1978, pp. 31–36, at p. 31.

5. John Locke, *Second Treatise on Civil Government*, chapter II, "Of the State of Nature," paragraph 6.

6. Ibid., chapter 5, "Of Property," paragraph 27. Emphasis added.

7. Later, in discussing the extent of legislative power, Locke denies to the legislative, though it be the supreme power in every commonwealth, arbitrary power over the individual and, in particular, power to destroy his life. "For nobody can transfer to another more power than he has in himself; and nobody has an absolute arbitrary power over himself, or over any other to destroy his own life, or take away the life or property of another." *Second Treatise*, chapter XI, "Of the Extent of the Legislative Power," paragraph 135.

Because the state's power derives from the people's, the person's lack of arbitrary power over himself is the ground for restricting the state's power to kill him.

8. See, for example, note 9 of the *Discourse on the Origin and Foundations of Inequality among Men*, especially paragraphs 4 and 5.

9. Immanuel Kant, *The Metaphysical Principles of Virtue*, trans. by James Ellington (Indianapolis: Bobbs-Merrill, 1964), pp. 83–84. My purpose in citing Kant here is not to defend Kantian morality—and I am not myself a Kantian—but simply to show that the thinker who thought most deeply about rights in relation to *reason* and *autonomy* would have found the idea of a "right to die" utterly indefensible on these grounds.

10. The attempt to ground a right to die in the so-called right to privacy fails for the same reasons. A right to make independent judgments regarding one's body in one's private sphere, free of governmental inference, cannot be the basis of the right of someone else, appointed by or protected by government, to put an end to one's bodily life.

11. Mansfield, chapter 5. This permanent instability of "the self" defeats the main benefit of a rights-based politics, which knows how to respect individual rights precisely because they are understood to be rooted in a common human nature, with reliable common interests, both natural and rational. The self-determining self, because it is variable, also turns out to be an embarrassment for attempts to respect prior acts of self-determination, as in the case of living wills. For if the self is truly constantly being re-created, there is no reason to honor today "its" prescriptions of yesterday: for the two selves are not the same.

12. 110 S. Ct. 2841 (1990).

13. Ibid., p. 2852.

14. Ibid., p. 2856.

15. Justice William Brennan, in his dissenting opinion, denies that the state has even a legitimate interest in—much less a duty toward—someone's life that could ever outweigh the person's choice to avoid medical treatment. And in the presence of a patient who can no longer choose for herself, the state has an interest *only* in trying to determine as accurately as possible "how she would exercise her rights under these circumstances. . . . *Until* Nancy's wishes have been determined, the only [!] state interest that may be asserted is an interest in safeguarding the accuracy of that determination"—by the way, a seemingly impossible task, given the view of the self that is implicit in Justice Brennan's reasoning. Not the security of life but the self-assertion of the self-determining *will* is, for Justice Brennan, the primary interest of the state. We see here how Nietzschean thinking threatens to replace classical American liberalism, even in constitutional interpretation.

16. 110 S. Ct. 2841 (1990), p. 2863.

17. Ibid., p. 2859.

18. A notable exception is Yale Kamisar, professor of law at the University of Michigan Law School, in my view our finest legal commentator on this subject. See his "When Is There a Constitutional 'Right to Die'? When Is

There *No* Constitutional 'Right to Live'?" *Georgia Law Review*, vol. 25, 1991, p. 1203.

CHAPTER 5: RESPONSIBILITY VERSUS SELF-EXPRESSION

1. A good part of it can be found in Allan Bloom's *The Closing of the American Mind*.

CHAPTER 6: NEW WHITE RIGHTS

1. People for the transcription of Jesse Helms's television commercial American Way.

2. The analysis that follows is equally applicable to affirmative action for women. Indeed, several of the cases discussed below involved just such programs. For simplicity, however, the analysis in this chapter refers primarily to race-based programs, since they are most frequently the focus of public and legal debate.

3. In Hughes v. Superior Court, 339 U.S. 460 (1950), a local community group picketed a Lucky grocery store, insisting that blacks be hired to fill any vacancies at the store until 50 percent of the employees were black. The California state courts enjoined the picketing on the ground that it sought to achieve an "unlawful purpose." The state Supreme Court characterized the pickets as seeking

> an arbitrary discrimination upon the basis of race and color alone, rather than a choice based solely upon individual qualification for the work to be done. . . . They would, to the extent of the fixed proportion, make the right to work for Lucky dependent not on fitness for the work nor on an equal right of all, regardless of race, to compete in an open market, but, rather, on membership in a particular racial group.

339 U.S. at 463–64. The United States Supreme Court upheld the injunction in 1950, rejecting objections that it violated the First Amendment.

4. 110 Cong. Rec. 8500 (1964); see also ibid. at 9034 (Senator Tower) (bill will induce employer to hire on the basis of "the various ratios in each group in the community, rather than on the basis of experience and ability").

5. H.R. Rep. 914, 89th Cong., 1st sess. 71–73 (1963). See also ibid.:

> Assume two women of separate races apply to [a] firm for the position of stenographer; further assume that the employer . . . prefers one above the other . . . because of personality, superior alertness, intelligence, work history, or general neatness. . . . If his firm is not "racially balanced," . . . he has no choice, he must employ the person of that race which, by ratio, is next up, even though he is certain in his own mind that the woman he is not allowed to employ would be a superior employee.

6. Alexander Bickel, *The Morality of Consent* (1975), pp. 133–34.

7. Alan Bakke, for example, asserted that the special admissions program to which he objected "resulted in the admission of minority applicants less qualified than plaintiff and other nonminority applicants who were therefore rejected." Complaint, pp. 2–3, Bakke v. Regents of the University of California, No. 31287 (Superior Ct. Yolo County). White firefighters who objected to a 1981 consent decree regarding promotions in the Cleveland Fire Department insisted

> Promotions based upon any criterion other than competence, such as a racial quota system, would deny those most capable from [sic] their promotions and would deny the residents of the City of Cleveland from maintaining the best possible fire fighting force.

Firefighters v. Cleveland, 478 U.S. 501, 507 (1986).

8. In University of California Regents v. Bakke, one opinion observed that

> racial . . . classifications . . . are contrary to our deep belief that "legal burdens should bear some relationship to individual responsibility . . ." and that advancement sanctioned, sponsored, or approved by the State should ideally be based on individual merit or achievement . . . .

438 U.S. 265, 360–61 (1978) (opinion of Justices Brennan, White, Marshall, and Blackmun). In Fullilove v. Klutznick, Justice Marshall acknowledged that

> governmental classification on the immutable characteristic of race runs counter to the deep national belief that state-sanctioned benefits and burdens should bear some relationship to individual merit and responsibility.

448 U.S. 448, 519 (1980) (Marshall, J., concurring). See also United Jewish Organizations of Williamsburg v. Carey, 430 U.S. 144, 173 (1977) (Brennan, J., concurring).

9. 416 U.S. 312 (1974).
10. 416 U.S. at 339.
11. 416 U.S. at 337.
12. 416 U.S. at 344.
13. 416 U.S. at 337.
14. 416 U.S. at 334.
15. 416 U.S. at 331.
16. 416 U.S. at 331.
17. 416 U.S. at 341.
18. 416 U.S. at 331.
19. 438 U.S. 265 (1978).
20. 438 U.S. 306 n. 43 (emphasis added).
21. 438 U.S. at 311 and n. 46.
22. 452 U.S. 105 (1981).
23. 452 U.S. at 109.

24. 452 U.S. at 111 n. 11.

25. 452 U.S. at 114.

26. 452 U.S. at 127.

27. 452 U.S. at 128–29.

28. 476 U.S. 267 (1986).

29. 476 U.S. at 298 (Marshall, J., dissenting).

30. 476 U.S. at 270–73.

31. 476 U.S. at 315. The difference between Justice Stevens's opinions in Bakke and Wygant arises in part because his analysis in Bakke was an interpretation of Title VI, while in Wygant his discussion concerns the constitutional limits on affirmative action.

32. 476 U.S. at 276. Several years earlier, in Mississippi University for Women v. Hogan, 458 U.S. 718 (1982), Justice Powell had argued that the need for faculty "role models" justified excluding male students from a traditionally single-sex school. 458 U.S. at 735.

33. 476 U.S. at 315.

34. 476 U.S. at 295–96.

35. Justice O'Connor's position in this regard is not necessarily the same as that of the plurality. Although agreeing that the role model justification was inadequate as a matter of law, she distinguished that proffered justification from "the very different goal of promoting racial diversity among the faculty." 476 U.S. at 288 note "*".

36. 458 U.S. at 718 (1982).

37. 458 U.S. at 739 n. 5.

38. 458 U.S. at 731.

39. 111 L. Ed. 2d 445, 493–504 (1990).

40. 111 L. Ed. 2d at 506.

41. Fullilove v. Klutznick, 448 U.S. 448, 525 (dissenting opinion).

42. Wygant v. Jackson Board of Education, 476 U.S. at 313–14 (footnotes omitted).

43. 111 L. Ed. 2d at 466.

44. See Richmond v. Croson Co., 488 U.S. 469, 521 (1989) (Scalia, J., concurring).

45. 401 U.S. 424 (1971).

46. 401 U.S. at 426.

47. Eric Schnapper, "The Varieties of Numerical Remedies," *Stanford Law Review*, vol. 39 (1987), pp. 851, 889–93.

48. This would be equally true under Griggs if there were merit differences among the members of the pool, but the employer had not yet developed a reliable method for identifying which applicants were in fact better qualified.

49. Consent decrees obtained by the department that contained such provisions are summarized in the brief amicus of the NAACP Legal Defense and Educational Fund, Inc., in Firefighters v. Cleveland, No. 84–1999, pp. 24–38.

50. 480 U.S. 149, 161–62, 179–80 (1987).

51. 430 U.S. 144 (1977).

52. 430 U.S. at 165–66.

53. 438 U.S. at 321–23.

54. 438 U.S. at 319.

55. 438 U.S. at 367; see also ibid. (plan would be justifiable if there were a statute that "mandated that universities refrain from applying any admissions policy that had a disparate and unjustified racial impact)."

56. 438 U.S. at 403.

57. Justice Marshall referred in his dissenting opinion to the fact that it would have been entirely constitutional for the school board, in order to maintain the proportion of minority teachers, to base layoffs on a lottery. 476 U.S. at 310.

58. *Washington Monthly* (March 1991), p. 6.

59. In separate opinions Justices Powell and O'Connor insisted that Wygant was in fact subject to the same standard and method of analysis as Fullilove, even though in Fullilove v. Klutznick, 448 U.S. 448 (1980), the adversely affected white subcontractors at times would be better qualified, that is, less expensive, than the preferred minority-owned firm.

60. 476 U.S. at 309.

61. 443 U.S. 193 (1979).

62. The differing outcomes of Wygant and Weber arise in part because Weber did not involve a layoff and was decided under Title VII rather than the Fourteenth Amendment.

63. 480 U.S. 618 (1987).

64. 480 U.S. at 623–25; 480 U.S. at 663 (Scalia, J., dissenting).

65. 480 U.S. at 648.

66. 480 U.S. at 655–56.

67. 480 U.S. at 641 n. 17.

68. 480 U.S. at 662–63; see also ibid. at 674 (Joyce "the less qualified candidate").

69. 480 U.S. at 674–75 (emphasis in original).

70. 480 U.S. at 641 n. 17.

71. 480 U.S. at 675 n. 5.

72. Ibid.

73. 430 U.S. 144 (1977).

74. 430 U.S. at 176 (concurring opinion).

75. 430 U.S. at 154 n. 14 (plurality opinion).

76. 430 U.S. at 186 (dissenting opinion).

77. 424 U.S. 747 (1976).

78. 424 U.S. at 778.

79. 424 U.S. at 780–81 (emphasis added).

80. 476 U.S. 267 (1986). The plurality opinion of Justice Powell did not decide whether such discrimination had in fact occurred. 476 U.S. at 277–78.

81. 476 U.S. at 283 (emphasis added) (footnote omitted). The plurality opinion, unlike Burger's view in Franks, approved competitive seniority relief for "actual, identified victims." 475 U.S. at 284 n. 12.

82. 476 U.S. at 287 (emphasis added).
83. 480 U.S. at 183.
84. 480 U.S. at 201.
85. 480 U.S. 616 (1987).
86. 480 U.S. at 637.
87. 480 U.S. at 638.
88. 480 U.S. at 649–50.
89. 448 U.S. 469 (1989); 488 U.S. at 549.
90. 111 L. Ed. 2d 445 (1990). See Metro Broadcasting v. FCC, 111 L.Ed. 2d at 804 (O'Connor, J., dissenting); 809 (Rehnquist, J., dissenting); Richmond v. Croson Co., 102 L.Ed. 2d at 896 (Stevens, J., dissenting).
91. 424 U.S. at 778.
92. 448 U.S. at 484.
93. 438 U.S. at 365.
94. 467 U.S. 561 (1984); 467 U.S. at 587.
95. 480 U.S. at 183 n. 33.
96. 480 U.S. at 638.
97. 488 U.S. at 549.
98. 111 L.Ed. 2d at 483.
99. 431 U.S. 324 (1977).
100. 443 U.S. at 224 (dissenting opinion).
101. 443 U.S. at 215.
102. 476 U.S. at 283.
103. 476 U.S. at 282 n. 10.
104. 443 U.S. at 208.
105. 476 U.S. at 283.
106. Fullilove v. Klutznick, 448 U.S. at 495 (Powell, J., concurring); University of California Regents v. Bakke, 438 U.S. at 310 (opinion of Powell, J.).
107. United States v. Paradise, 480 U.S. at 170 (majority opinion), 193 n. 2 (Stevens, J., concurring); Firefighters v. Cleveland, 478 U.S. 501, 512 (1986); Richmond v. Croson Co., 102 L.Ed. 2d at 910 (Brennan, J., dissenting); Fullilove v. Klutznick, 448 U.S. at 485 (plurality opinion); Richmond v. Croson Co., 102 L.Ed. 2d at 854 (Blackmun, J., dissenting).
108. See Johnson v. Santa Clara Transportation Agency, 480 U.S. at 676 (dissenting opinion) (likelihood adversely affected whites will "have profited from societal discrimination in the past"); Richmond v. Croson Co., 102 L.Ed. 2d at 902 (concurring opinion) (state may dismiss wrongfully hired white worker in order to hire black applicant improperly denied job at issue).
109. 102 L.Ed. 2d at 901.
110. 438 U.S. at 306.
111. 438 U.S. at 306 n. 43.
112. 438 U.S. at 307–08.
113. 438 U.S. at 296 n. 36.
114. 448 U.S. at 504 (emphasis added).
115. 448 U.S. at 505.
116. 448 U.S. at 505. The plurality opinion relied on this same passage. 448 U.S. at 466 n. 48.

117. 476 U.S. at 274.
118. 476 U.S. at 274–76.
119. 476 U.S. at 289 (emphasis added).
120. 488 U.S. 469 (1989).
121. 488 U.S. at 491–92. Justice Scalia would have adopted the more restrictive standard of the Fourth Circuit. 102 L.Ed. 2d at 901.
122. 488 U.S. at 498.
123. 488 U.S. at 490.
124. 488 U.S. at 499.
125. 488 U.S. at 524.
126. 448 U.S. at 532, n. 15, quoting Olmstead v. United States, 277 U.S. 438, 485 (1928) (Brandeis, J., dissenting).

CHAPTER 7: "KANTIANISM" AND CONSTITUTIONAL RIGHTS

1. There has recently arisen, against the dominant "Kantian" strain in contemporary constitutional scholarship that we here address, a number of alternative or competing approaches. The casual peruser of the most recent constitutional scholarship cannot help but be struck by the sheer variety of such efforts to flesh out or otherwise support constitutional doctrine in one or another extraconstitutional teaching—be it "romanticism," a "reconstructed" or "anti-Augustinian" Locke, the Stoic natural law tradition, the Augustinian critique of the Stoic natural law tradition, "neo-Aristotelianism," or Rortyian "pragmatism." See, for example, Steven H. Shiffrin, *The First Amendment, Democracy, and Romance* (Cambridge, Mass.: Harvard University Press, 1990); Rogers M. Smith, *Liberalism and American Constitutional Law* (Cambridge, Mass.: Harvard University Press, 1988); David A. J. Richards, *Foundations of American Constitutionalism* (New York: Oxford University Press, 1989); Lloyd L. Weinreb, *Natural Law and Justice* (Cambridge, Mass.: Harvard University Press, 1987); Graham Walker, *Moral Foundations of Constitutional Thought: Current Problems, Augustinian Prospects* (Princeton: Princeton University Press, 1990); Michael J. Perry, *Morality, Politics, and the Law* (New York: Oxford University Press, 1988); and Sanford Levinson, *Constitutional Faith* (Princeton: Princeton University Press, 1988). For more sober and far-reaching assessments of the relation between American constitutional doctrine and earlier liberal thought, see, for example, Thomas L. Pangle, *The Spirit of Modern Republicanism: The Moral Vision of the American Founders and the Philosophy of Locke* (Chicago: University of Chicago Press, 1988); and Robert K. Faulkner, *The Jurisprudence of John Marshall* (Princeton: Princeton University Press, 1968). For a "Kantian" interpretation of constitutional issues very different from the one addressed below, see Hadley Arkes, *Beyond the Constitution* (Princeton: Princeton University Press, 1990). Arkes's otherwise relatively traditional natural law approach is leavened by a Kantian understanding of rational personality as rooted in the (equal) capacity to have a concept of law. See *First Things* (Princeton: Princeton University Press, 1986), p. 8.

2. For the relevant history, see William M. Wiecek, *Liberty under Law: The*

Supreme Court in American Life (Baltimore: The Johns Hopkins University Press, 1988). See also Walker, *Moral Foundations,* pp. 9ff, and Smith, *Liberalism and American Constitutional Law,* p. 65.

3. Lochner v. New York, 1905, struck down, in the name of "liberty of contract," a New York state law limiting the working hours of bakers.

4. Wechsler's notion of "neutral principles," along with Hart's emphasis of "universalizability" and Meiklejohn's understanding of constitutionally protected speech as essentially "public," in some ways anticipates the later turn to Kant for a principled (but epistemologically and morally minimalist) counter to prevailing conventionalist orthodoxies.

5. John Rawls, *A Theory of Justice,* (Cambridge, Mass.: Harvard University Press, 1978).

6. See Ronald Dworkin, *Taking Rights Seriously* (Cambridge, Mass.: Harvard University Press, 1977); *A Matter of Principle* (Cambridge, Mass.: Harvard University Press, 1985); *Law's Empire* (Cambridge, Mass.: Harvard University Press, 1986). Dworkin's more recent work has shifted emphasis away from rights, decreasing some of his affinity with Rawls. Nevertheless, his thought remains in an important sense within the Kantian orbit, as I argue below.

7. The literature on Rawls is voluminous, to say the least. For a recent and trenchant survey and critique of Rawls's thought, see Clifford Orwin and James R. Stoner, Jr., "Neo-Constitutionalism? Rawls, Dworkin, Nozick," in Allan Bloom, *Confronting the Constitution* (Washington, D.C.: American Enterprise Institute Press, 1990). For an amusing discussion of Rawls's treatment of natural talents as a "common asset," see Michael Sandel, *Liberalism and the Limits of Justice,* (Cambridge: Cambridge University Press, 1982). Rawls's insistence on the priority of "equality of fair opportunity" over the "difference principle" (which states that inequalities must benefit the least well off) is only apparently at odds with his treatment of talents as a "common asset." For equality of opportunity is justified not, as in more traditional liberal theory (including that of Kant), as flowing from the right of individuals to the fruits of their labor and talents. Rather it is justified by the fact that it improves the range of desirable choices for the least well off. See Rawls, *A Theory of Justice,* pp. 300ff.

8. Although Rawls's usage in *A Theory of Justice* inexplicably varies, he generally speaks of favoring the "least" rather than the "less" well off.

9. See Sandel, *Liberalism and the Limits of Justice.*

10. According to Rawls, distributive justice has to do not with "desert," but with the "legitimate expectations" to which following the rules originally laid down is said to give rise. The "premiums earned by scarce natural talents," for example, are justified wholly in terms of the contribution of such premiums to the "common interest." "The distributive shares that result do not correlate with moral worth, since the initial endowment of natural assets and the contingencies of their growth and nurture . . . are arbitrary from a moral point of view." (Rawls, *A Theory of Justice,* pp. 311–12; see also p. 103.) The only sort of "moral desert" that Rawls seriously entertains is one attaching to a person on the basis of a quality or an act of which he is the sole cause. It is clear, however (for example, from his treatment of "effort"), that for Rawls none of us is the cause, in the strong sense required, of any of our own qualities or acts. It would seem to follow

that no one is or can be truly, that is, morally, deserving of anything. Rawls later argues that people are "owed" justice inasmuch as they are "moral beings," that is, "capable of having . . . a conception of the good," and "capable of having . . . a sense of justice" (p. 505). Since such capacities are no more our own doing than our ability to make an effort, it remains unclear how they can perform the function Rawls thrusts upon them. For an extended critique from a somewhat different point of view of Rawls's treatment of desert, see George Sher, *Desert* (Princeton: Princeton University Press, 1987). As Onora O'Neill has observed, Rawls's subsequent Dewey Lectures attempt to provide a more substantial Kantian ideal of the moral person, an ideal whose "heteronomy" still falls far short of Kant. See *Constructions of Reason: Explorations of Kant's Practical Philosophy* (Cambridge: Cambridge University Press, 1989), p. 210. For a related discussion of the difference between Kant and Rawls, see William A. Galston, *Justice and the Human Good* (Chicago: University of Chicago Press, 1980), pp. 170ff.

The original position is thus a "purely hypothetical position characterized so as to lead to a certain conception of justice." This formulation suggests that Rawls already has a just outcome in mind, and deliberately constructs the original position so as to ensure that just outcome. At the same time, that outcome is itself justified on the grounds that it follows from an initial position "that is fair [unlike ordinary life?] between individuals as moral persons." It thus presupposes or trades on an implicit notion of desert: that is, a prior notion of what fairness between moral persons consists in (pp. 12–13).

11. As a number of critiques have pointed out, it is not clear on the basis of Rawls's argument why our bodies should not also be regarded as "common assets," as is for all practical purposes the case in Hobbes's state of nature.

12. See, for example, Rawls's designation of "self-respect and a sure confidence in the sense of one's own worth" as "perhaps the most important primary good." Ibid., p. 396. Rawls's later works make increasingly clear his conviction as to the social basis of rights. See, for example, his "Kantian Constructivism in Moral Theory," *Journal of Philosophy*, vol. 77 (1980), pp. 515–72; and "Justice as Fairness: Political, Not Metaphysical," *Philosophy and Public Affairs*, vol. 14 (1985), pp. 223–51.

13. For a different application of Rawls's theory of justice to constitutional questions, see Frank Michelman, "In Pursuit of Constitutional Welfare Rights: One View of Rawls's *Theory of Justice*," *University of Pennsylvania Law Review*, vol. 121 (1973), pp. 990–01.

14. See Dworkin, *Taking Rights Seriously*, pp. 190ff.

15. Ibid., pp. 205–06.

16. Dworkin, *Law's Empire*, pp. 177–275. Compare Dworkin's claim that "a community that accepts integrity has a vehicle for organic change, even if it is not always effective, that it would not otherwise have at all"; Dworkin, *Taking Rights Seriously*, p. 189.

17. Walker, *Moral Foundations*, pp. 42–46.

18. Dworkin, *Law's Empire*, p. 189.

19. Ibid., p. 222.

20. Ibid., pp. 95–96.

21. Compare Dworkin's references to Habermas and Gadamer: ibid., pp. 62, 420n., 422n.

22. The substitution of "concern" (for the earlier "respect and concern") in the most recent version of Dworkin's egalitarian formula points revealingly to his increased commitment to communitarian values at the expense of individual rights as classically conceived. "Taking rights seriously" has been all but reduced to the practice of refraining from making unprincipled exceptions. (The implications of this "historicized" neo-Kantianism are considered briefly below.)

23. This description of his earlier book appears in Richards, *Foundations*, which aims to apply that methodology more generally (p. vi). In *Toleration and the Constitution*, Richards makes a more explicit appeal to Kant. See, for example, pp. 133ff., where the author buttresses his theoretical construction and historical retrieval of Locke with an account of Kantian "practical reason" as "self-direction," a gloss that assimilates Kantian moral autonomy and something resembling Rawlsian "life-planning." Compare Richards, p. 134, and Kant, *Critique of Practical Reason*, tr. Lewis Lehite Beck (Indianapolis: Bobbs-Merrill, 1956), p. 31.

24. Richards, *Foundations*, pp. 285–86.

25. For alternative accounts of the foundations of Lockean rights of "self-possession" or man's natural freedom, see Pangle, *Spirit of Modern Republicanism*, pp. 268ff.; and Ruth Grant, *John Locke's Liberalism* (Chicago: University of Chicago Press, 1987), pp. 27ff. See also Nathan Tarcov, *Locke's Education for Liberty* (Chicago: University of Chicago Press, 1984). Compare Richards's own suggestion (in tension with his conclusion) that Lockean right is rooted in a substantive account of individual self-determination. See Richards, *Foundations*, pp. 85ff.

26. See, for example, the work of Perry, who contrasts attention to the aspirations "symbolized" by the Constitution with what he calls "originalism"; Perry, *Morality, Politics, and the Law*, pp. 133ff. According to Perry, among the multiple (legitimate) means of the Constitution (only one of which is "originalist") is that arising from its status "as a symbol of fundamental aspirations of the political tradition." The precise contours of that tradition, which Perry *opposes* to original meaning, is left deliberately vague, though the content of its aspiration is said to be both "transformative" (pp. 153ff.) and "prophetic" in the sense of "disturbing" (p. 137) the life of the community. For a different version of the appeal to fundamental constitutional aspirations in light of a fundamental community of moral and intellectual discourse, see Sotirios A. Barber, *On What the Constitution Means* (Baltimore: The Johns Hopkins University Press, 1984); according to Barber, "The Constitution makes sense only in light of an ideal state of affairs to which those who fully understand and accept the Constitution's claim to supremacy aspire" (p. 169). This "ideal society" seems to be one in which "we enjoy just those amounts and kinds of other good things (security, comfort, etc.) as are compatible with honoring constitutional rights, a practice that manifests our devotion to thinking and therefore our concern for all who are capable of

thinking." Barber would substitute the "dignified self-restraint" that flows from the original idea of a people "who have the moral and intellectual strength to give and exchange reasons" for the "willfulness" that accompanies current litigation concerning constitutional rights (p. 179). Barber's formulation is notable for its treatment of individual dignity as bound up with community without becoming a mere product of communal approval— that is, as a *ground* of right rather than an *object* of willful assertion.

On John Hart Ely's critique of the aspirational approach on the grounds that it cannot adequately determine judicial outcomes, see Barber, pp. 19ff., and Ely, "Constitutional Interpretivism: Its Allure and Impossibility," *Indiana Law Journal*, vol. 53 (1978), pp. 399ff. On Alexander Bickel's differing critique (along legal realist lines) see Robert Faulkner, "Bickel's Constitution," *American Political Science Review*, vol. 72 (September 1978), pp. 925ff.

27. See Justice William J. Brennan, Jr., speech presented "To the Text and Teaching Symposium, Georgetown University, October 12, 1985, Washington, D.C.," Occasional paper no. 2 (Washington, D.C.: The Federalist Society, 1986), p. 11.

28. Ibid., p. 16.

29. Ibid., p. 17.

30. Brennan quotes from Justice Robert Jackson, *Board of Education v. Barnette* (1943).

31. Ibid., p. 23.

32. Ibid., p. 25.

33. Long before Marcuse, Kant assumed that one can be free only "with the others."

34. Kant's only controversial "metaphysical" assumption is that moral freedom is in fact possible: that is, that we can reasonably be held accountable as causes of our own acts. Lacking this freedom, Rawlsian individuals also lack the basis of moral personality in a more truly Kantian sense.

35. The new judicial philosophies tend to treat "self-respect" (or the bases thereof) as something one receives from others, and to which one may claim a right. There is some foundation for this in Kant, for whom all rights reduce fundamentally to a right to respect: that is, a right to be treated not only as a means but also as an end in oneself. That very distinction, however, rests in turn on the self-sufficiency of our moral personality. We do not *need* respect for the sake of our dignity. We deserve respect on account of it. As a result Kant retains, and in some ways exaggerates, that emphasis on self-reliance intrinsic to liberalism in both its original Lockean and more recent American formulations.

36. One virtue of Kant's moral grounding of human dignity lies in its peculiar facility in reconciling equality of right with inequality of merit. Many critics of liberalism worry that material inequality in particular will cause the less well off to question their intrinsic worth as human beings. Kant's account radically detaches nonmoral achievement (that is, getting rich) from intrinsic moral worth, even as it separates intrinsic moral worth from the moral merit of our actions. Insofar as we are all capable of responding to the moral law,

of which we—or our better selves—are author, each of us has worth infinitely beyond anything in nature. But insofar as we remain unequal to that law (either directly, that is, by violating another's rights, or indirectly, that is, by failing to develop our talents), we may be said to deserve greater or lesser amounts of moral (dis)credit. Kant's grounding of moral personality in the capacity to be held morally accountable for one's actions depends less upon a recondite "metaphysical idealism" than upon a practical logic that we take seriously (however paradoxical it may ultimately be) in our daily lives. This fact substantially weakens Rawls's defense, in the name of avoiding that metaphysics, of a demoralized understanding of Kantian justice.

For a different critique of Rawlsian equality of worth on the basis of its "shallow and unsupported view of human dignity," see Smith, *Liberalism and American Constitutional Law*, pp. 170, 185ff. Smith correctly points to dangers flowing from Rawls's consequent inability to reconcile equality of respect with inequality of achievement, but he concludes by seeking all the more vigorously to provide equality of respect by external means. For an alternative resolution, in terms of a more traditional conception of moral "character," of the tension between equality of fundamental right and inequality along other dimensions, see Robert Faulkner, "Bickel's Constitution," p. 933.

37. Kant, *Critique of Pure Reason*, A, p. 316, B, pp. 372–73.

38. Immanuel Kant, *Metaphysical Elements of Justice* [Part One of the *Metaphysics of Morals*], tr. John Ladd (Indianapolis: Bobbs-Merrill, 1963); see also "On the Common Saying, 'This May Be True in Theory, but It Does Not Apply in Practice,' " in *Kant's Political Writings*, ed. Hans Reiss (Cambridge: Cambridge University Press, 1971), pp. 73ff., and Kant, "An Answer to the Question: "What Is Enlightenment?" pp. 54ff.

39. Kant, *Theory and Practice*, p. 75.

40. Compare Lincoln's hope that American workers would not remain paid laborers all their lives, a condition of dependency that he evidently considered to be at odds with the requirements of American citizenship in the fullest sense. Lincoln, of course, would not (like Kant) make exercise of the franchise conditional on self-employment. See, for example, his "Speech at Kalamazoo, Michigan," August 27, 1856; and his "Speech to the Wisconsin Agricultural Fair," September 30, 1859. Needless to say, Kant's animadversions against active female citizenship found a stronger echo in the historical American understanding of equal liberty.

41. See, for example, Kant, *What Is Enlightenment?*, pp. 59ff.

42. To be sure, this ideal remains in an important sense "indeterminate," that is, dependent in its particulars on personal choice. The duty of benevolence, for example, can be adhered to in a variety of ways, among which the individual is privileged to select.

43. See, for example, Kant, *Theory and Practice*, p. 80: "No generally valid principle of legislation can be based on happiness. For both the current circumstances and the highly conflicting and variable illusions as to what happiness is (and no one can prescribe to others how they should attain it) make all fixed principles impossible, so that happiness *alone* can never be a

suitable principle of legislation" (emphasis added). Thus if the supreme power makes laws primarily directed toward happiness (that is, the affluence of its citizens, or increased population), "it cannot be regarded as the *end* for which a civil constitution was established, but only as a means of *securing the rightful state,* especially against external enemies of the people." Kant's stipulation that a person "remain free to pursue happiness in whatever way he thinks best," so long as he does not violate "the lawful freedom and rights" of others, must be understood in the light of his general hostility toward "paternalistic" government and, in particular, toward the presumed authority of monarchs to override the will of their subjects in the name of their subjects' own "happiness."

44. See, for example, Kant, *Critique of Practical Reason,* pp. 114ff.

45. See, for example, Kant, *Perpetual Peace,* in Reiss, pp. 93–130.

46. Those who defend welfare as a matter of entitlement often do so on the grounds that to do otherwise makes the poor into objects of charity and thus robs them of their "human dignity." The traditional American equation of dignity and self-reliance is thus turned against itself. A laudable disinclination to accept "charity" becomes, ironically, a motive for dependence, it being more honorable to claim one's due than to beg succor. Kant's conception of welfare as a public investment (like the purchase of police cars) suggests a way out of this dilemma—a rationale for aid that is less abrasive than either private charity or public entitlement to the ideal of self-reliance. Treating, say, maternal and infant nutrition programs as a public investment rather than a handout, whether voluntary or compelled, encourages recipients to feel both that they are worth the investment and that they owe a return both to themselves and to the community at large. So conceived, welfare need be no more demeaning than federal highway aid or the Chrysler bailout, both justified (reasonably or not) not as entitlements, but as investments in legitimate public goods.

47. In the small town where I live, housewives—women, that is, not gainfully employed outside the home—hold virtually all the "public" offices, as well as running the local network of "private" charities. Though ostensibly "at home," they are publicly more visible than men. This points to the sort of helpful slippage between public and private that Kant's thought to some extent initiates. For a less happy view of the sexual division of labor in liberal societies, see Carol Pateman, "Feminist Critiques of the Public-Private Dichotomy," in *Public and Private in Social Life,* S. I. Benn and G. F. Gaus, eds. (London: Croom Helm, 1983).

48. Kant, *What Is Enlightenment?,* p. 59.

49. See, for example, Kant, *Theory and Practice,* p. 100: "As far as right is concerned, republicanism is in itself the original basis of every kind of civil constitution. . . ."

50. Governments, in other words, are to evolve through "metamorphosis" rather than "palingenesis" (see Kant, *Metaphysical Elements of Justice,* p. 111).

51. All of this leaves aside Kant's views on the role of the judiciary in a properly constituted state. A few observations, however, may be in order.

Kant, laboring within the confines of the Roman law tradition (which he was not loath to breach when reason dictated), opposed courts of equity, except in cases where the rights of the judge were touched upon, or the Crown was otherwise involved (Kant, *Metaphysical Elements of Justice*, p. 40). Kant stipulates that there be three "distinct authorities," of which the judiciary is one (p. 83). His further insistence that "the constitution itself cannot contain any article that would allow for some authority in the state that could resist or restrain the chief magistrate in cases in which he violates constitutional laws" suggests that Kant did not contemplate anything resembling American "judicial review," though the American Constitution is itself not a little ambiguous on this point. See also his description of the judicial role as one of adjudication performed "on a subject," that is, someone "belonging to the people." Kant cautions judges to be guided by what is lawful in a positive sense, rather than what is "just in itself." He follows that caution, however, with a lengthy and detailed outline of the requirements of private right (see p. 69, and 37–40, omitted from Ladd's translation). This, along with the importance he accords the system of legal justice (without which man, however "socialized," remains in a state of nature), suggests an active, if not overriding, role for judges.

52. See Lincoln's "Speech on the Dred Scot Decision," Springfield, Illinois, June 26, 1857:

> I think the authors of [the Declaration] intended to include *all* men. . . . They did not mean to say all were equal in color, size, intellect, moral developments, or social capacity. They defined with tolerable distinctness, in what respects they did consider all men created equal—equal in "certain inalienable rights, among which are life, liberty, and the pursuit of happiness." This they said and this they meant. They did not mean to assert the obvious untruth, that all were then actually enjoying that equality, nor yet, that they were about to confer it immediately upon them. In fact they had no right to confer such a boon. They meant simply to declare the *right*, so that the *enforcement* of it might follow as fast as circumstances should permit. They meant to set up a standard maxim for free society, which should be familiar to all, and revered by all; constantly looked to, constantly labored for, and even though never perfectly attained, constantly approximated, and thereby constantly spreading and deepening its influence, and augmenting the happiness and value of life to all people of all colors everywhere."

Here, as in his speech in Chicago, Illinois, July 10, 1858, Lincoln links the mandate to work for the elimination of slavery to the beliefs both of the framers and of the general public at the time of the adoption of the Constitution that "slavery was on course of extinction."

As Lincoln suggests, the accident of slavery gave the American Constitution an aspirational thrust that a constitution adopted without the need to compromise on slavery would have lacked. As a consequence human equality, originally conceived as securing the basis of legitimate government, becomes the latter's goal as well. See Harry Jaffa, *Crisis of the House Divided* (New York: Doubleday, 1959), p. 321.

CHAPTER 8: IMPLIED PROTECTIONS AND PROTECTIONS PRESUPPOSED

1. United States, Department of State, *Foreign Relations of the United States, 1952–1954,* vol. II, National Security Affairs, part 2 (Washington: Government Printing Office, 1984), p. 1070.

2. Philip Alston, "Conjuring Up New Human Rights: A Proposal for Quality Control," 78 *American Journal of International Law* 607 at 618 and 619.

3. Harvey C. Mansfield, Jr., "Responsibility versus Self-Expression," chapter 5 of this volume.

4. Ibid.

5. Ibid.

6. On the Humean elements in Rawlsian theory, see Brian Barry, *Theories of Justice,* vol. 1 of *A Treatise on Social Justice* (Berkeley, Calif.: University of California Press, 1989), chapter 4.

7. Mansfield, "Responsibility versus Self-Expression."

8. John Rawls, *A Theory of Justice* (Cambridge, Mass.: Belknap Press of Harvard University Press, 1971), p. 201.

9. Samuel D. Warren and Louis D. Brandeis, "The Right to Privacy," *Harvard Law Review,* vol. IV (December 15, 1890), p. 205.

10. At the beginning of his chapter Mansfield gives this account of the line between "new" and "old": "Fairly recently—perhaps in the New Deal, perhaps in the 1960s—a new conception of rights has taken hold." Mansfield, "Responsibility versus Self-Expression." That would make the Warren-Brandeis conception of the right to privacy clearly an old right, since it arrived under the wire in the nineteenth century. One could try to apply the Nietzschean standard by trying to show that the "new" Warren-Court conception is Nietzschean in respects that the Warren-Brandeis conception of 1890 is not. That would at least be the kind of substantive argument about specific conceptions of a right that is needed. If the new conception took hold in the New Deal, then Mansfield takes Rawls's book published in 1971 simply to play the venerable role of the owl of Minerva, I suppose. Monumental developments in conceptions of rights took place between the time of the New Deal and the 1960s—for example, the increasingly broad acceptance of the "International Bill of Rights," including the *International Covenant on Civil and Political Rights,* with its *Optional Protocol* providing individuals with a means of redress against their own governments; the *International Covenant on Economic, Social, and Cultural Rights;* and the *International Convention on the Elimination of All Forms of Racial Discrimination.*

11. Mansfield, "Responsibility versus Self-Expression." A more standard definition of a natural right is given in Norman E. Bowie and Robert L. Simon, *The Individual and the Political Order* (Englewood Cliffs, N.J.: Prentice-Hall, 1977), p. 62. Also see *Encyclopedia of Ethics,* Lawrence and Charlotte Becker, eds. (New York: Garland Publishing, 1992), *s.v.* human rights; rights, theories of.

12. John Stuart Mill, *Utilitarianism*, chapter 5 (Indianapolis: Bobbs-Merrill Co., 1957), p. 66.

13. Henry Shue, *Basic Rights: Subsistence, Affluence, and U.S. Foreign Policy* (Princeton, N.J.: Princeton University Press, 1980), chapter 1.

14. Wesley Hohfeld, *Fundamental Legal Conceptions* (New Haven, Conn.: Yale University Press, 1923).

15. Obviously this is not a complete analysis of the concept of a right. I have presented a fuller account in *Basic Rights*, chapters 1 and 2.

16. In the case of this moral right we have good, additional reasons to pursue legal protection. Whether that legal protection requires legislative action is a separate matter. Harvey C. Mansfield, Jr., writes vaguely of unnamed people who believe that "human rights become civil or constitutional rights immediately, with no sense of having to pass through a form of government for their securing and specification." Mansfield, "Responsibility versus Self-Expression." Until one knows specifically whose views are being criticized for this belief in magical, nongovernmental legal rights, it is impossible to know whether the criticism hits any target.

17. For a preliminary discussion of the concept of a standard threat, see Shue, *Basic Rights*, pp. 29–34. The concept has been developed in a provocative direction by David Luban in "The Warren Court and the Concept of a Right," Bertram Morris Colloquium, 1991, photocopy.

18. Mansfield, "Responsibility versus Self-Expression."

19. Robert H. Bork, *The Tempting of America: The Political Seduction of the Law* (New York: Free Press, 1990), p. 97.

20. Luban, "The Warren Court."

21. 381 U.S. 474 at 484.

22. Bork, *The Tempting of America*, p. 97.

23. Ibid., p. 98. Judge Bork is of course far from alone in ascribing this untidy picture to Douglas; Walter Berns has portrayed Douglas as having found the right to privacy "lurking in shadows cast by a potpourri of constitutional provisions"—see "Taking Rights Frivolously" in *Liberalism Reconsidered*, edited by Douglas MacLean and Claudia Mills, Maryland Studies in Political Philosophy (Savage, Md.: Rowman & Littlefield, 1983), p. 63.

24. Luban, "The Warren Court," p. 23.

25. Richard D. Mohr, *Gays/Justice: A Study of Ethics, Society, and Law* (New York: Columbia University Press, 1988), p. 72; originally published in 1986 in somewhat different form as Richard Mohr, "Mr. Justice Douglas at Sodom: Gays and Privacy," *Columbia Human Rights Law Review*, vol. 18, p. 43.

26. I have tried to demonstrate the role of this form of reasoning in Rawls's *A Theory of Justice* in "Justice, Rationality and Desire: On the Logical Structure of 'Justice as Fairness,' " *Southern Journal of Philosophy*, vol. 13 (1975–1976), pp. 89–97.

27. Compare the sympathetic reinterpretation of the notion of "original intent" in David Lyons, "Basic Rights and Constitutional Interpretation," *Social Theory and Practice*, vol. 16 (Fall 1990), pp. 337–57.

Index

Affirmative action
    changes in basis of objections
        to, 122–23
    merit-based, 124–31, 144–47
    objections to, 112–14
    societal discrimination justifies,
        140
    transformation of jurisprudence
        of, 24–29
    See also Merit equivalence; Race
Alston, Philip, 165
Animal rights, 48, 71, 105–6
Anti-Federalists, 3
Antinomian doctrine of rights, 3
Aristotelianism, 22, 47
Atlantic Charter, 53
Author of Nature belief, 46–47
Autonomy
    Kantian meaning of, 87
    modern interpretation of, 87–88
    of natural reason, 4
    in question of right to die, 32
    See also Moral autonomy, indi
        vidual; Self; Suicide, assisted

Bacon, Francis, 92
Bakke. See University of California Re-
    gents v. Bakke
Barber, Benjamin, 57
Best way of life (Kant), 19, 159
Bickel, Alexander, 113
Bill of Rights
    arguments against, 42–43, 63
    as constitutional law, 41
    is civil rights, 98
Black, Hugo, 149
Blackmun, Harry A., 127, 135

Bork, Robert, 11, 174, 176–77
Brandeis, Louis D., 9, 146, 167
Brennan, William J.
    in *Bakke* decision, 127, 135
    on idea of human dignity, 16,
        18, 149, 155–56
    in *Johnson* decision, 27–28, 134–
        35
    in *Metro Broadcasting* decision,
        136
    in *United Jewish Organizations* de-
        cision, 27, 132
    in *United States v. Paradise* deci-
        sion, 134, 135–36
    view of Constitution, 18
Burger, Warren
    in *Bakke* decision, 119
    in *Franks* decision, 27, 132–33
    in *Fullilove* decision, 135–36
    in *United Jewish Organizations* de-
        cision, 27, 132
    in *Wygant* decision, 27, 121,
        133–34

Centralization of power, 3
Charity, 105
Civil rights
    development of, 45
    evolution of, 22
    exchange of natural rights for,
        5, 98
    group rights within, 24
    under new rights, 8
Civil Rights Act (1964)
    Title VI, 119
    Title VII, 113, 125, 129, 131–33,
        136–37

as guard to life and liberty, 98,
106
man's property in his own person (Locke), 86
meaning of ownership in, 43–44
in relation to due process, 44
See also Limited liability concept;
Self-ownership
Property, private
under new and old rights, 7–8
to reify property rights, 43–44
Property rights
as constitutional rights, 21–22,
44
in form of entitlements, 23, 49
of Locke and Kant, 160–61
in U.S. Constitution, 54
See also Taking (of property)
Protection
equal, 44
in Fourth Amendment, 63
of old right by new right, 173–
74
in response to new threats, 173
rights as, 51, 66–67
of rights in colonial America,
20–21
rights of personal, 14, 68
Protestantism, 12, 54
Prudence, 41
Public policy, 64
Publius, 101

Quotas
relation between group rights
and, 72
in selection procedures, 125

Race
as argument to correct past discrimination, 139–44
challenge to hiring criteria related to, 25–26
in determination of qualifications, 25, 112–24
expectations because of, 131–39
in layoffs of minority teachers,
26
seniority because of, 132–34

Rawls, John
concept of least advantaged,
103, 151, 166
critique of utilitarianism, 62
difference principle of, 70
influences on, 9, 55, 166–67
justice as fairness concept, 16–
17, 150–52
position on rights and duties, 65
self-worth concept of, 17
Theory of Justice, 149
Raz, Joseph, 65
Rehnquist, William
in *Bakke* decision, 119
in *Cruzan* decision, 33, 89–90, 91
in *United Jewish Organizations* decision, 126
in *Weber* decision, 136–37
in *Wygant* decision, 121, 133–34
Relativism, 23
Religion, 3
Republicanism (Kant), 162
Respect, 152
Responsibility
under affirmative action legislation, 107
in context of rights and interests, 100–102
definition and exercise of, 6–7
entitlements secure from, 109
under environmentalism, 106
perception of new rights, 106
Rhetoric
of claiming rights, 78
of rights, 34
of welfare rights, 78
Richards, David A. J., 18, 154–55
Richmond v. Croson Co., 29, 135, 139,
142–44
Right
concept and content of a, 168–
69
concept of claiming a, 6–7
distinction from a permission,
9–10, 168–69
human dignity as a, 36
as justified claim, 78
meaning of, 77
as a permission, 5, 9, 97
to take one's life, 77

A Note on the Book

*This book was edited by Cheryl Weissman
of the staff of the AEI Press.
The index was prepared by Shirley Kessel.
The text was set in Palatino, a typeface designed by
the twentieth-century Swiss designer Hermann Zapf.
Coghill Composition Company
set the type, and Edwards Brothers Incorporated,
of Ann Arbor, Michigan, printed and bound the book,
using permanent acid-free paper.*

The AEI Press is the publisher for the American Enterprise Institute for Public Policy Research, 1150 17th Street, N.W., Washington, D.C. 20036: *Christopher C. DeMuth,* publisher; *Edward Styles,* director; *Dana Lane,* assistant director; *Ann Petty,* editor; *Cheryl Weissman,* editor; Mary Cristina Delaney, editorial assistant (rights and permissions). Books published by the AEI Press are distributed by arrangement with the University Press of America, 4720 Boston Way, Lanham, Md. 20706.